Isabelle Roelofs & Fabien Petillion

Mastering Color Mixing with Watercolors

Mastering Color Mixing with Watercolors
Isabelle Roelofs and Fabien Petillion

Project editor: Maggie Yates
Project manager: Lisa Brazieal
Marketing coordinator: Mercedes Murray
Graphic design and layout: Zaoum
Layout production: WolfsonDesign
Cover design: Aren Straiger

ISBN: 978-1-68198-779-8
1st Edition (1st printing, July 2021)

Original French title: Maîtriser le mélange des couleurs à l'aquarelle
© 2021 Éditions Eyrolles, Paris, France
Translation copyright © 2021 Rocky Nook, Inc.
All illustrations by Isabelle Roelofs, except for the following:
Marie Boudon: pages 76 and 79
Manù: pages 82, 86, 90, 94, and 97
Cindy Barillet: pages 109, 112, 114, 116, and 117
Fabien Petillion: front cover illustration and pages 100, 102, 104, 107, 122,
125, 129, 132, and 136

Rocky Nook Inc.
1010 B Street, Suite 350
San Rafael, CA 94901
USA
www.rockynook.com

Distributed in the UK and Europe by Publishers Group UK
Distributed in the U.S. and all other territories by Ingram Publisher Services

Library of Congress Control Number: 2020952747

*We want to thank Nathalie for listening,
Cindy, Marie, and Manù for giving us their time,
and our loved ones for their support.*

Foreword

In this book, we would like to familiarize you with watercolor mixtures.

First, we will detail some of the theoretical notions that are necessary for understanding watercolor mixtures. We will then suggest a palette of 11 colors, made up exclusively of primary and monopigment colors, offering a very extensive chromatic range.

The works of four watercolorists will then guide you with respect to the nuances to be favored in order to build balanced thematic palettes. These will allow for easy and harmonious color mixing. Our 11 colors will form the basis of a large number of mixtures, without however being exhaustive, because others will also be added to support them. Then, a detailed analysis of the step-by-step development of several different watercolor paintings will help you to put the theory of color mixing into practice. It is not enough just to learn how to overcome the specific, common technical weaknesses that we will highlight.

Finally, we want to emphasize the fact that this volume should be read as a guide, one that we hope will make you want to open yourself up to a multitude of experimentations.

In watercolors, nothing stands still, and there is no absolute truth; when it comes to mixing colors, you can try anything. Every artist complements their basic colors with other colors that correspond to their own artistic affinities. This book will allow you to correctly choose your own colors, to appreciate their full potential, and, most of all, not to buy colors for which you will ultimately have no use.

Isabelle Roelofs and Fabien Petillion

Contents

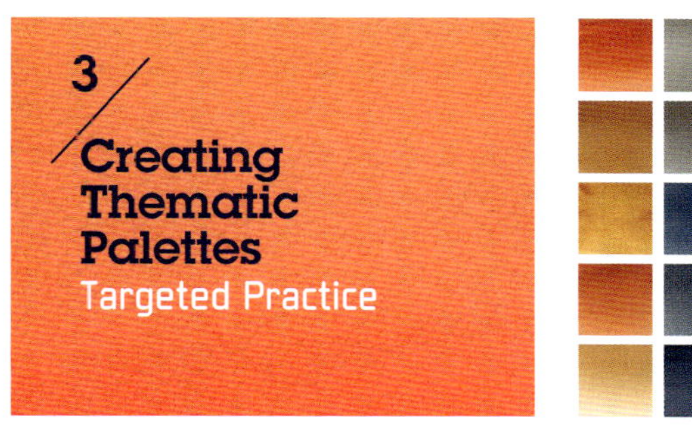

3
Creating Thematic Palettes
Targeted Practice

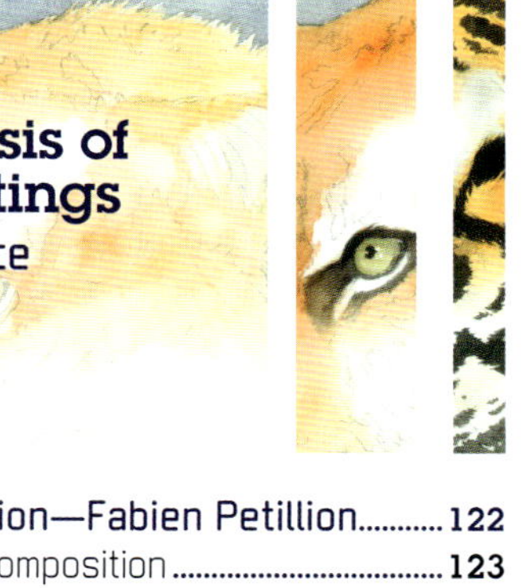

4
An Analysis of Five Paintings
Global Practice

1 / Understanding a Watercolor

Basic Concepts

This chapter lays out some of the basic concepts that you will need in order to better understand the characteristics of watercolors, such as the nature of the pigments, their granularity, opacity, and transparency, and monopigment colors. We will then look at the specific characteristics of the 11 colors that we recommend you use in order to build up a balanced basic palette.

The Nature of Pigments

Watercolors are made from colored powders called pigments. These are mixed with a water-based binding agent consisting of gum arabic or dextrin. The formulation is completed with additives known for their qualities of plasticity and retaining moisture, such as glycerin and honey, as well as preservative agents.

Each pigment has intrinsic qualities that define what an artist can expect of a particular color. Opacity, transparency, granularity, and coloring power all depend on the nature of the pigments that are used in making the watercolors. This is why a good knowledge of the pigments that enter into the composition of watercolors will allow you to use them to their full potential.

Pigments fall into two main categories: **mineral pigments** and **organic pigments**. These two categories are then each also subdivided into two further categories: **natural pigments** and **synthetic pigments**. Nowadays, artists' colors are mostly made using synthetic pigments, whose chemical composition is more or less complex.

MINERAL PIGMENTS

Earth tones and ocher colors are the only natural mineral pigments that are still used on an industrial basis today and that you will currently find in the assortment put out by color manufacturers.

The other mineral pigments, also called inorganic pigments, are produced artificially, based on metallic compounds. In a color chart, you will be able to find mineral-based pigments relatively easily. The name of the color indicates which metallic compound it contains, the most common ones being cobalt, titanium, zinc, cadmium, barium, chrome, nickel, and iron.

Watercolors based on mineral pigments are opaque and sometimes granular.

ORGANIC PIGMENTS

It is rare these days to find watercolors based on natural organic pigments. They are no longer manufactured industrially; they are only made "artisanally" and are correspondingly expensive to buy. These pigments, of animal or plant origin, are mostly lacquers. "Lacquers" means that the dyes contained in the organic matter have been extracted. Then this dye concentrate is combined with a neutral base (usually an aluminum or iron

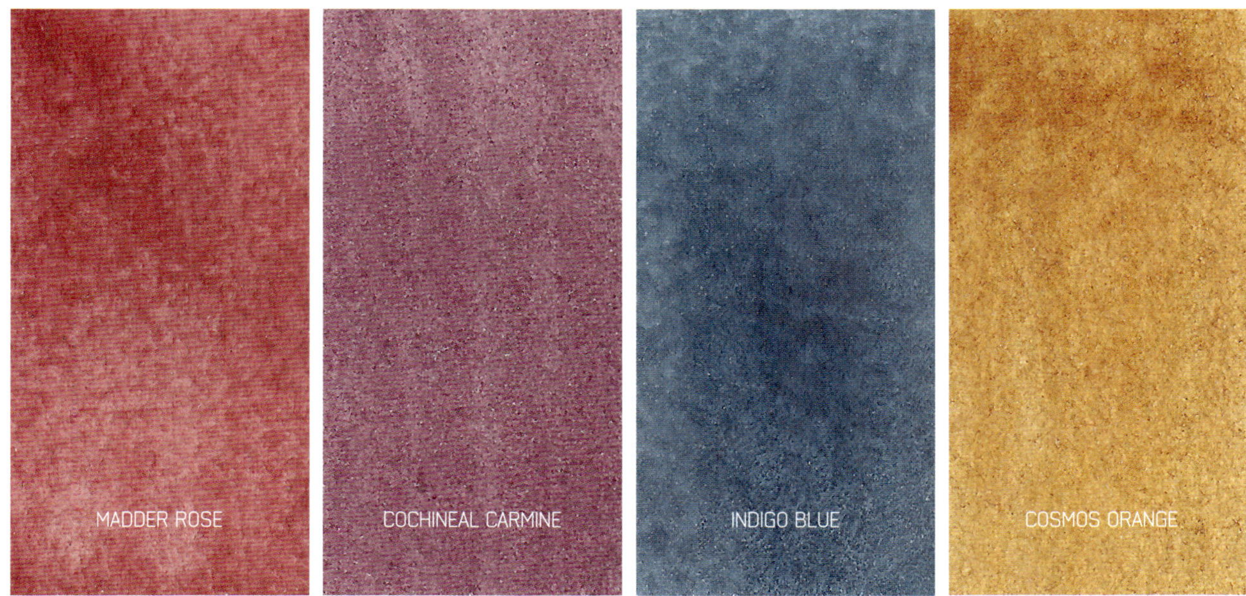

NATURAL COLORS FROM
THE LUTEA ASSORTMENT.

sulphate), which makes it possible to obtain a powdered color that can be used to make artists' paints. Madder rose, cochineal carmine, indigo blue, and even cosmos orange are colors that will delight purists looking for more muted shades that will delicately complement each other. Remember that these watercolors are more sensitive to ultraviolet than are their synthetic counterparts. Works painted using these colors should therefore be kept away from too much exposure to light. A varnish or anti-ultraviolet glass will also help to protect the permanence of these colors.

The manufacture of synthetic organic pigments, meanwhile, is based on the specific chemical properties of the carbon atom. These pigments are produced using the complex connection between carbon molecules and hydrogen molecules, nitrogen molecules, or sometimes (very rarely) also metallic compounds such as copper (in which case what we have then are organcmetallic pigments). They can be found in abundance in the color assortments of watercolor manufacturers. Their chemical compounds, which often have complicated names (dioxazine, quinacridone, diketopyrrolopyrrole, phthalocyanine, perylene), are seldom included in the name of the color. Referring to the pigment nomenclature given on the labels of color tubes will help you to identify these.

GRANULAR COLOR
ON RAG PAPER
CERULEAN BLUE (PB35 OR PB36)

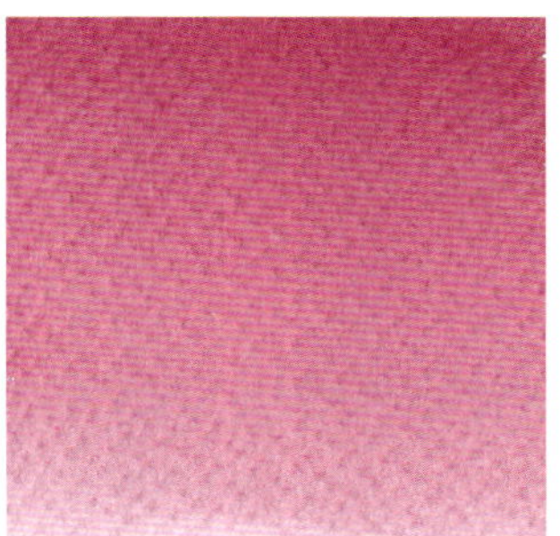

NON-GRANULAR COLOR
ON RAG PAPER
ISARO ROSE (PR122)

GRANULAR COLOR MIXED WITH
NON-GRANULAR COLOR
ON RAG PAPER
ISARO ROSE (PR122)
+ CERULEAN BLUE (PB35 OR PB36)

Synthetic organic pigments are highly valued in the manufacture of watercolors because they are transparent and their coloring power is often impressive. They also form uniform washes and only very rarely granulate.

Granularity

In watercolor painting, some colors provide uniform washes, as if they were just dyeing the paper, while others create an effect that looks like inlays.

This affect is accentuated on rag paper. From a technical standpoint, the granularity is related to the nature of the pigment. Even after careful grinding, some of the elementary particles of the pigments retain the tendency to clump and bond, which prevents an even distribution of the pigment. This produces varied washes, which are preferred by those who value colors with structured washes.

Mineral pigments, whose particles are not as fine as those of organic pigments, are more prone to granularity. Earth tones, ultramarines (blue, violet, and pink), cobalt-based colors (blue, green, and violet), emerald green, and manganese violet are the colors to choose if you would like to work with this effect.

COLORING POWER

Some pigments have a great deal of coloring power. Generally speaking, the smaller the pigment's elemental particle, the stronger its coloring power will be. Synthetic organic pigments have finer pigment particles than mineral pigments do. These extremely fine pigments can very easily travel through and penetrate a paper's fibers. Watercolors made using synthetic organic pigments therefore have a stronger coloring power than that of watercolors made up of mineral pigments. The pigment families of phthalocyanine, quinacridone, dioxazine, and DPP (diketopyrrolopyrrole) have an extraordinary coloring power, and once you have applied those colors to your paper, they are very difficult to erase and will not allow you much chance to change your mind.

Transparency and Opacity

The transparency of a color is connected to the structure of the pigment particles of which it is composed. If we look at them through a microscope, we will see that certain pigments, such as cadmiums and iron oxides, are very dense. Other pigments, however, will look almost translucent (phthalocyanine, quinacridone, Prussian blue (PB27)). In watercolors, it is important how you play with transparency. Keeping in mind that mineral pigments are opaque and that synthetic organic pigments are transparent will allow you to begin to imagine what you might be able to expect of a color. In order to make a more detailed study of the level of transparency of the colors that you already own, take the time to draw a black line on a piece of watercolor paper and to apply your colors to it, with very little dilution. The more the color lets the black line show through, the more transparent it is.

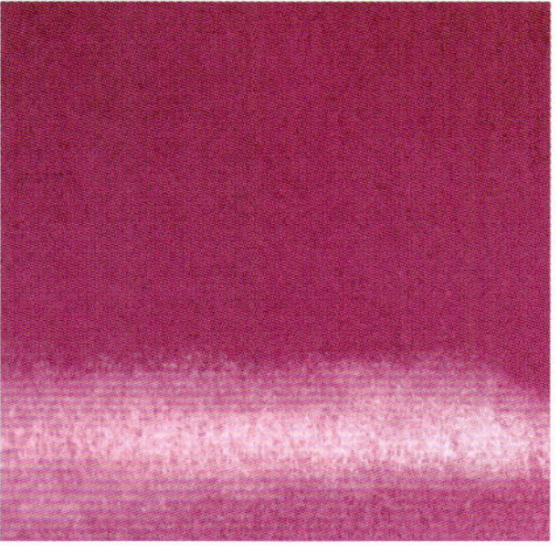

EVEN THOUGH SOME KINDS OF PAPER MAKE REMOVAL MORE POSSIBLE, MINERAL PIGMENTS (HERE ULTRAMARINE BLUE (PB29)) ARE EASIER TO ERASE THAN ORGANIC PIGMENTS (HERE ISARO ROSE (PR122) OR QUINACRIDONE ROSE).

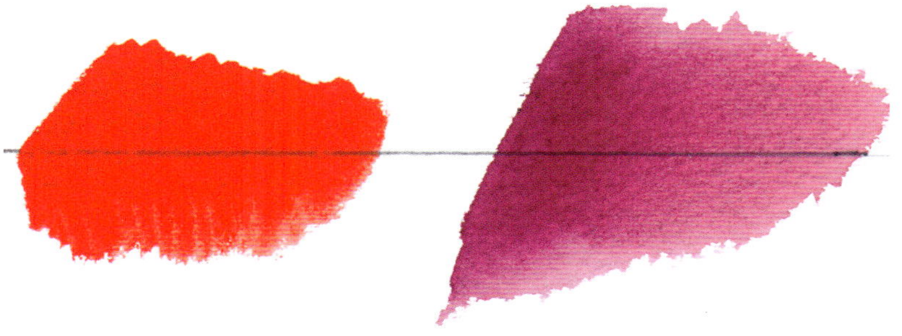

AT LEFT, AN OPAQUE COLOR (CADMIUM RED); AT RIGHT, A TRANSPARENT COLOR (ISARO ROSE (PR122)).

Capacity for removal

Because of their solidity, some kinds of paper make removal more easily possible. These papers will allow you to go over the same area with a wet brush several times without pilling on the surface. Thus, you can allow the white of the paper, or a previously applied underlayer, to show through.

Monopigment Colors

Monopigment colors are colors made from a single pigment. The benefit of working with these colors is that in painting, we are subject to subtractive synthesis. You will surely already have noticed that the more you mix your colors, the more you lose in luminance or brightness, until finally, they will tend toward black. By choosing to paint with monopigment colors, you will be able to retain greater brightness as you create your secondary and tertiary colors.

Variations in Shade between Brands

Between one brand or manufacturer and another, the same color can have a different shade, even when you compare monopigment colors. Thus, even when referring to the same color name, the shades will change depending on the manufacturer.

The families of pigments often spread across a very broad chromatic palette. Thus, iron oxides can come in an enormous variety of shades, ranging from yellow to brown and passing through oranges, reds, and violets along the way. The same is true for earth tones, cadmiums, and diketopyrrolopyrroles, for example.

As for the colors that are made up of several different pigments, such as Payne's gray, indigo blue, or certain greens, the variations in shade can be even greater.

It is essential to refer to the manufacturers' color charts, to find out what pigments went into the composition of any given color, in order to fully appreciate that color's intrinsic qualities. However, you will also need to test the shades that they propose to make sure they meet your own expectations. With practice, you will be able to create your own non-monopigment colors.

Lightening a Color

Unlike other kinds of painting, such as oil and acrylic, where white is used to lighten a color, in watercolors we use the white of the paper. Therefore, we proceed by diluting the color with the water, allowing the white of the page to show through more or less intensely.

You can work directly on your palette, adding more or less water to the color, or else you can lighten the color after it is already on the paper by using a brush filled with water.

By learning to lighten your colors using water, you will enlarge the tonal range of your palette.

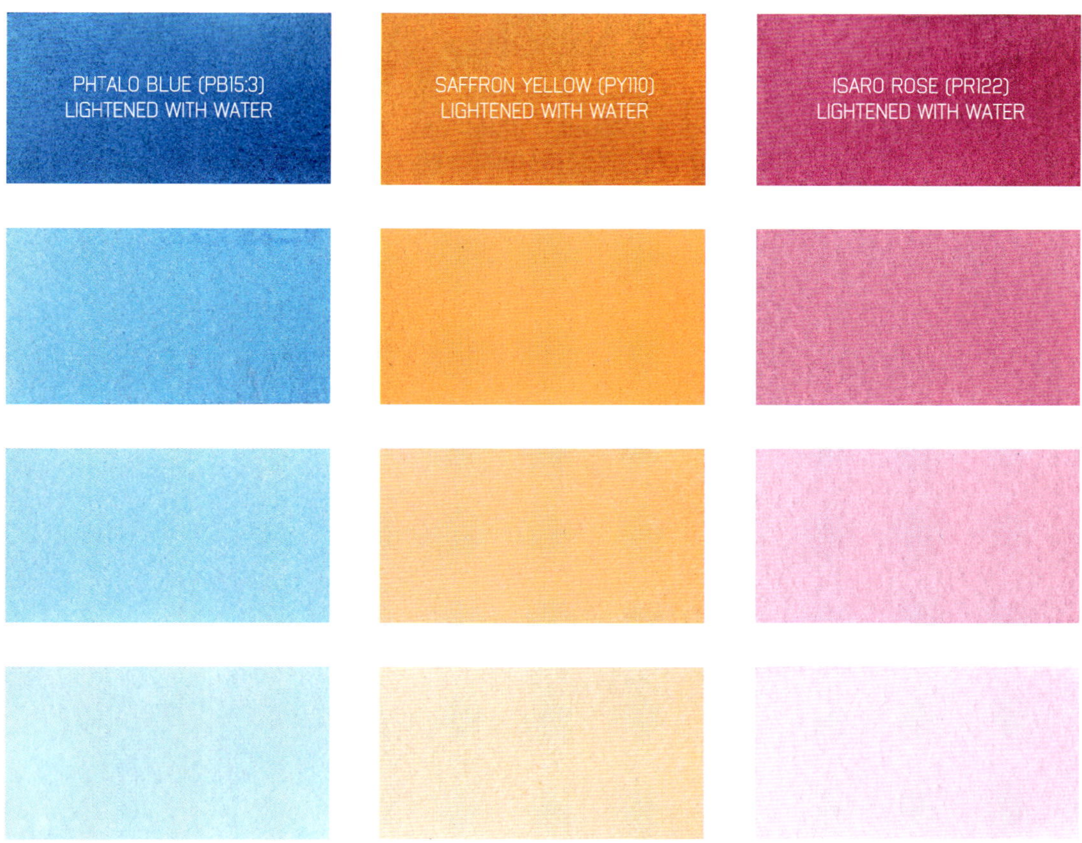

Painting Techniques

Painting with watercolors means learning to tame water and to correctly understand the moisture of the paper.

There are two main techniques for working in watercolor. They complement each other, because most watercolorists first work wet-on-wet and then add details on dry paper.

WET-ON-WET

This technique requires you to wet the paper first, before you add any colors. This allows you to obtain magnificent fades, to create diffuse mixtures, and to delicately merge the colors.

You must learn to master the moisture of the paper. The wetter it is, the more the colors will spread and diffuse, in an uncontrolled fashion. If the paper is less wet, the colors will be easier to control, but they will also be less likely to spread.

WET-ON-DRY

As the name indicates, this technique involves applying color to dry paper. It allows you to lay colors on top of each other in order to get the effects of mixture through transparency.

This way of working also allows for greater precision and is particularly suitable for detailed renderings.

Techniques for Mixing Colors

You can mix your colors on your palette and in this way find the shade that you would like to work with. A simple plate will work just fine for making your mixtures. You can also work directly on the lids of the watercolor boxes that are intended for this purpose. Many watercolorists use the hermetically sealable travel palettes and fill them with watercolors from tubes. They have larger receptacles for the colors than the classic cups, which are not easy to work in if you have a large brush. This technique will be presented by illustrations showing four squares of color in the section "Creating the Range of Secondary Colors" (see page 41).

You can also mix your colors right on the paper, working either wet-on-wet or on semi-wet. This will allow the colors to merge into each other, and the mixture will be less homogeneous and more vibrant. This technique will be presented by gradients in the section "Creating the Range of Secondary Colors" (see page 41).

ULTRAMARINE BLUE (PB29) +
ISARO ROSE (PR122)
(MIXED ON THE PALETTE AND
LAID DOWN ON DRY PAPER)

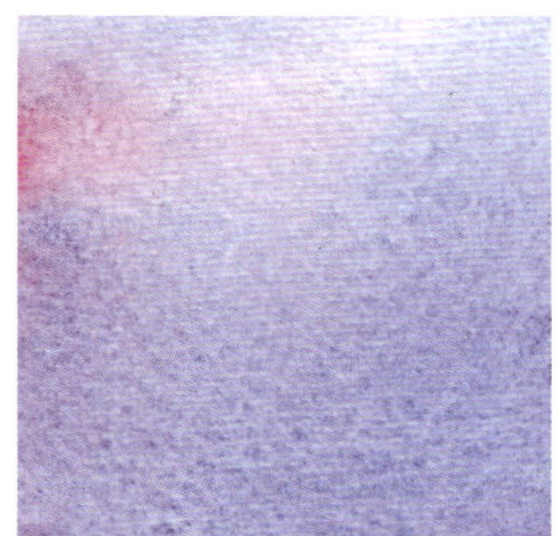

ULTRAMARINE BLUE (PB29) +
ISARO ROSE (PR122)
(MIXED ON PAPER THAT WAS
ALREADY WET)

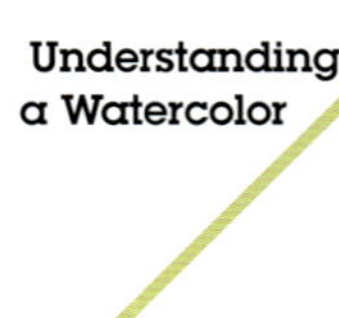

Paper

GRAIN

There are three kinds of paper surface.

• Satin grain: This paper has a very smooth surface, with almost no roughness. It is hard to work with for a beginner.

• Fine grain: This paper has a very lightly marked surface. A little rougher than satin-grain paper, it is very popular, and considered to be the most versatile. It is suitable for both beginners and experienced artists.

• Cloth grain: This paper is textured. It allows for beautiful color and relief effects. It requires a certain level of technical mastery in order to use it to its full potential.

QUALITY

There are two kinds of watercolor paper: cellulose (wood pulp) paper and cotton paper.

The first kind, 100 percent cellulose, is made out of wood fibers. This is lower-quality paper, industrially manufactured. Wood fibers are easy to produce and inexpensive, which explains why this paper costs less than cotton paper.

The second kind, made from plant fibers such as cotton, hemp, linen, or abaca, is a higher-quality paper and more expensive than cellulose paper. This category also includes what is called "rag" paper. This last kind is rare nowadays, because it is hard to get textiles that do not include traces of synthetic fiber or detergent. These papers can be either industrially produced or else artisanally handmade.

The choice of plant is what gives the paper its characteristics. For example, cotton flowers have long fibers that add a lot of resistance to the paper. Cotton paper is also a naturally low-acid paper. 100 percent-cotton watercolor paper is very popular with watercolor artists.

CLOSE-UP, CANSON HERITAGE SATIN GRAIN PAPER

CLOSE-UP, CANSON HERITAGE FINE GRAIN PAPER

There are several ways to make paper:

• Flat-table manufacturing is the fastest and cheapest. Once the wood pulp fibers have been bound and the paper has been sufficiently drained, a synthetic felt makes it possible to create the grain. Then the paper goes into a press to squeeze out the water, and then a layer of gelatin (which prevents too much of the watercolor from penetrating the fibers) or of starch is added, and the paper goes through a final drying stage.

• Moldmade paper, using a cylindrical mold, involves a manufacturing process that is closer to that of handmade paper. Here, the bonding agent is either added directly to the pulp or placed onto the surface of the paper.

• There are still some artisanal paper makers who use old-fashioned techniques and create papers in qualities that greatly distinguish them from traditional papers. These artisans have technical skills that allow them to create custom papers and fulfill special orders. They always work from plant fibers.

CLOSE-UP, CANSON HERITAGE CLOTH GRAIN PAPER

WEIGHT

Watercolor paper comes in various weights, measured in weight per square inch of paper. The weight of watercolor paper ranges from 185 g/m2 to 850 g/m2. Of course, the higher the weight, the thicker the paper.

• Less than 300 g/m2—the thinner the paper, the more it will tend to curl up when it is wet. Thus, it is strongly recommended that you stretch it or that you use it in the form of a notepad glued down on the edges.

• 300 g/m2—this is a thicker weight and it is the most popular for watercolorists. It is less likely to curl up and therefore you do not need to stretch it unless you like to work under very wet conditions.

• More than 300 g/m2—these are papers that can take a lot of water. They will also stay wet longer and the colors on them will dry more slowly.

Reminder
In order to review the basics for preparing your watercolor materials, you can follow the clear and succinct explanations available at: www.cansonstudio.com/preparing-your-watercolor-materials

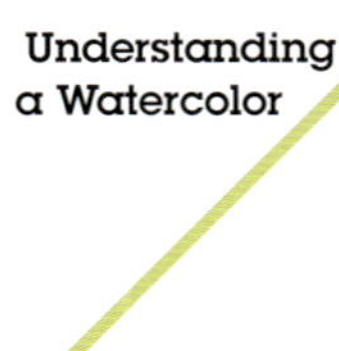

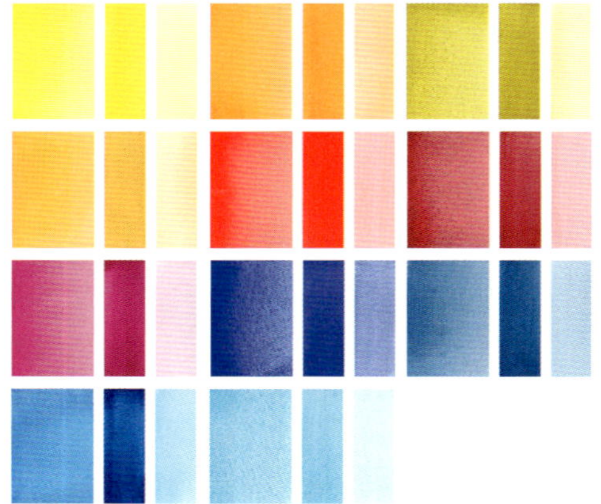

Presentation of
the Chosen Colors

The basic palette that we have chosen here includes **eleven colors**. In order for you to be able to identify them on the color charts of various manufacturers, we also include their pigmentary description.

While the names of colors can vary from one brand to the next, the pigments that are used in watercolor tubes have to be listed on the labels, or at least on the manufacturer's color chart or web site. The pigmentary description will allow you to correctly find the colors you are looking for.

This pigmentary description is universal. In its simplified form, it always follows the following structure:

• First, P, for pigment;

• then, the first letter of the color in English: Y for *yellow*, R for *red*, O for *orange*, B for *blue*, G for *green*, Bk for *black*, Br for *brown*, V for *violet*, and W for *white*;

• and finally, two or three digits that identify the pigment or the pigment family. These numbers do not give any further information but just refer to the order in which the pigments are recorded in the Color Index.

Thus, PR255 informs that you dealing with **Pigment Red 255**. This is a red in the family of diketopyrrolopyrroles.

Please note that all of these pigments are listed in the Color Index. The Color Index uses a double system of classification, including both the generic name of the pigment and its five- or six-digit composition code. This code gives professionals information about the pigment's chemical composition and molecular structure. Thus, to revisit the previous example, PR255 is listed in the Color Index under the reference C.1 Pigment red 255 (complete generic name) and also the reference 561050 (composition code). In this book, we only use the simplified generic name.

On the facing page, please see a chart that shows the most important pigments used by painters. This is not an exhaustive list.

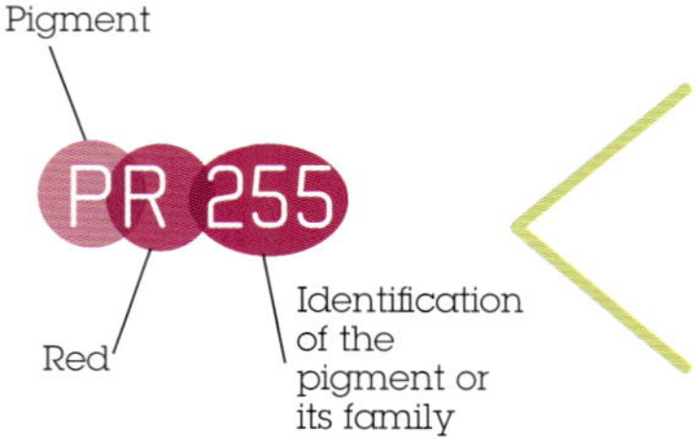

WHITE	
Titanium White	PW6
Zinc White	PW4

YELLOW	
Cadmium Yellow	PY35, PY37
Aureoline Yellow	PY40
Azo Yellow (Hansa, Benzimidazolone, and Disazoic)	PY1, PY3, PY65, PY74, PY83, PY97, PY151, PY154, PY175
Natural Iron Oxide (Yellow Ocher)	PY43
Synthetic Iron Oxide Yellow	PY42
Nickel Rutile Yellow	PY53
Isoindolinone Yellow	PY110, PY139
Copper Azomethine Green	PY129
Chrome Rutile Yellow	PBr24
Bismuth Vanadate Yellow	PY184

ORANGE	
Cadmium Orange	PO20
Azo Orange (Bezimidazolone)	PO36, PO62
Diketopyrrolopyrrole Orange	PO71, PO73

RED	
Synthetic Iron Oxide Red	PR101
Natural Iron Oxide Red (Calcined Natural Ocher)	PR102
Cadmium Red	PR108
Alizarin Red	PR83
Azo Red (Naphthol)	PR112, PR170, PR188
Perylene Red	PR149, PR179
Anthraquinone Red	PR168, PR177
Quinacridone Red	PR122, PR207, PR209
Diketopyrrolopyrrole Red	PR254, PR255, PR264
Ultramarine Red	PR259

VIOLET	
Iron Oxide Violet	PR101
Cobalt Violet	PV14
Manganese Violet	PV16
Ultramarine Violet	PV15
Dioxazine Violet	PV23
Perylene Violet	PV29
Quinacridone Violet	PV19

BLUE	
Cobalt-based Blue	PB28, PB35, PB36, PB72, PB73, PB74
Ultramarine Blue	PB29
Phthalocyanine Blue	PB15, PB15:1, PB15:2, PB15:3, PB15:4, PB15:5, PB15:6, PB16
Prussian Blue	PB27
Indanthrene or Indanthrone Blue	PB60
GREEN	
Phthalocyanine Green	PG7, PG36
Chrome-based Green	PG17, PG18
Green Earth Tone	PG23
Cobalt-based Green	PG26, PG50
BROWN	
Natural Earth Tone	PBr7
Synthetic Iron Oxide Brown	PR101
BLACK	
Carbon Black	PBk6, PBk7, PBk9
Iron Oxide Black	PBk11
Perylene Black	PBk31

Multiple Pigments for One Color?

Every manufacturer can let their imagination run wild in naming a color. This is how a watercolor produced from the same pigment can have different names, and how the same color name can indicate a color using a different pigment, depending on which brand you are using.

In this book, the colors of the Isaro brand will be our reference point. However, you will find a table of equivalences at the end of this chapter (see page 35). This table will help you to identify the colors we discuss here in the assortments of different manufacturers.

As for the colors that we have chosen, you will notice that they are not limited to the three primary colors. The purpose of the palette that we propose here is, in fact, to offer a wide choice of mixtures that can be made by combining two colors. The goal is to allow you a great deal of artistic freedom without you having to go hunting for how to create secondary and tertiary colors. That is definitely what would happen if we proposed a much more restricted palette. To these eleven colors, depending on the themes that you want to paint, you can add more either for convenience or because certain colors are particularly well suited to certain subjects.

Yellow PY154
Isaro Yellow Light

Synthetic organic pigment from the benzimidazolone family.

This yellow holds up well in the light and should be preferred to the pigment PY1 (from the family of azo yellows), also known as Hansa yellow, which has a much lower UV resistance.

Benzimidazolone yellows are more transparent than cadmium yellows (PY35), and in watercolors, transparency is often very much desired.

This non-granular yellow, with its strong coloring power, thus has all the necessary qualities for playing the role of an excellent primary yellow.

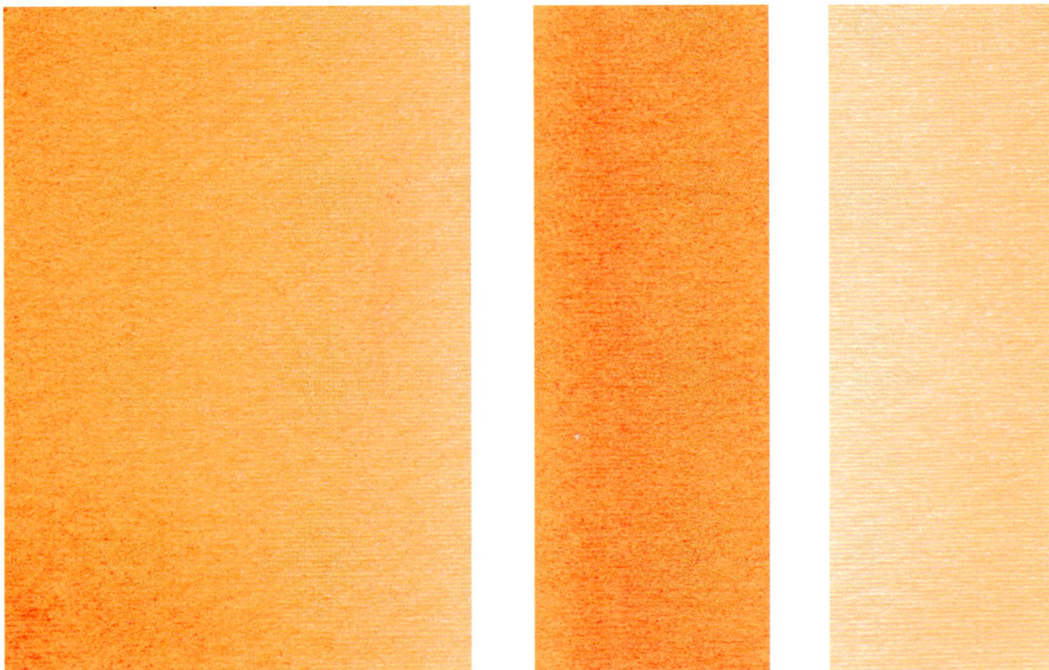

Yellow PY110
Saffron Yellow

Synthetic organic pigment from the isoindolinone family.

This is one of the rare pigments in this family that has the advantage of a very great resistance to light. This orangeish yellow is more transparent than dark cadmium yellow (PY35), and is therefore often preferred to it.

This non-granular yellow, with its strong coloring power and its warm tonality, is a perfect complement to Isaro yellow light (PY154), which is more neutral.

Chartreuse Yellow

Synthetic organic pigment from the copper azomethine family.

This cool yellow holds up well in the light and tends strongly toward a greenish yellow. Beautifully transparent and with excellent coloring power, this tone is a valuable ally for creating a magnificent range of greens.

This color granulates very lightly when it is applied to the page to saturation.

Yellow PY42 or PY43
Yellow Ocher

Natural or synthetic inorganic pigment from the iron oxide family.

The pigment PY43 identifies a natural earth color, while PY42 is its synthetic counterpart. Natural earth colors have slightly less coloring power than synthetic iron oxides. The shade of yellow ocher, whether natural or synthetic, can vary slightly from manufacturer to manufacturer.

It is better to choose a bright yellow ocher, and one that is not too opaque, in order to keep your mixtures from becoming muddy.

By definition, all iron oxides are magnificently light resistant. They are commonly found in industrial painting because they are so remarkably weather resistant. Depending on the brand, this color can be more or less granular.

Red PR255
Scarlet Red

Synthetic organic pigment from the diketopyrrolopyrrole family.

This is a warm, lightly orangeish, medium red. It has excellent resistance to light. This pigment is more transparent than light or medium cadmium red (PR108) and is therefore often preferred to it. As a vibrant red, PR254, which belongs to this same family of pigments, can also be used. Deciding between these two is a personal choice.

This red, which is relatively transparent, non-granular, and which has a very nice coloring power, is the most neutral one in the palette.

Red PR264
Pyrrole Red Deep

Synthetic organic pigment from the diketopyrrolopyrrole family.

This red is very light resistant and can definitely be substituted for the madder reds (PR83), which are less UV-stable.

Like all diketopyrrolopyrroles, it has a remarkable coloring power, is beautifully transparent, and is non-granular.

This is a relatively dark cool red that harmoniously complements scarlet red (PR255).

Rose PR122
Isaro Rose

Synthetic organic pigment from the quinacridone family.

This pigment, which is listed as a red pigment, should instead be classified as one of the rose, or pink, pigments. Cool and bluish, this rose color is perfect for creating a lovely range of bright, straightforward violets. It is therefore an essential part of a watercolorist's palette, because the two previous reds cannot produce such pure violets.

It is non-granular, has a remarkable coloring power, is transparent, and possesses excellent light resistance.

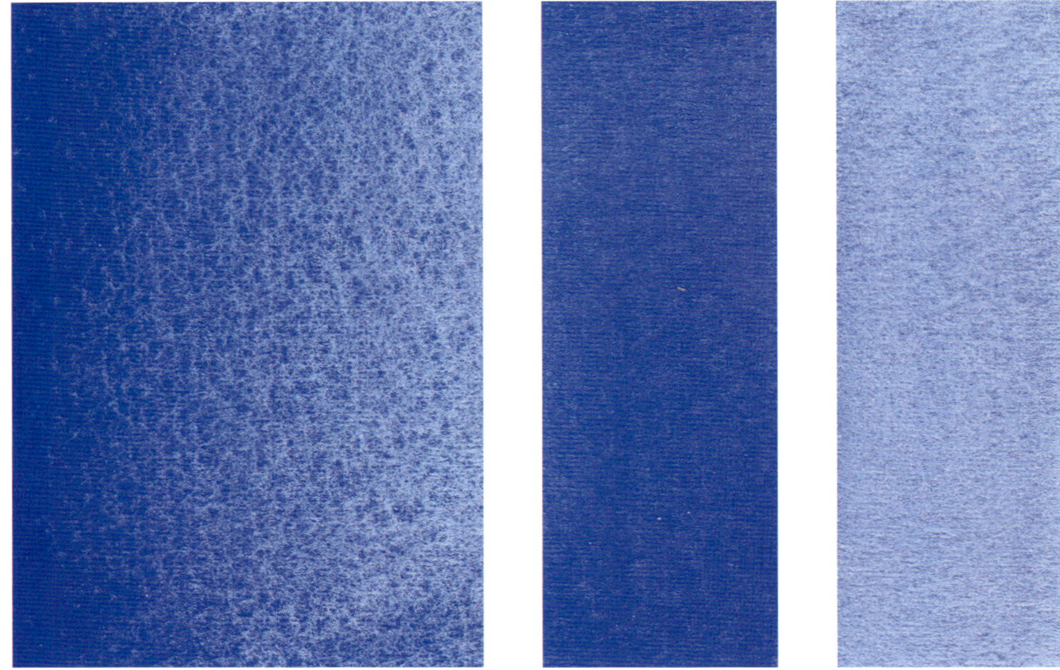

Blue PB29
Ultramarine Blue

Synthetic inorganic pigment from the polysulfurized sodium aluminosilicate family.

Perfectly stable in the light, and relatively opaque, this blue, which tends toward violet, can be found on the palettes of almost all watercolorists.

It granulates and also causes the colors that it is used with to granulate. Its unique shade and its granularity make it particularly interesting.

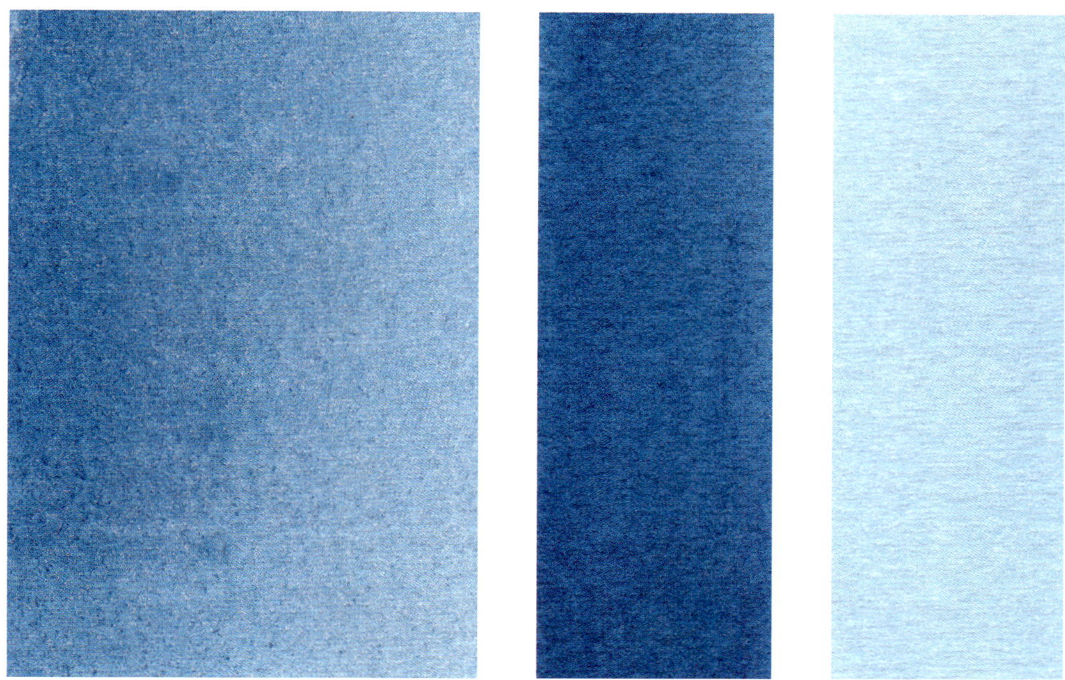

Blue PB27
Prussian Blue

Synthetic inorganic pigment from the polysulfurized ferric ferrocyanide family.

This dark blue has an interesting cool tone with hints of green. For this reason, it is essential for composing greens.

This color is very stable in light and is characterized by a lovely transparency and a strong coloring power. It is not granular.

Blue PB15:3
Phtalo Blue

Synthetic organic pigment from the copper phthalocyanine family.

Known mostly as phtalo blue, this color exists in two different shades, one tending toward red and the other toward green.

The copper phthalocyanine blues are identified under the nomenclature of PB15, which exists in six varieties, ranging from PB15:1 to PB15:6. Each shade is slightly different. We have chosen PB15:3, the greenest of the copper phthalocyanine blues.

This blue is like all the phthalocyanines: magnificently transparent, with remarkable coloring power, and with excellent light resistance. It is not granular.

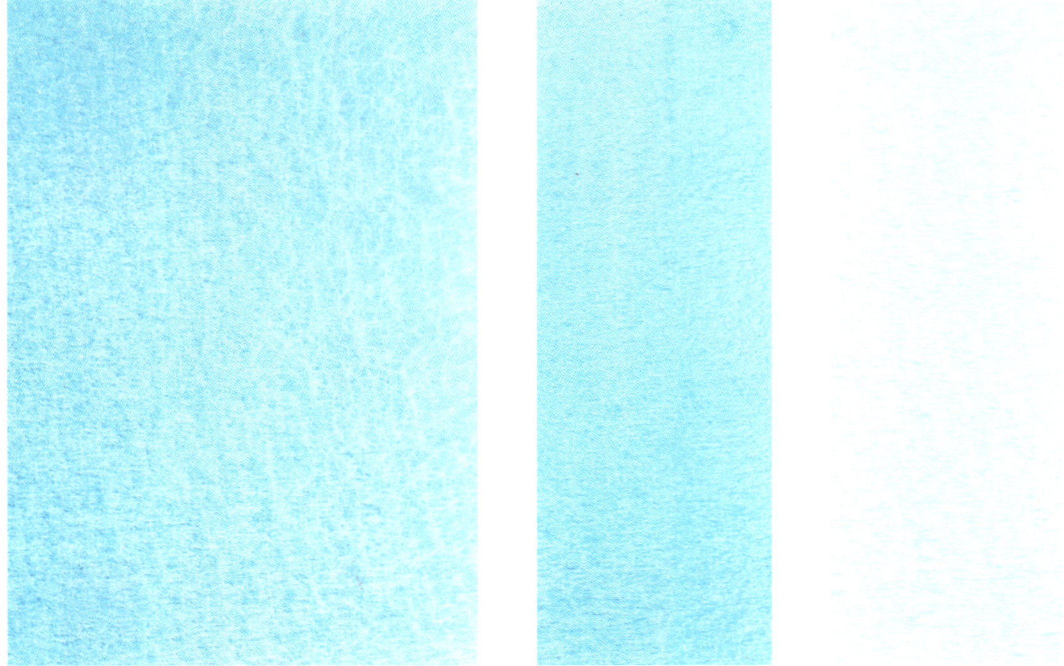

Blue PB35 or PB36
Cerulean Blue

Synthetic inorganic pigment from the family of cobalt stannates or of chromium and cobalt oxides.

Best known as true cerulean blue.

This pigment, which is based on cobalt, has as its foremost characteristic the fact that it granulates strongly. It is also a light blue that is reminiscent of sky blue. Some manufacturers offer imitations, because cobalt pigments are very expensive. But the pigmentary nomenclatures PB35 and PB36 will allow you to correctly identify the pigment. You have to be careful to choose a light shade of blue so that it will be clearly distinguished from the three other blues.

This blue is semi-transparent and excellently light resistant, but its coloring power is not as strong as that of the organic blues.

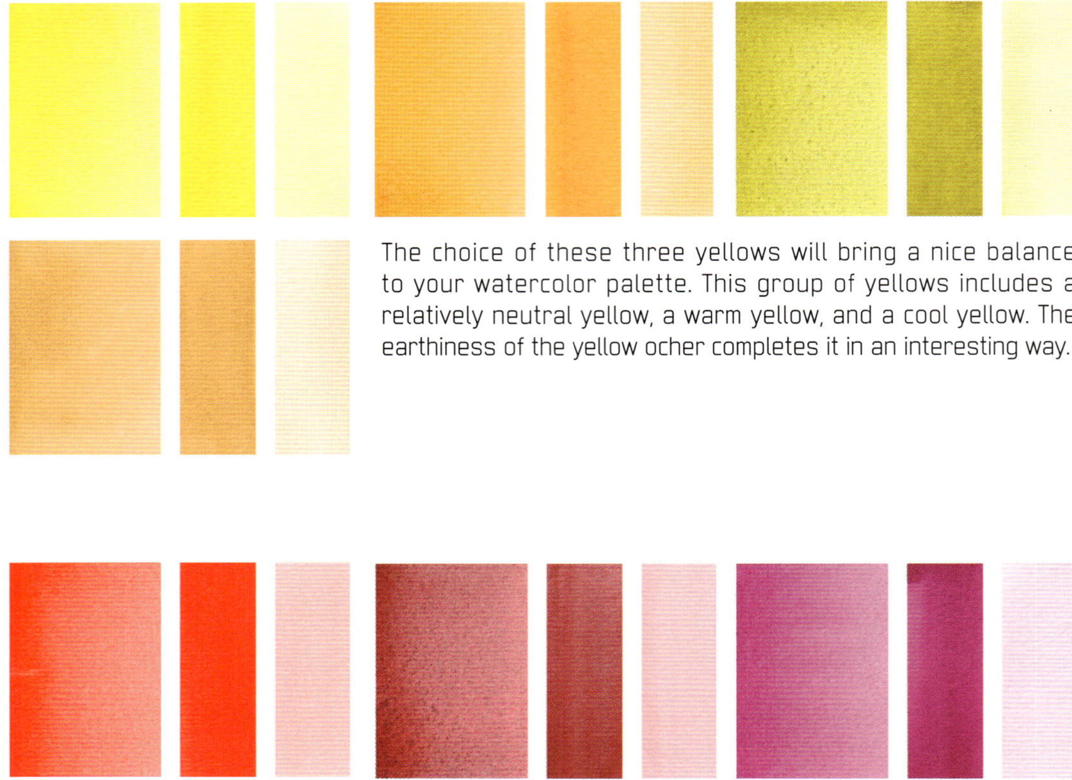

The choice of these three yellows will bring a nice balance
to your watercolor palette. This group of yellows includes a
relatively neutral yellow, a warm yellow, and a cool yellow. The
earthiness of the yellow ocher completes it in an interesting way.

These three reds complement each other beautifully. The scarlet
red (PR255) is indisputably the warmest and the most forthright.
The pyrrole red deep (PR264), which is cooler, will allow you to
obtain more restrained shades. As for the Isaro rose (PR122),
it has a shade that uniquely distinguishes it from the other two
reds and makes it essential for creating violet colors.

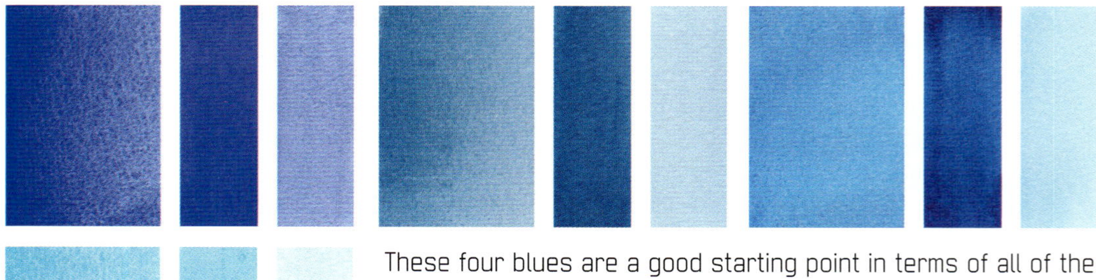

These four blues are a good starting point in terms of all of the
secondary colors that they will allow you to obtain. Phtalo blue
(PB15:3) is the most neutral, ultramarine blue (PB29) the warmest,
and Prussian blue (PB27) the coolest. Cerulean blue (PB35 or
PB36), with its lightness, counterbalances the deep color of the
phtalo blue and the Prussian blue.

The Basic Palette,
by Manufacturer

The following table will allow you to find the equivalents of the colors that were presented on the preceding pages. When the name of the color is given in pink, that means that the shade is similar to the colors we have discussed but is not identical to them. In some cases, no equivalence is given. In that case, that means that the manufacturer offers a similar color but one that is not monopigmentary, or else that the shade is not part of that manufacturer's offerings at all.

		BLOCKX	DANIEL SMITH	ISARO	REMBRANDT	SCHMINCKE	SENNELIER	WINSOR & NEWTON
PIGMENTARY NOMENCLATURE	PY154	Primary Yellow	Hansa Yellow Light (PY3)	Isaro Yellow Light	Azo Yellow Light	Pure Yellow	Primary Yellow (PY74)	Winsor Yellow
	PY110	Gamboge (PY65)	Permanent Yellow Deep	Saffron Yellow	Azo Yellow Deep	Yellow Orange		Winsor Yellow Deep (PY65)
	PY129		Rich Green Gold	Chartreuse Yellow	Azomethine Green Yellow		Brown Green	Green Gold
	PY42 or PY43	Yellow Ocher	French Ocher		Raw Sienna	Yellow Ocher	Yellow Ocher	Yellow Ocher
	PR255	Pyrrolo Red	Pyrrol Scarlet	Scarlet Red	Permanent Red Medium	Vermilion	Rose Dore Madder Laker	Winsor Red (PR254)
	PR264	Crimson Lake	Pyrrol Crimson	Pyrrole Red Deep	Carmine	Ruby Red Deep		Winsor Red Deep
	PR122	Quinacridone Magenta	Quinacridone Lilac	Isaro Rose	Quinacridone Rose Magenta	Purple Magenta	Helios Purple	Quinacridone Magenta
	PB29	Fr. Ultramarine Blue Light or Deep	Ultramarine Blue	Ultramarine Blue	French Ultramarine	French Ultramarine	French Ultramarine Blue	French Ultramarine
	PB27	Prussian Blue	Prussian Blue	Prussian Blue	Prussian Blue	Prussian Blue	Prussian Blue	Prussian Blue
	PB15:3	Primary Blue	Phthalo Blue (GS)	Phtalo Blue	Phthalo Blue Greenish	Helio Cerulean	Phthalocyanine Turquoise	Winsor Blue
	PB35 - PB36	Cerulean Grey (PB35) or Cerulean Blue (PB36)	Cerulean Blue	Cerulean Blue	Cerulean Blue	Cobalt Cerulean (PB36) or Cobalt Azure (PB35)	Cerulean Blue (PB28)	Cerulean Blue

2

Experimenting with Color Mixing

A Theoretical Approach

It is hard to prescribe precise recipes for obtaining one particular mixture. In fact, depending on which brand of watercolors you choose, the pigmentary concentration may be lesser or greater. Every manufacturer has its own manufacturing secrets, which you will have to adapt to as you get to know the behavior and characteristics of the colors offered by that company.

When you create a mixture, the most important thing is to try to use as few colors as possible in your mixture.

The goal is to approximate the desired shades, because when you are painting, you don't have to create something that is identical to your model. A similar shade will often be perfectly adequate.

Expanding the Range of Primary Colors

Every color brings a chromatic richness to the other primary colors in the same shade. Because each primary color includes complementary hues, the chromatic range of reds, blues, and yellows is broadly covered.

BLUES

Prussian blue (PB27) gives an interesting depth to ultramarine blue (PB29). As for phtalo blue (PB15:3), when combined with ultramarine blue it creates a magnificent, deep, luminous ultramarine.

Cerulean blue (PB36) and ultramarine blue combine to create a blue that is very close to true cobalt blue.

The addition of a hint of phtalo blue or Prussian blue to cerulean blue creates shades of turquoise cerulean blue, which are similar to those offered in the color charts of some color manufacturers.

ULTRAMARINE BLUE (PB29) DEEPENED WITH PRUSSIAN BLUE (PB27)

ULTRAMARINE BLUE (PB29) DEEPENED WITH PHTALO BLUE (PB15:3)

TRUE COBALT BLUE

CERULEAN BLUE (PB36) DEEPENED WITH A HINT OF ULTRAMARINE BLUE (PB29)

CERULEAN BLUE (PB36) + PHTALO BLUE (PB15:3)

CERULEAN BLUE (PB36) + PRUSSIAN BLUE (PB27)

REDS

When they are mixed together, the three reds that have been chosen here offer the possibility of harmoniously expanding the red chromatic scale.

Scarlet red (PR255) and pyrrole red deep (PR264) make it possible to obtain a continuous range running from a vibrant red to a somber red.

Isaro rose (PR122) also nuances scarlet red very nicely and makes it possible to deepen it.

Isaro rose and pyrrole red deep, both of them cool colors, create a gamut of pink to red within which certain shades are reminiscent of strawberry red. Isaro rose can also be darkened using pyrrole red deep.

SCARLET RED (PR255) DARKENED USING PYRROLE RED DEEP (PR264) IN DIFFERENT PROPORTIONS

SCARLET RED (PR255) DEEPENED WITH ISARO ROSE (PR122)

ISARO ROSE (PR122) DARKENED WITH PYRROLE RED DEEP (PR264)

YELLOWS

The mixture of Isaro yellow light (PY154) and saffron yellow (PY110) makes it possible to achieve a wide range of bright, warm yellow.

Saffron yellow can be wonderfully mixed with yellow ocher. It accentuates the warm notes of this earthy yellow while retaining its brightness. Isaro yellow light, meanwhile, is perfect for lightening yellow ocher (PY42 or PY43).

A hint of chartreuse yellow (PY129) in the Isaro yellow light cools the latter down. And inversely, Isaro yellow light easily lightens the chartreuse yellow.

YELLOW OCHER (PY42 OR PY43) WITH A LITTLE BIT OF SAFFRON YELLOW (PY110) IN DIFFERENT PROPORTIONS

YELLOW OCHER (PY42 OR PY43) LIGHTENED WITH ISARO YELLOW LIGHT (PY154)

ISARO YELLOW (PY154) LIGHT AUGMENTED WITH A TOUCH OF CHARTREUSE YELLOW (PY129) TO COOL IT DOWN

CHARTREUSE YELLOW (PY129) LIGHTENED WITH ISARO YELLOW LIGHT (PY154)

Creating the Range of Secondary Colors

We will focus here on the production of the secondary colors, in other words the range of greens, violets, and oranges. The illustrations will give you an idea of the gamut of colors that can be obtained by combining two primary colors. However, please do note that depending on the brand of watercolors you use, the quality of your paper, and the proportion of water in your mixture, the shades that you obtain my vary lightly from the colors shown here.

IMPLEMENTATION

In the following pages, the proportions in the mixtures will be given in the form of percentages. We have worked using drops of color (also called parts) in order to indicate the dosages as accurately as possible. But there is nothing to stop you from working with colors in pots.

The main objective is to understand which colors should be chosen in order to produce the range of desired shades. If you want to get bright, vibrant secondary colors, you will not use the same primary colors as you would if you were wanting to create more subdued, less shimmering secondary colors.

How the dosages are indicated:

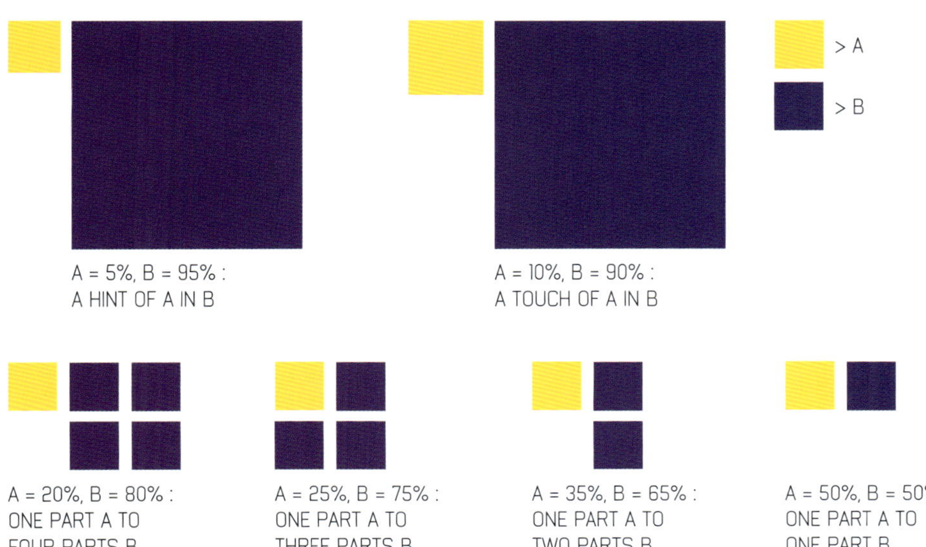

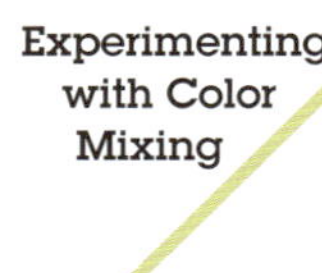

GREENS

The organic blues (Prussian and phtalo), combined with the organic yellows (Isaro light, orange saffron, and chartreuse), produce even, bright greens. The light cool notes of Isaro yellow light (PY154) and the stronger ones of chartreuse yellow (PY129) combine perfectly with these two blues. Phtalo blue (PB15:3) will produce the most vibrant greens, while Prussian blue (PB27) will create the most natural greens.

The red note contained in saffron yellow (PY110) softens the brightness of the mixtures and, thus, produces more muted greens.

The two mineral blues, ultramarine and cerulean, produce structured greens with interesting effects. The presence of red in the ultramarine blue (PB29) indirectly unbalances the harmony of the mixture. This is why, when using ultramarine blue, the range of greens that one obtains is always more restrained than those produced by Prussian blue and phtalo blue.

Yellow ocher (PY42 or PY43), combined with any blue, easily produces earthy, natural greens.

Of all the yellows, it is chartreuse yellow (PY129) that, combined with Prussian blue and phtalo blue, produces sumptuous greens of unique and singular vibrancy.

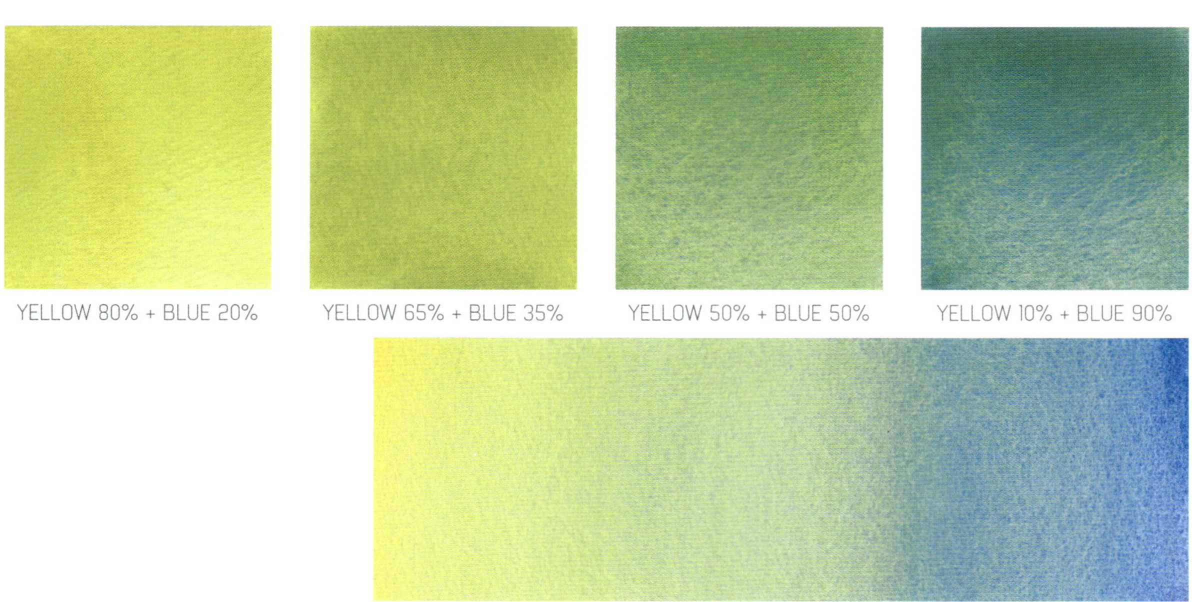

Isaro yellow light (PY154) + ultramarine blue (PB29)

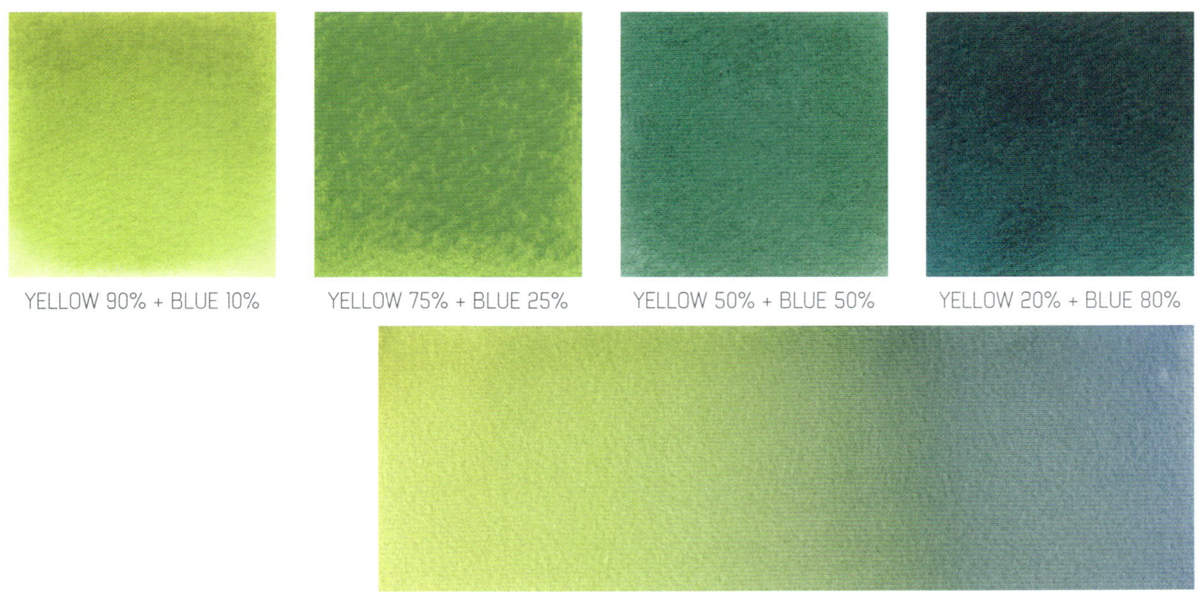

Isaro yellow light (PY154) + Prussian blue (PB27)

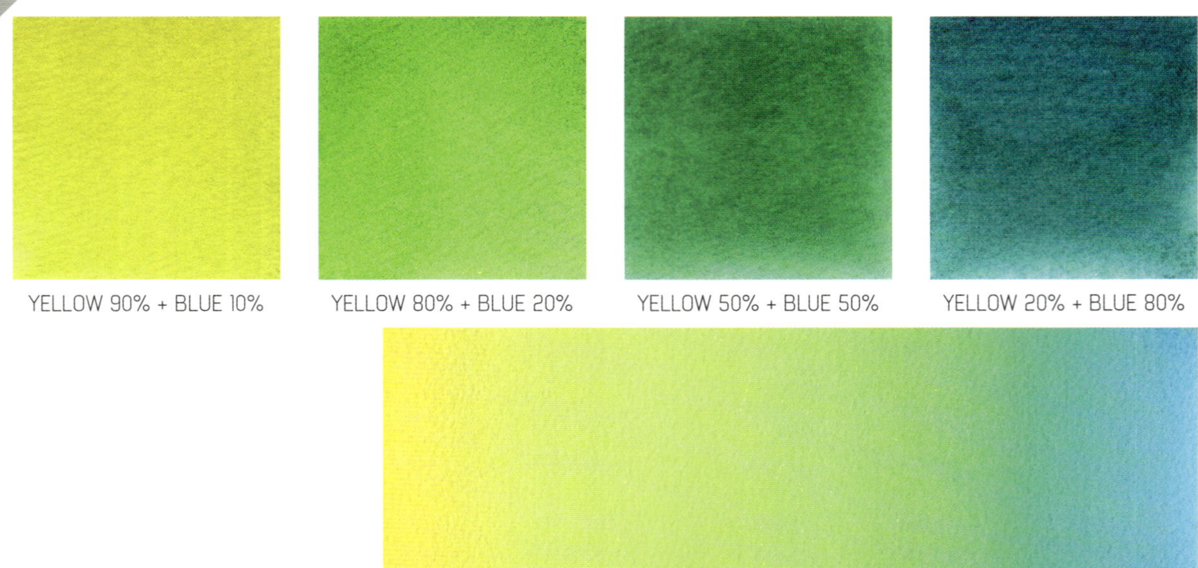

Isaro yellow light (PY154) + phtalo blue (PB15:3)

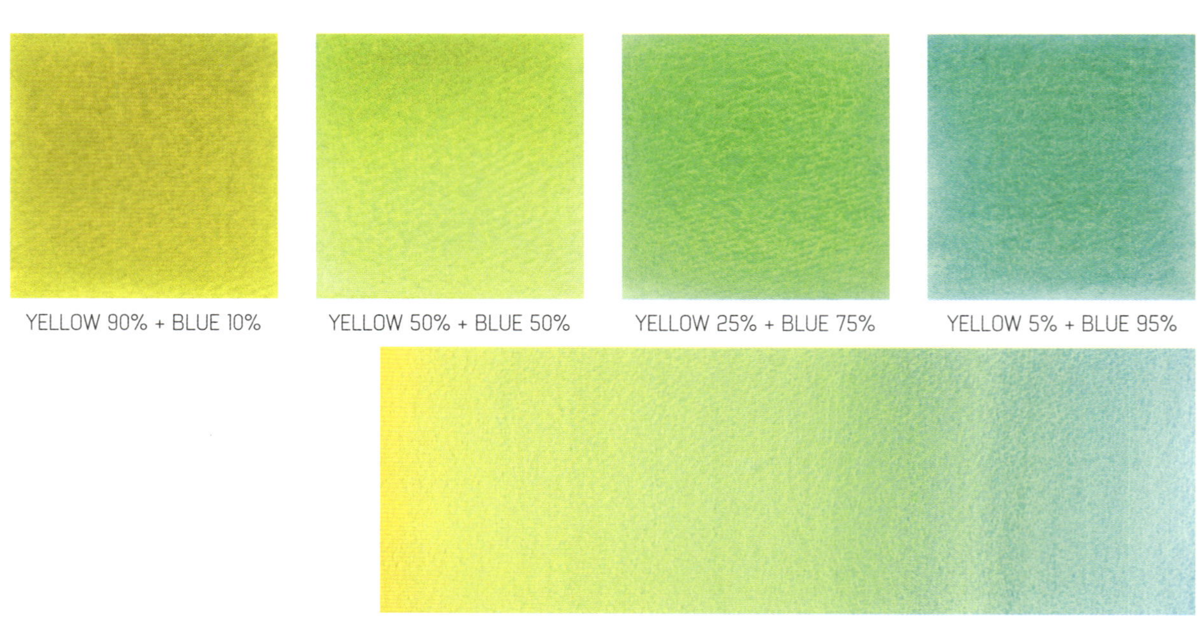

Isaro yellow light (PY154) + cerulean blue (PB35)

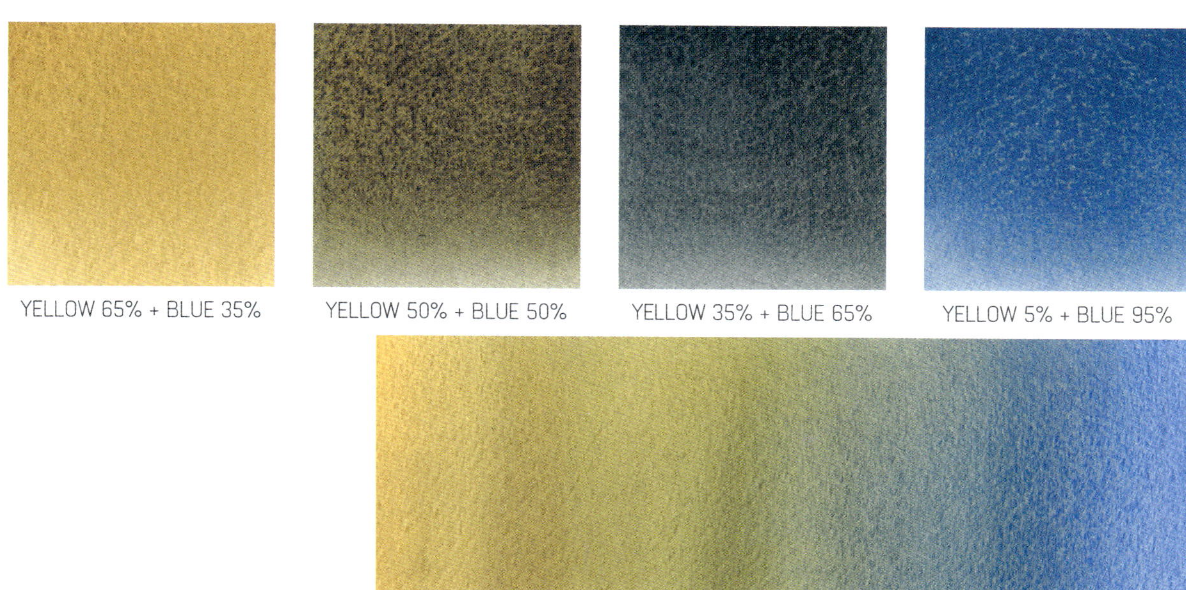

Saffron yellow (PY110) + ultramarine blue (PB29)

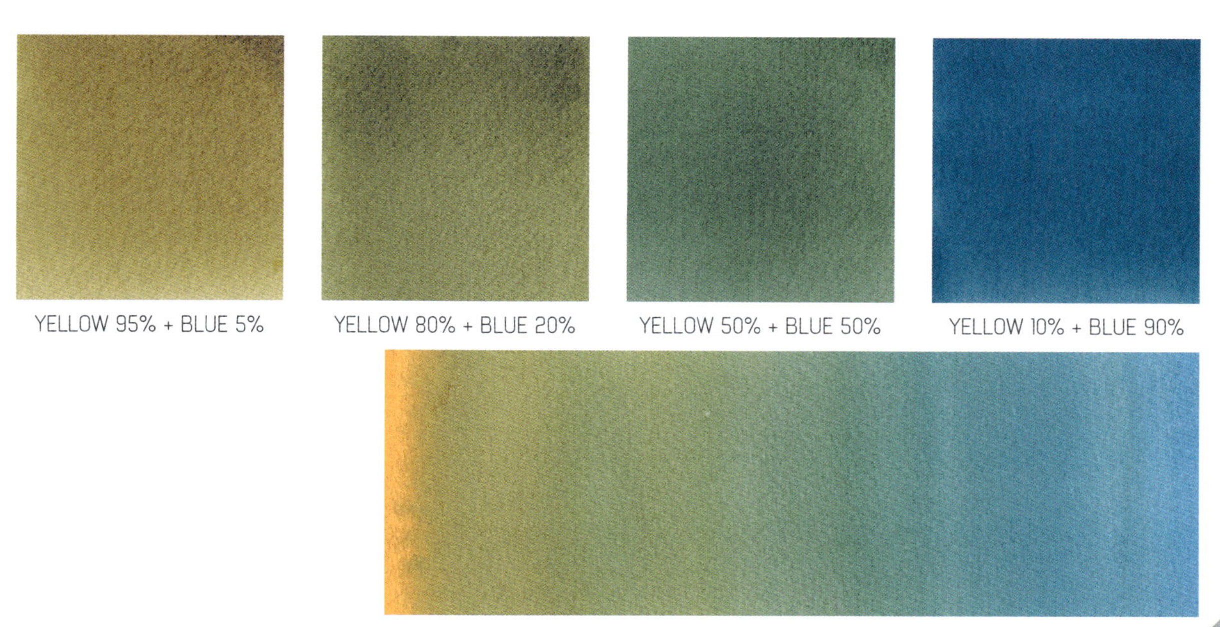

Saffron yellow (PY110) + Prussian blue (PB27)

YELLOW 90% + BLUE 10%

YELLOW 80% + BLUE 20%

YELLOW 50% + BLUE 50%

YELLOW 5% + BLUE 95%

Saffron yellow (PY110) + phtalo blue (PB15:3)

YELLOW 80% + BLUE 20%

YELLOW 65% + BLUE 35%

YELLOW 50% + BLUE 50%

YELLOW 5% + BLUE 95%

Saffron yellow (PY110) + cerulean blue (PB35)

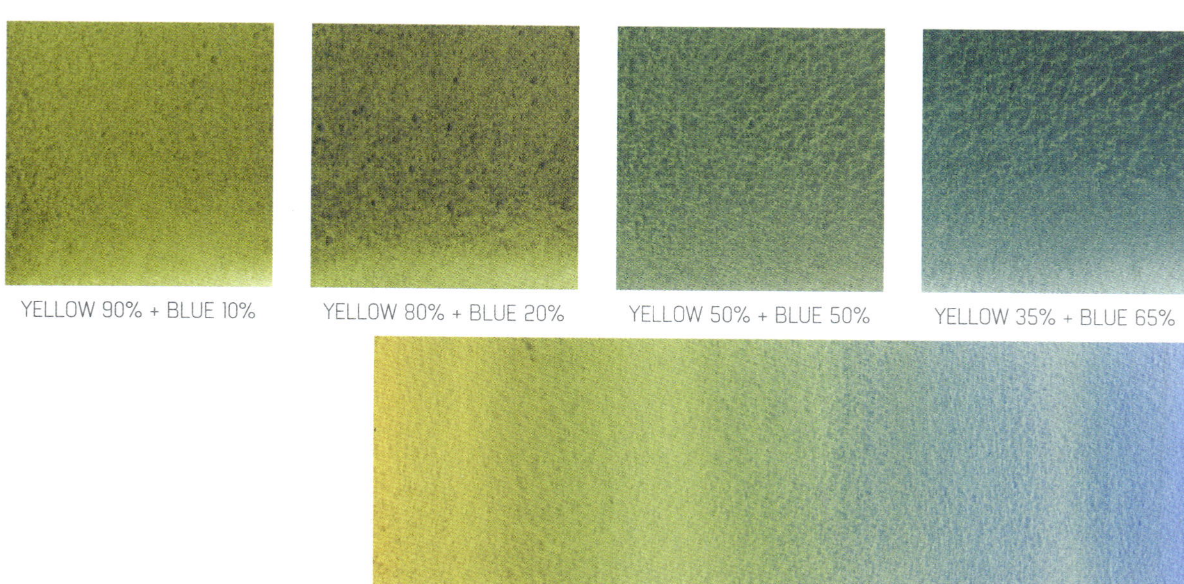

Chartreuse yellow (PY129) + ultramarine blue (PB29)

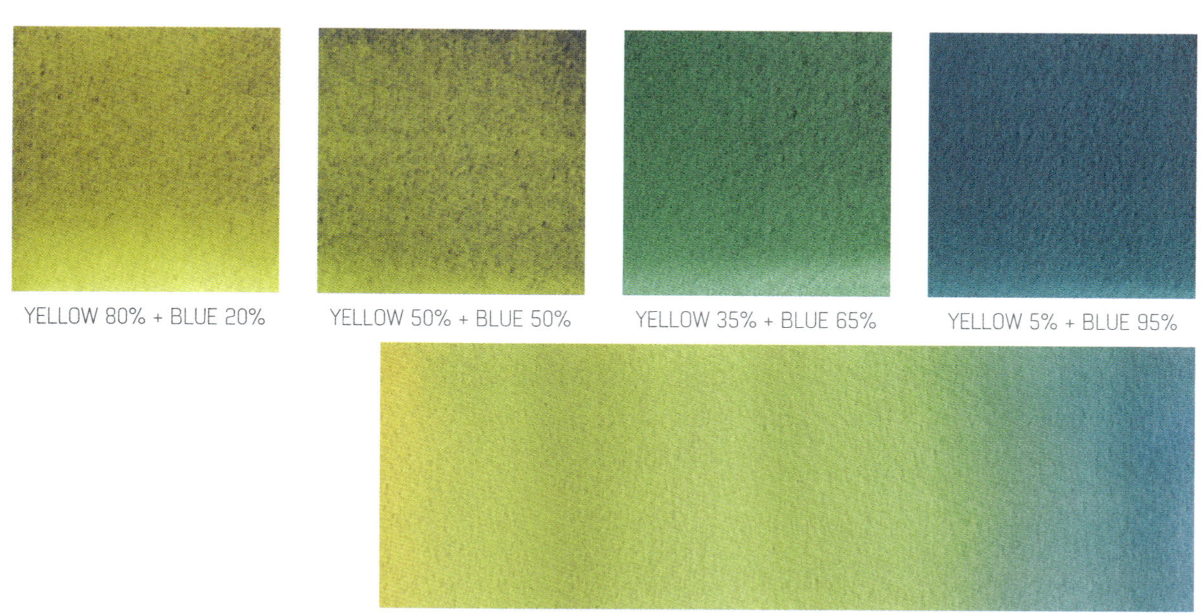

Chartreuse yellow (PY129) + Prussian blue (PB27)

YELLOW 95% + BLUE 5%　　YELLOW 80% + BLUE 20%　　YELLOW 50% + BLUE 50%　　YELLOW 20% + BLUE 80%

Chartreuse yellow (PY129) + phtalo blue (PB15:3)

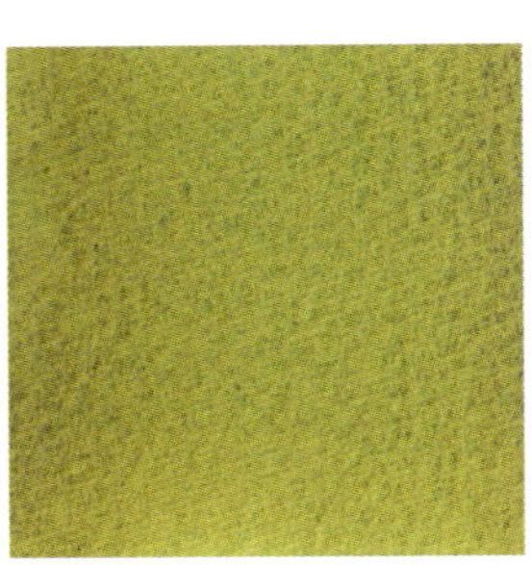

YELLOW 90% + BLUE 10%　　YELLOW 65% + BLUE 35%　　YELLOW 50% + BLUE 50%　　YELLOW 5% + BLUE 95%

Chartreuse yellow (PY129) + cerulean blue (PB35)

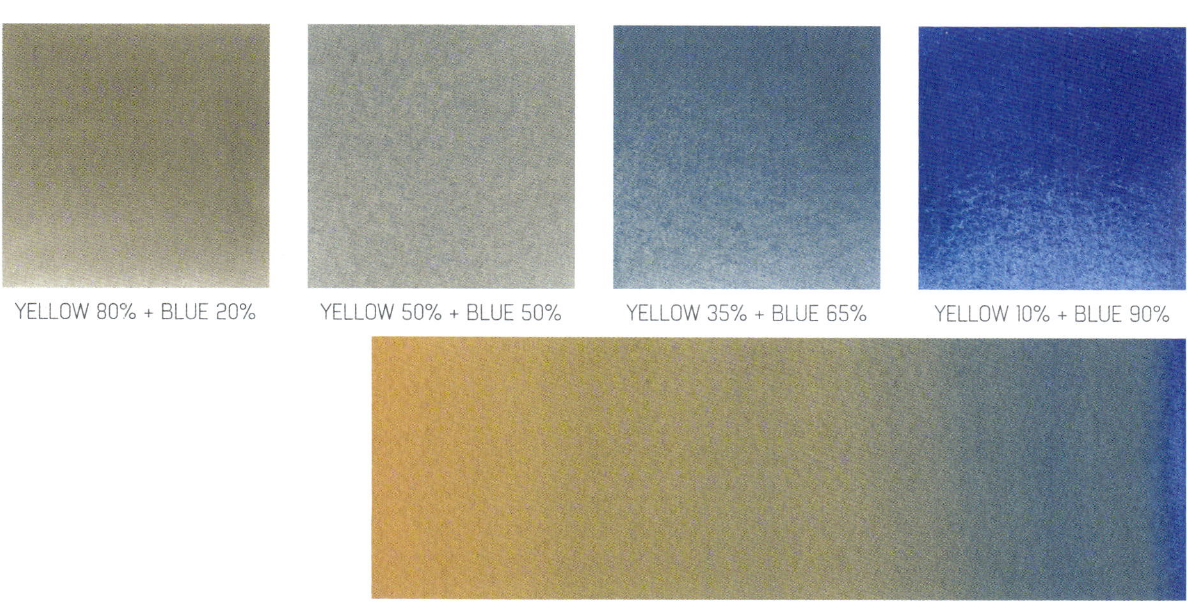

Yellow ocher (PY42) + ultramarine blue (PB29)

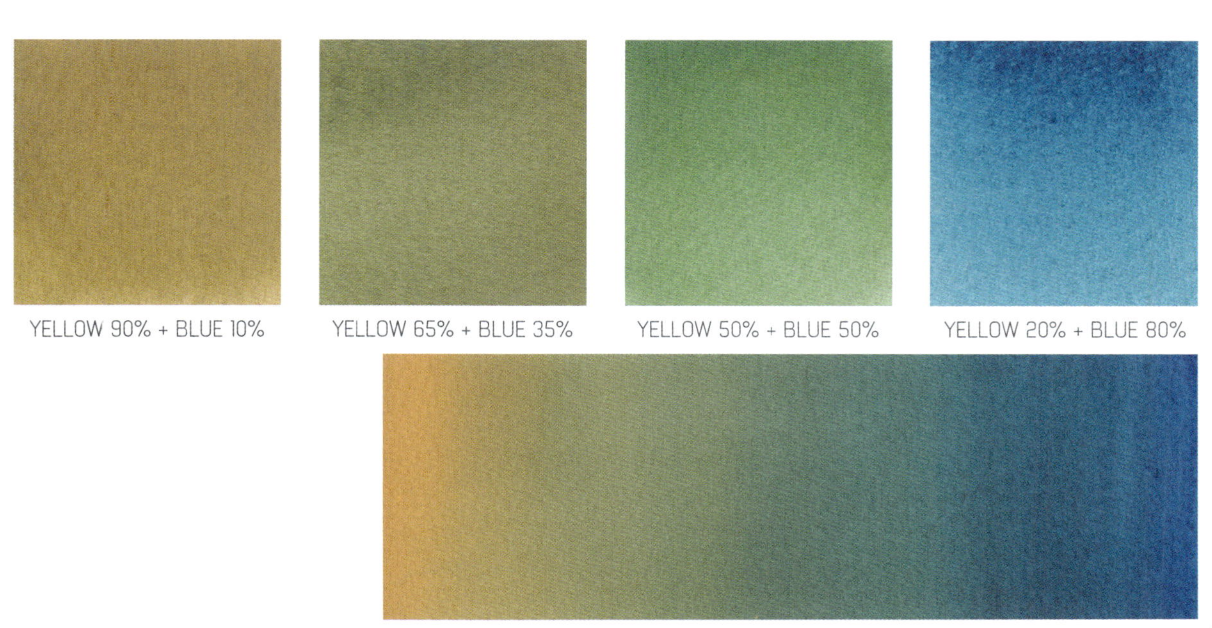

Yellow ocher (PY42) + Prussian blue (PB27)

YELLOW 95% + BLUE 5% YELLOW 80% + BLUE 20% YELLOW 50% + BLUE 50% YELLOW 20% + BLUE 80%

Yellow ocher (PY42) + phtalo blue (PB15:3)

YELLOW 80% + BLUE 20% YELLOW 50% + BLUE 50% YELLOW 35% + BLUE 65% YELLOW 10% + BLUE 90%

Yellow ocher (PY42) + cerulean blue (PB35)

VIOLETS

Indisputably, Isaro rose (PR122), combined with all of the blues, offers violets of great beauty, some of which possess a magnificent purity of tone.

Scarlet red (PR255) is the least suitable for creating violet colors. However, it does allow you to create violets that tend toward browns, which are reminiscent of the range of brown and violet iron oxides. This can be explained by the fact that scarlet red has an underlying note of yellow. Because yellow is the color opposite violet on the color wheel, the addition of this color, even indirectly, breaks up the shade.

As for pyrrole red deep (PR264), its rose note allows it, when mixed with the blues, to create a very lovely range of dark violet tending toward eggplant.

You will also notice that a touch of blue added to scarlet red or pyrrole red deep will deepen them. Blues can be deepened in the same way, by adding a hint of red.

The two mineral blues, which, as we have seen, are granular, create less uniform violets than those created using organic blues.

The chromatic range of the violets is broadly covered through the creation of deep, dark violets, brown violets, and bright violets.

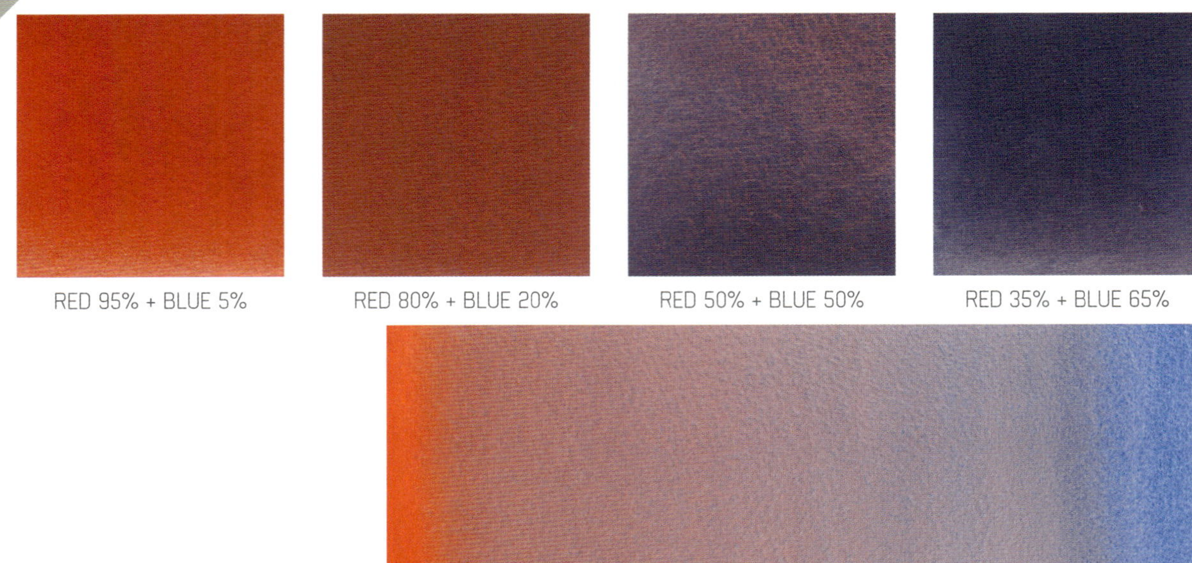

Scarlet red (PR255) + ultramarine blue (PB29)

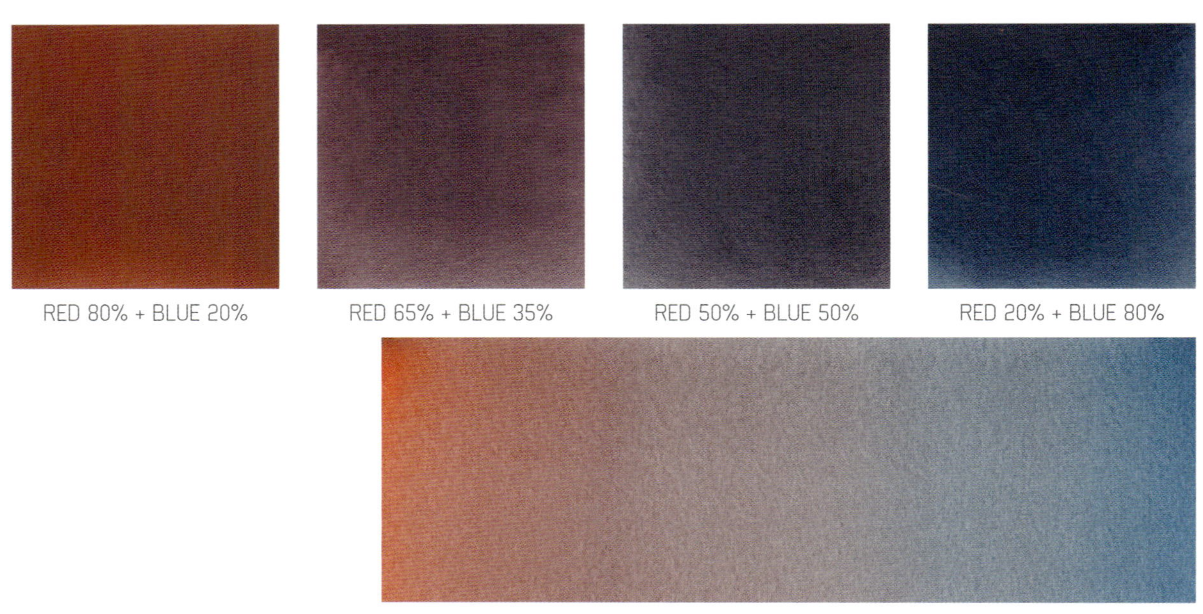

Scarlet red (PR255) + Prussian blue (PB27)

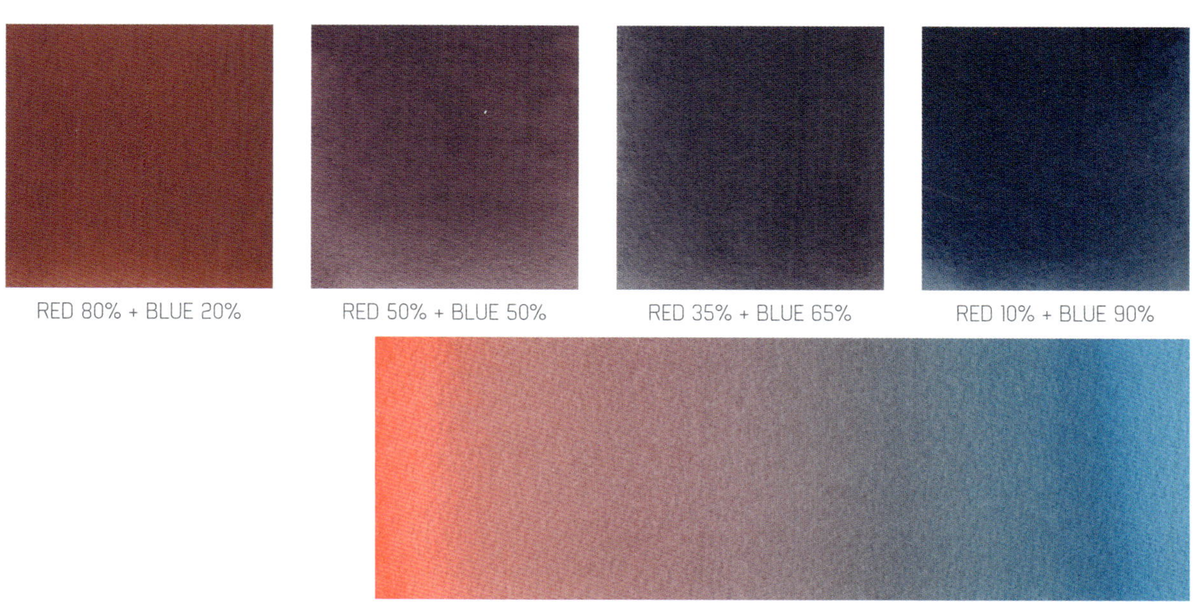

RED 80% + BLUE 20%   RED 50% + BLUE 50%   RED 35% + BLUE 65%   RED 10% + BLUE 90%

Scarlet red (PR255) + phtalo blue (PB15:3)

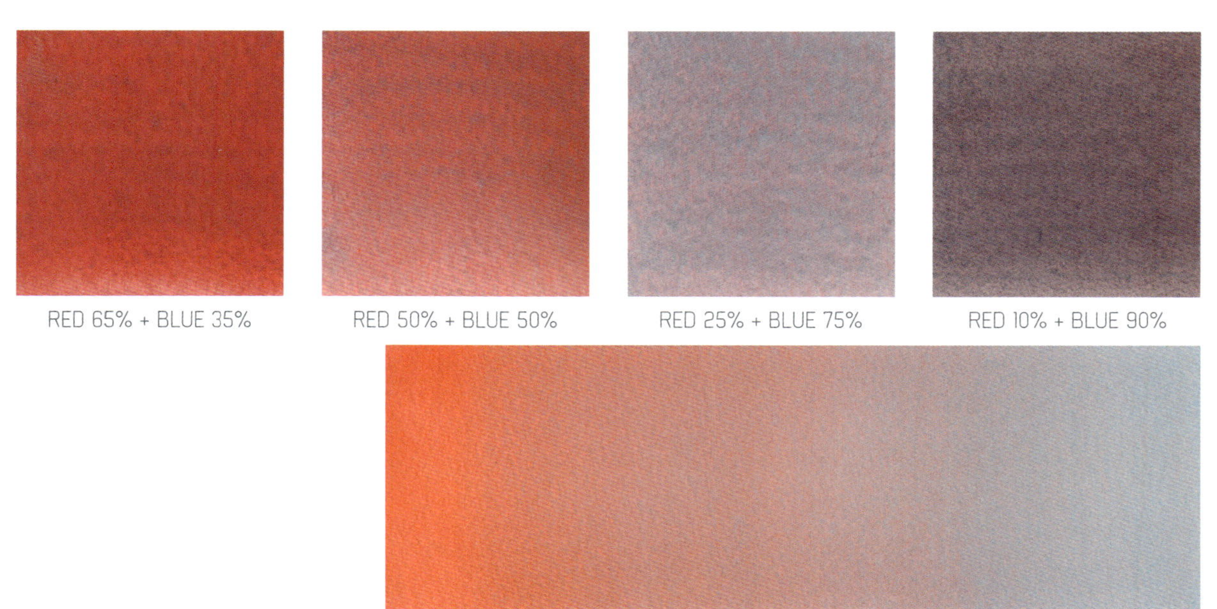

RED 65% + BLUE 35%   RED 50% + BLUE 50%   RED 25% + BLUE 75%   RED 10% + BLUE 90%

Scarlet red (PR255) + cerulean blue (PB35)

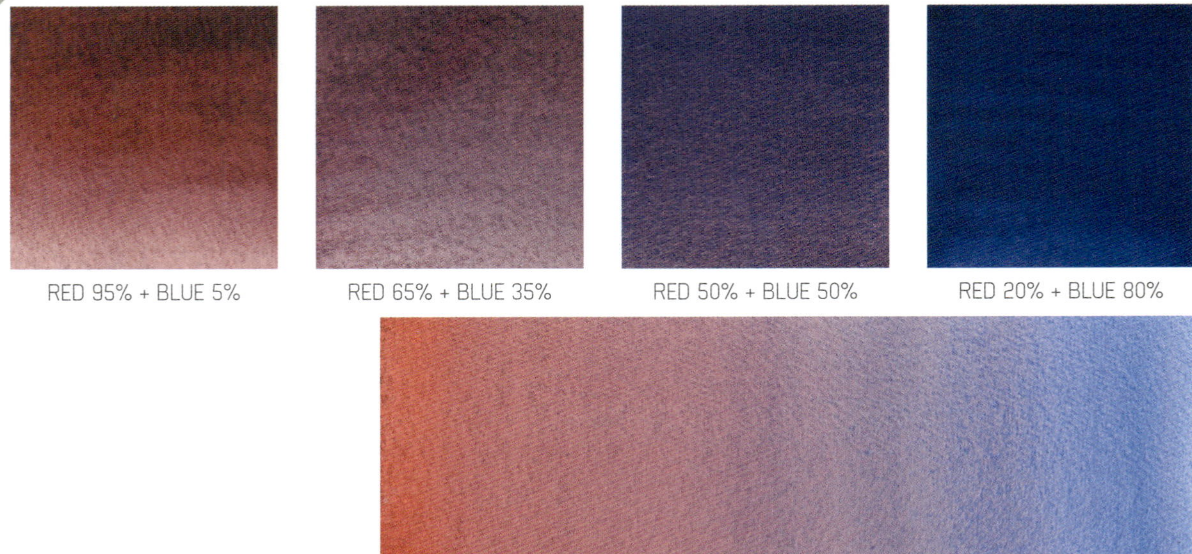

Pyrrole red deep (PR264) + ultramarine blue (PB29)

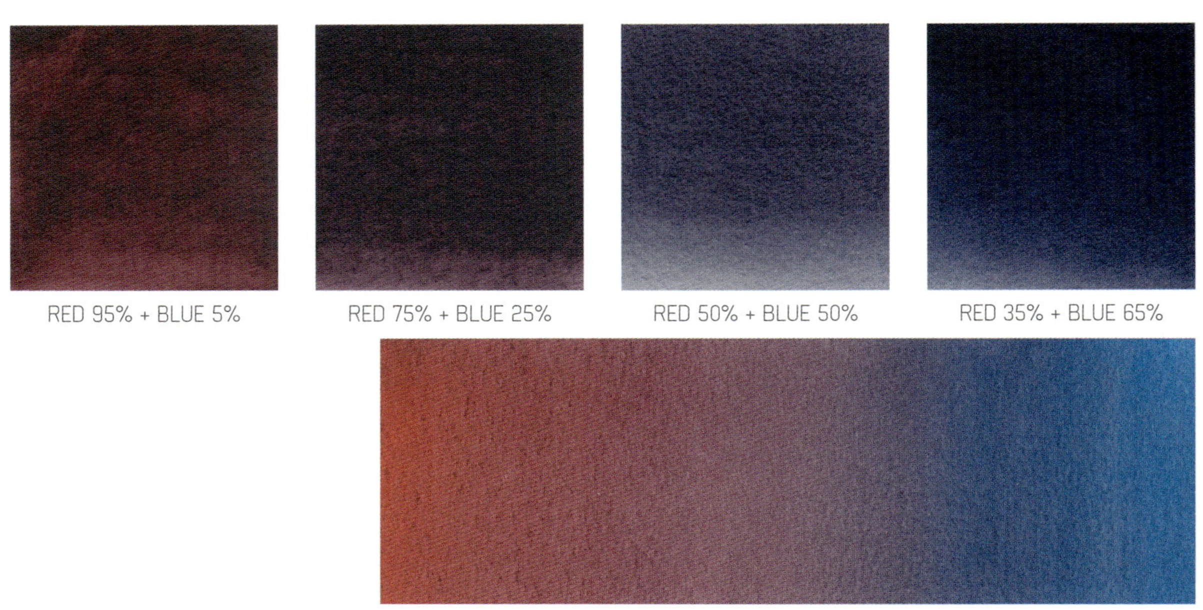

Pyrrole red deep (PR264) + Prussian blue (PB27)

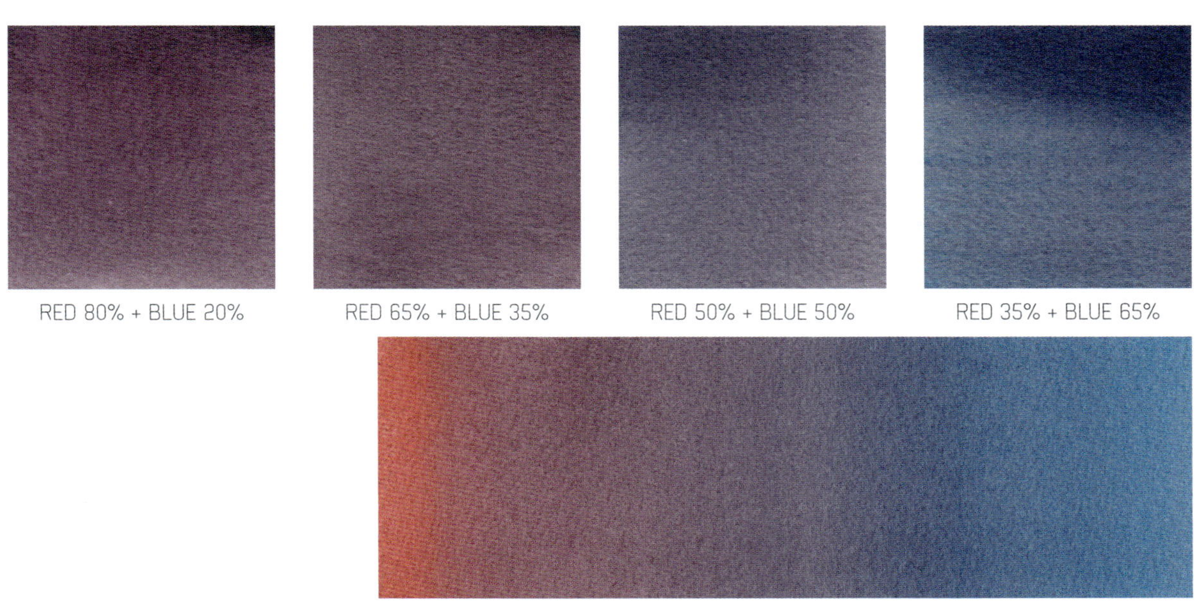

Pyrrole red deep (PR264) + phtalo blue (PB15:3)

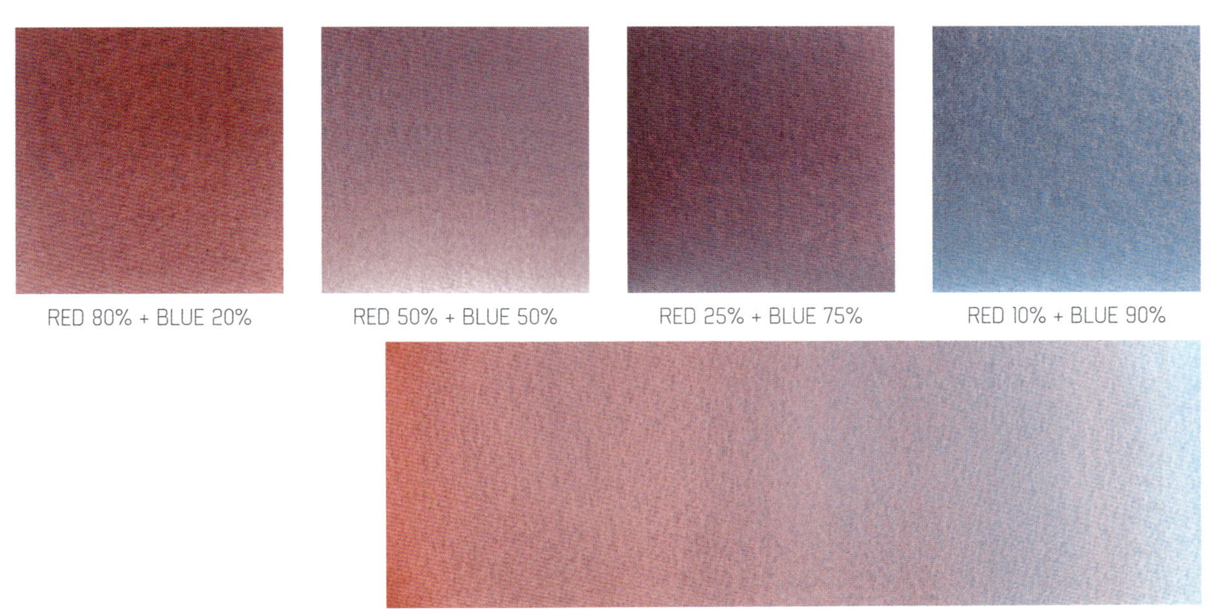

Pyrrole red deep (PR264) + cerulean blue (PB35)

ROSE 90% + BLUE 10%   ROSE 75% + BLUE 25%   ROSE 50% + BLUE 50%   ROSE 10% + BLUE 90%

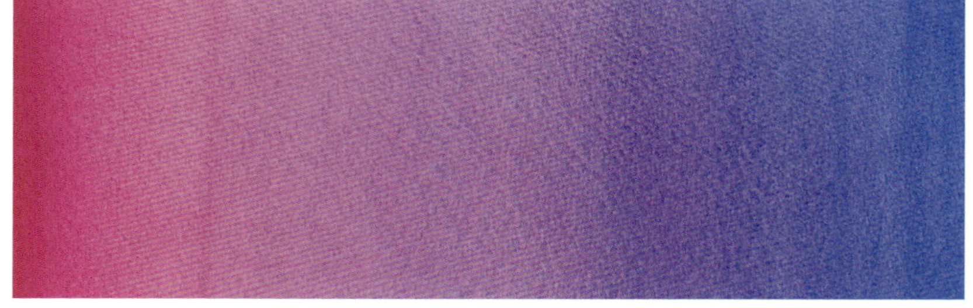

Isaro rose (PR122) + ultramarine blue (PB29)

ROSE 95% + BLUE 5%   ROSE 80% + BLUE 20%   ROSE 65% + BLUE 35%   ROSE 50% + BLUE 50%

Isaro rose (PR122) + Prussian blue (PB27)

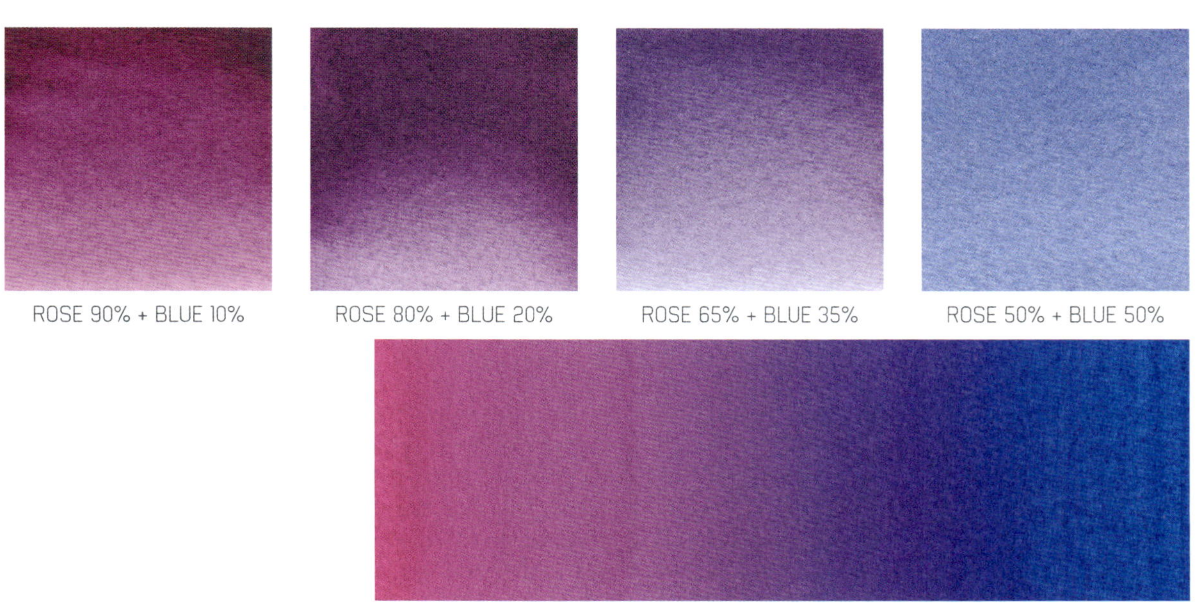

Isaro rose (PR122) + phtalo blue (PB15:3)

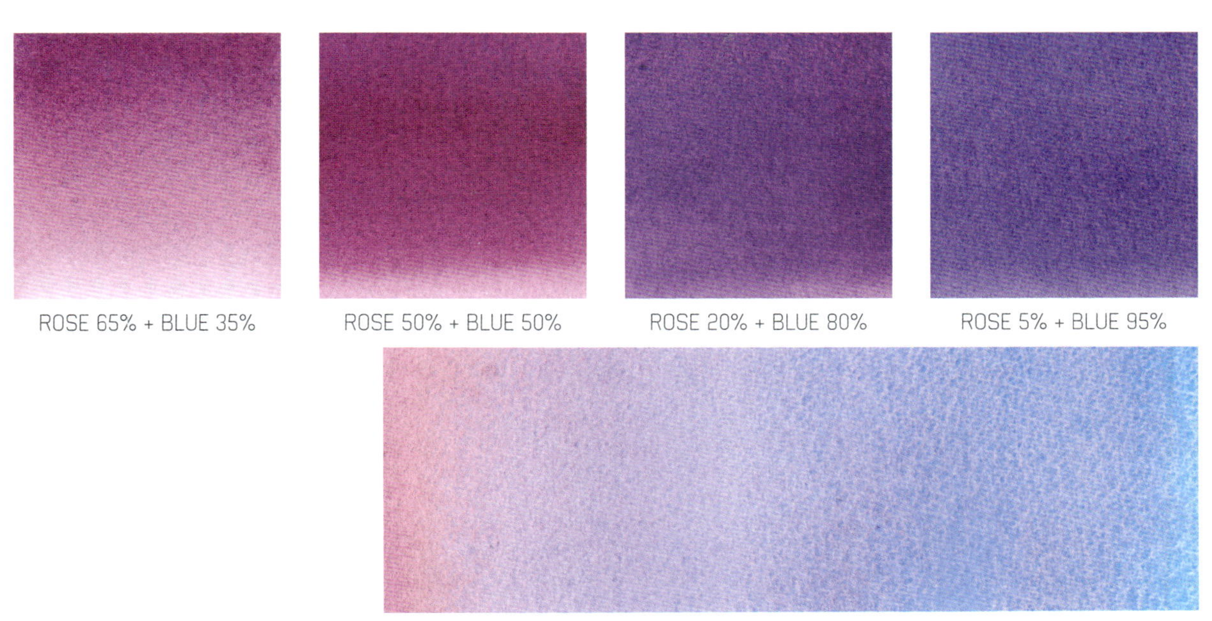

Isaro rose (PR122) + cerulean blue (PB35)

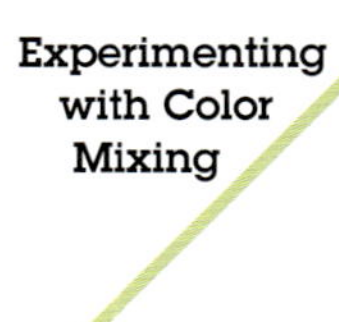

ORANGES

Of all the yellows that we have chosen, it is saffron yellow (PY110), with its very sustained note of orange, that makes it possible, when combined with scarlet red (PR255), to create very bright oranges. This same yellow, when combined with pyrrole red deep (PR264) or Isaro rose (PR122), produces interesting orangeish reds. With just the right proportions, a drop of pyrrole red deep in saffron yellow makes it possible to create an orange close to that of quinacridone, which is missing from manufacturers' color assortments because that pigment is no longer produced today.

Isaro yellow light (PY154) also offers a lovely range of bright oranges, especially when combined with scarlet red.

As for chartreuse yellow (PY129), its cool note pulls color mixtures toward interesting yellow-orangeish browns.

And with yellow ocher (PY42), the shades that you can produce are more or less bright earthy oranges.

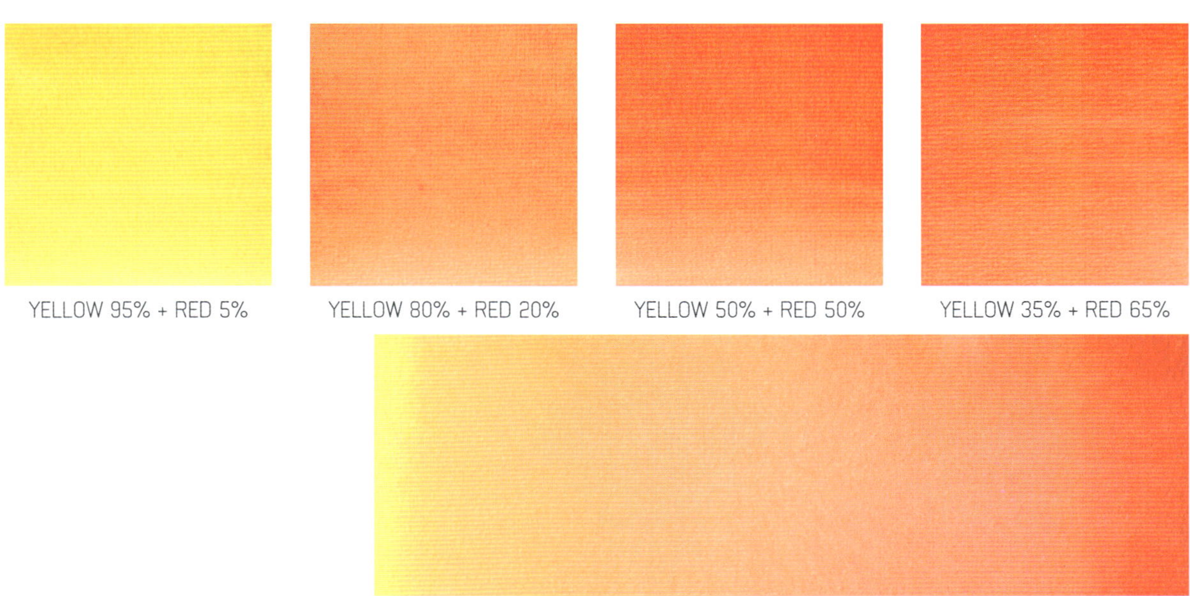

Isaro yellow light (PY154) + scarlet red (PR255)

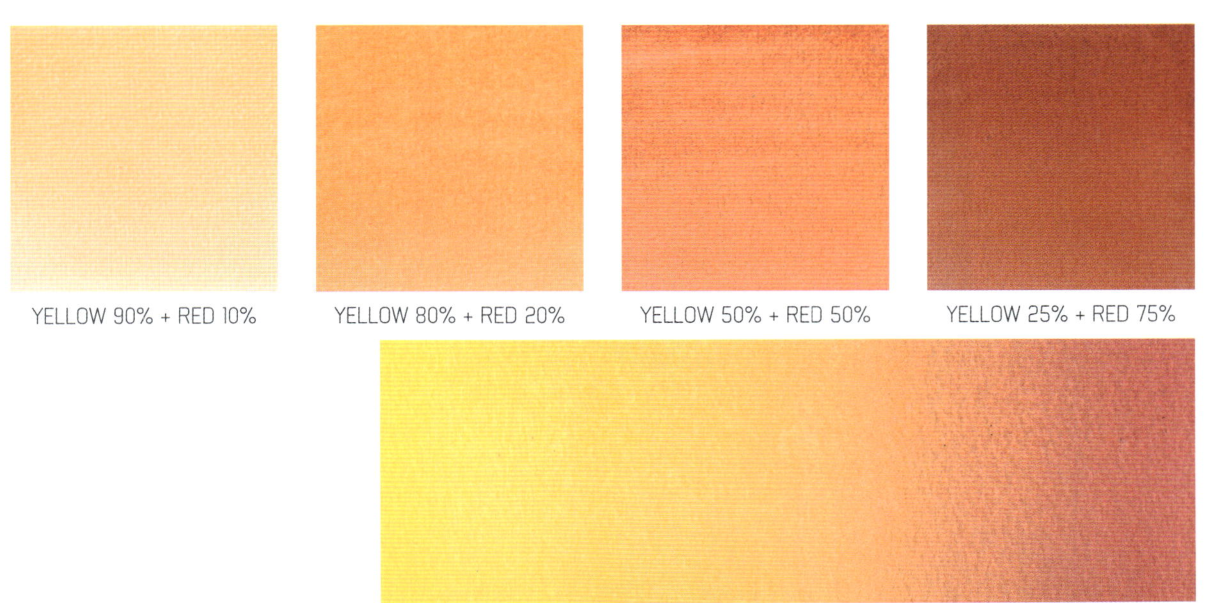

Isaro yellow light (PY154) + pyrrole red deep (PR264)

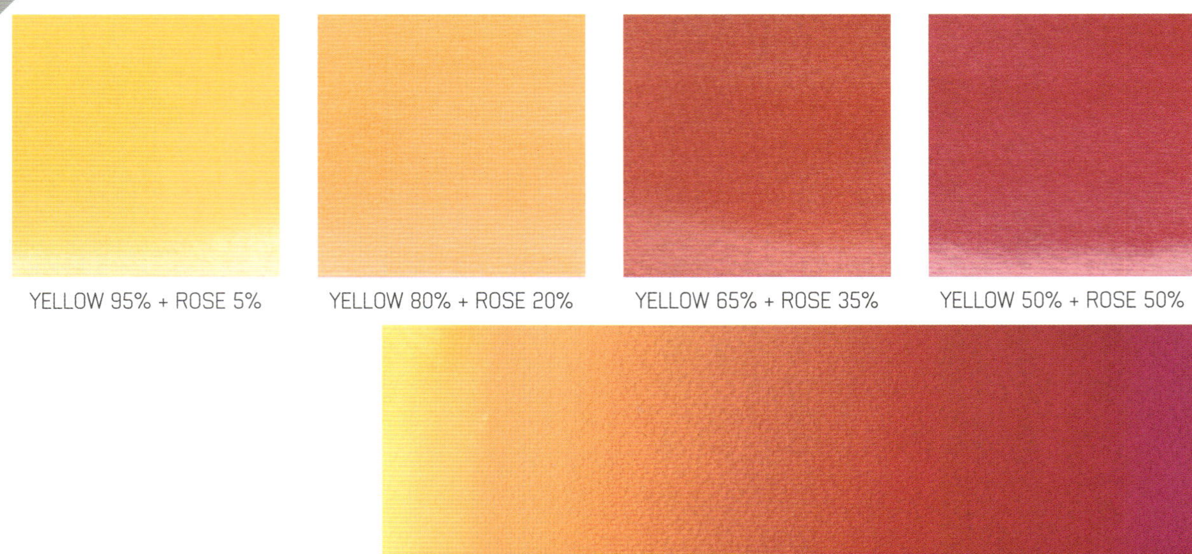

Isaro yellow light (PY154) + Isaro rose (PR122)

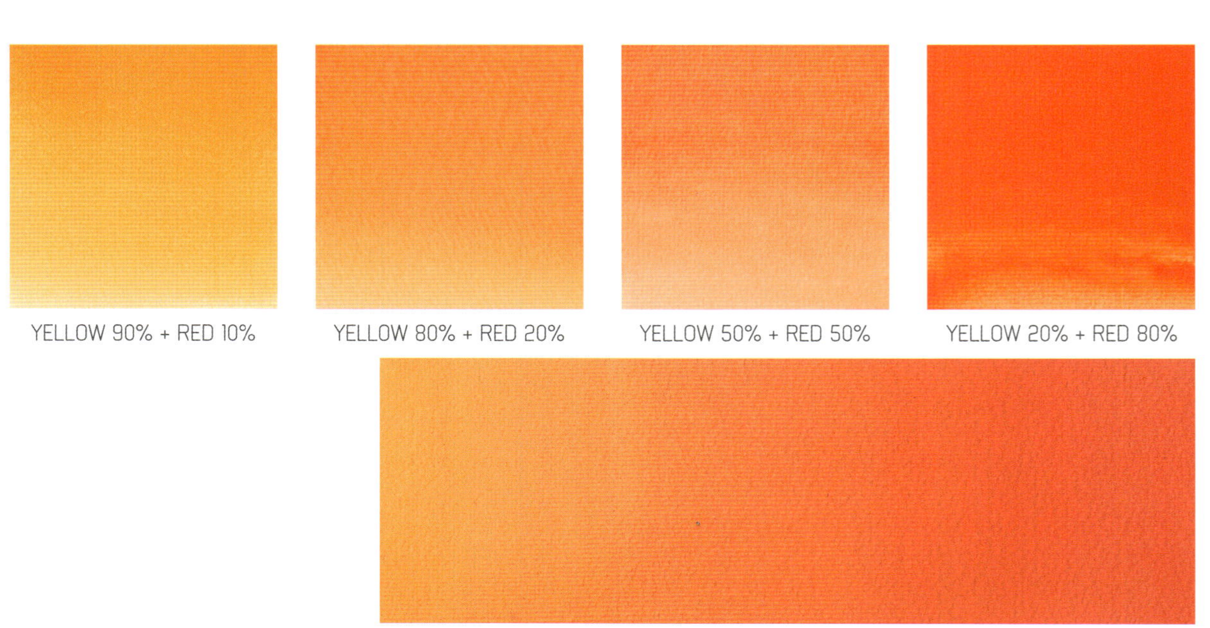

Saffron yellow (PY110) + scarlet red (PR255)

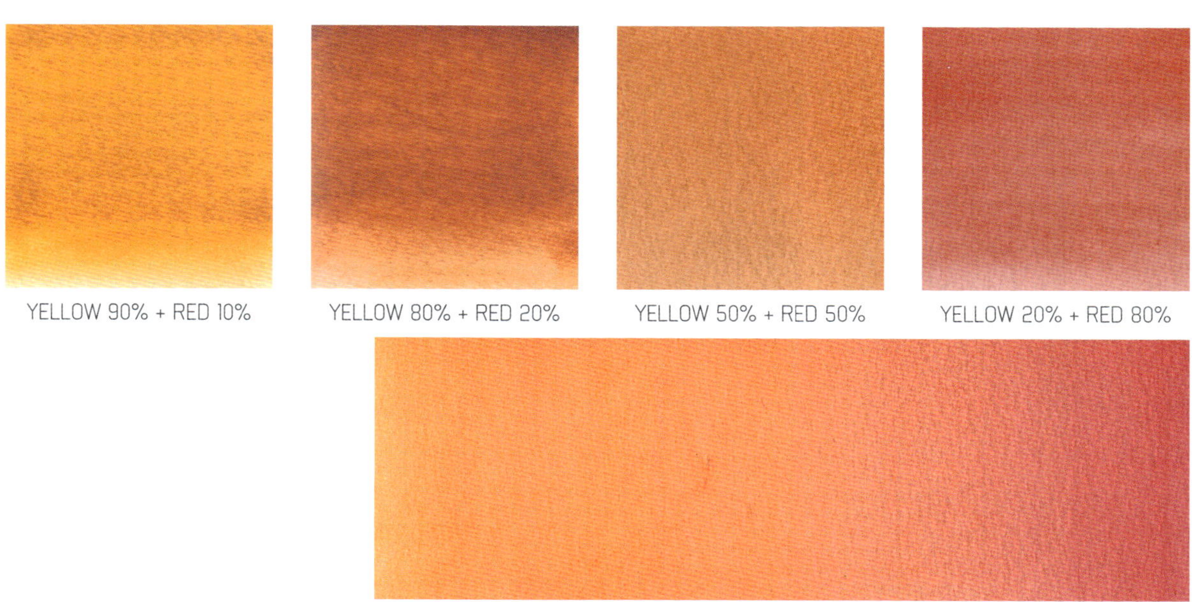

Saffron yellow (PY110) + pyrrole red deep (PR264)

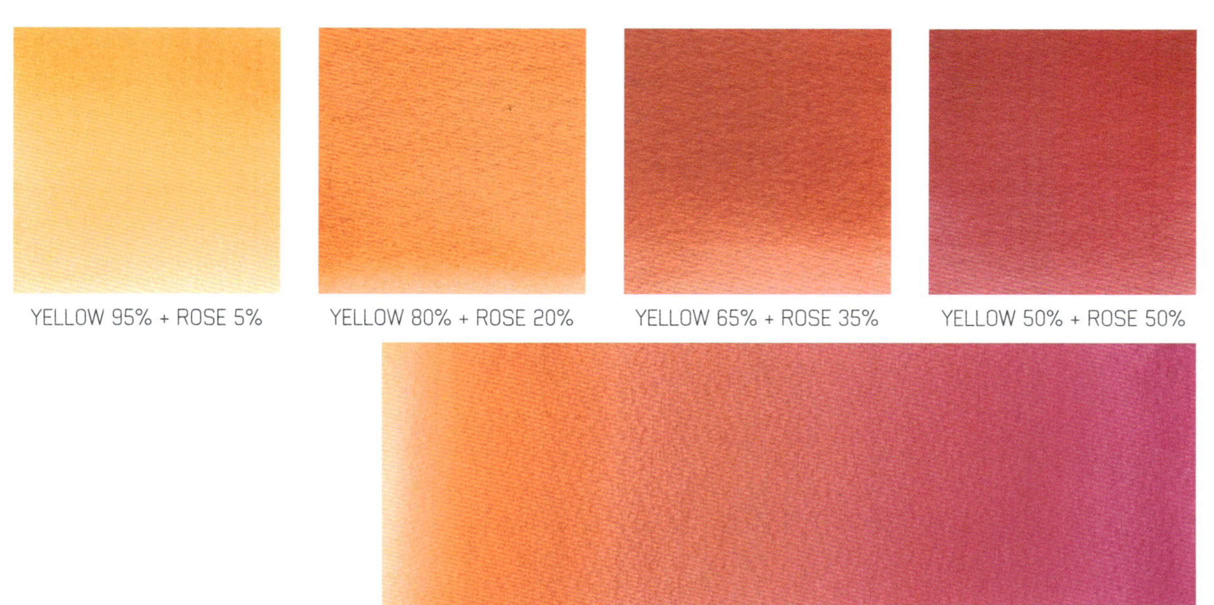

Saffron yellow (PY110) + Isaro rose (PR122)

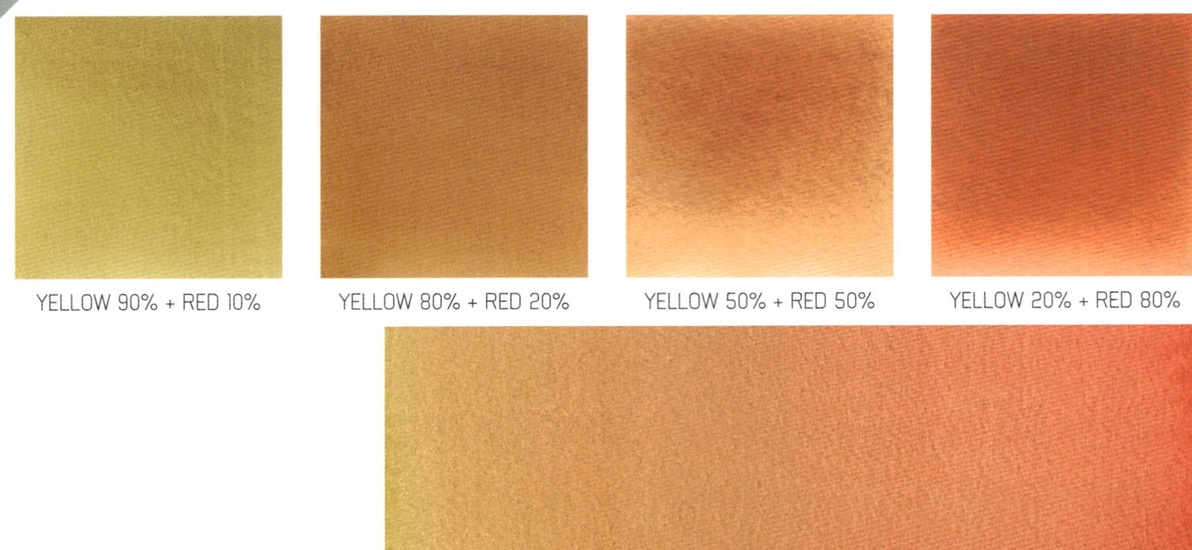

Chartreuse yellow (PY129) + scarlet red (PR255)

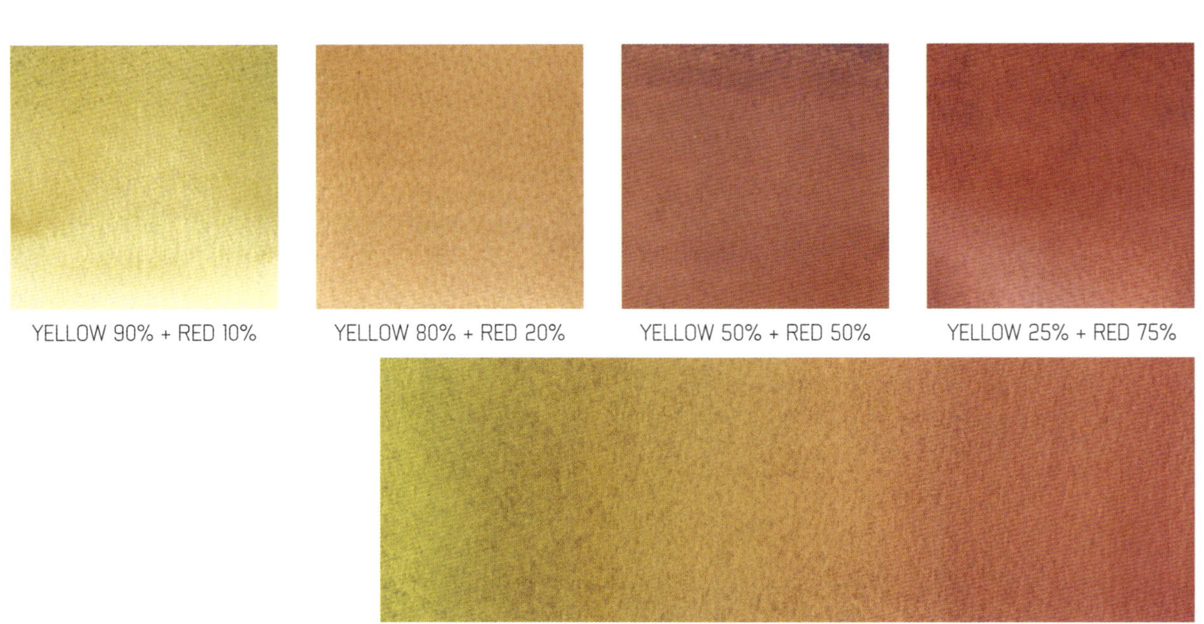

Chartreuse yellow (PY129) + pyrrole red deep (PR264)

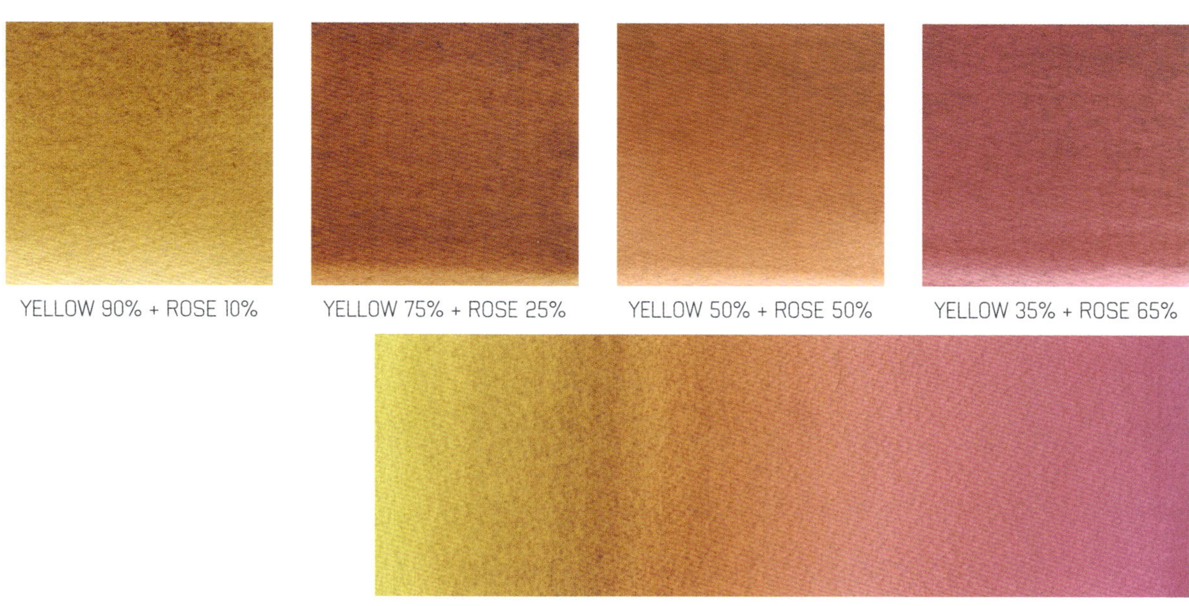

Chartreuse yellow (PY129) + Isaro rose (PR122)

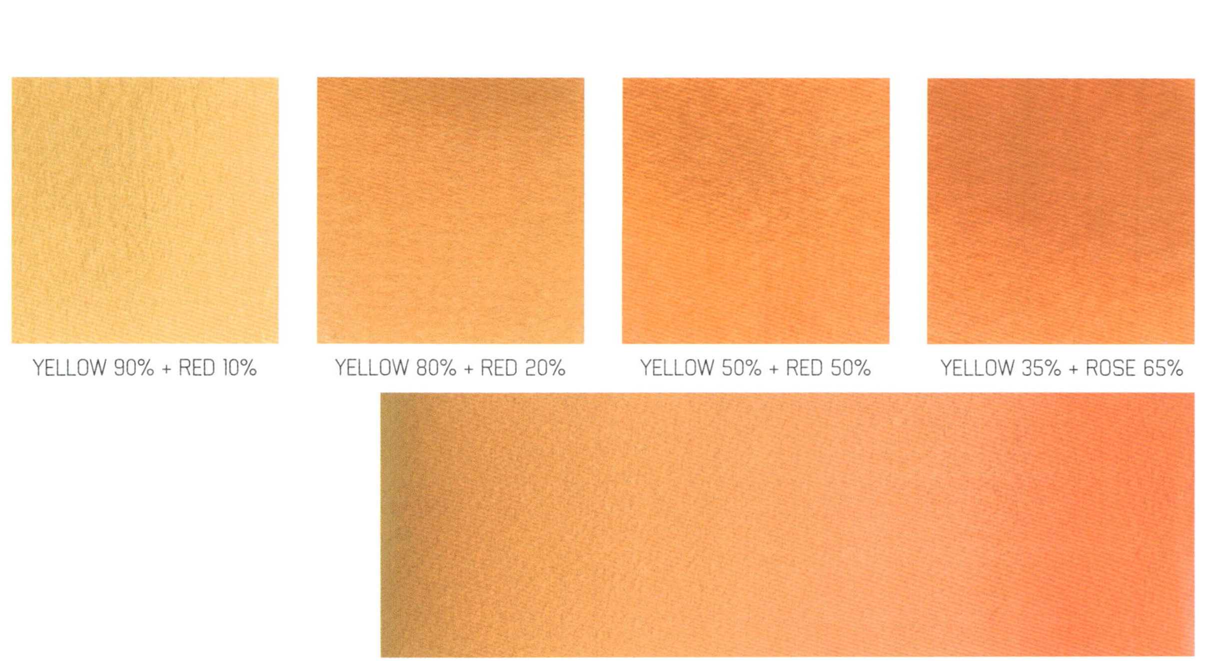

Yellow ocher (PY42) + scarlet red (PR255)

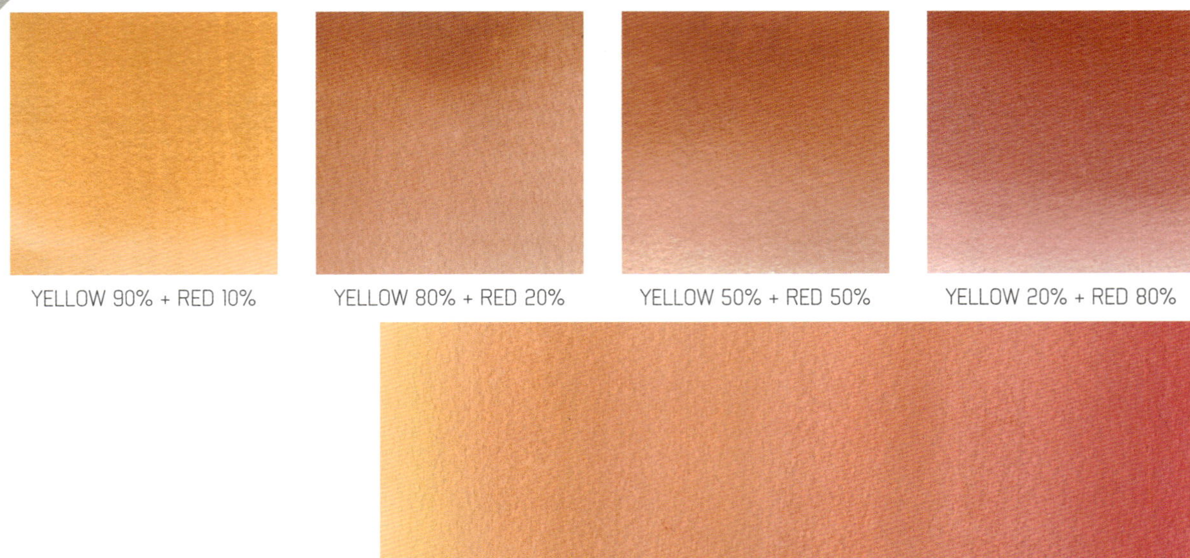

Yellow ocher (PY42) + pyrrole red deep (PR264)

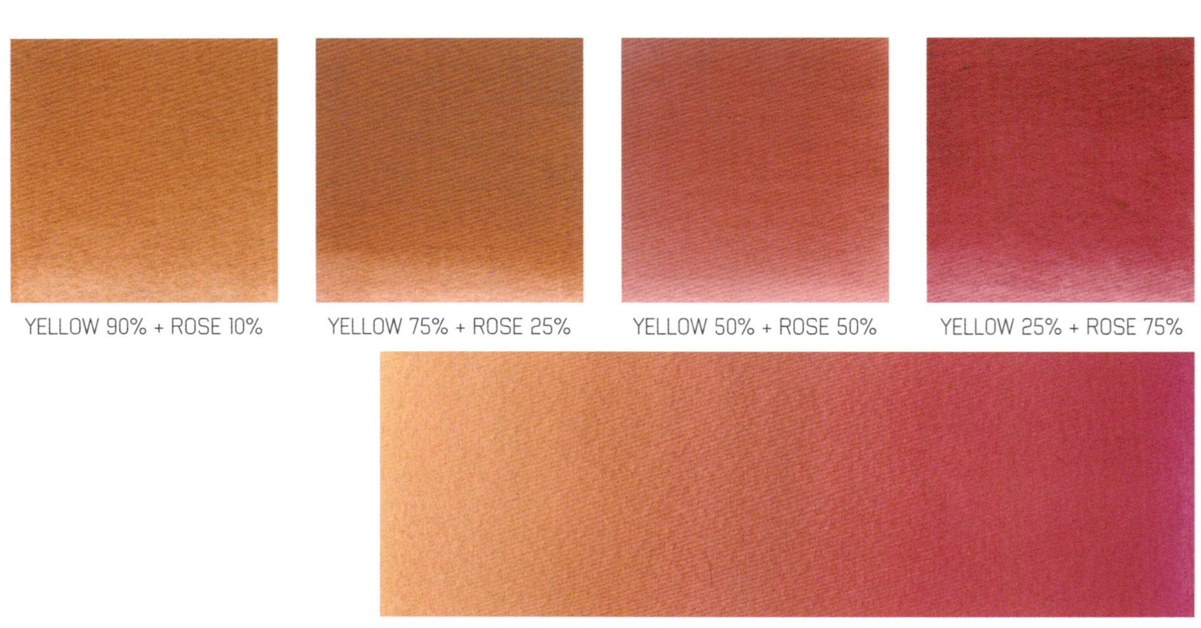

Yellow ocher (PY42) + Isaro rose (PR122)

Creating a Range of Essential Colors

In manufacturers' color charts, you will find that some of the colors on offer are not mono-pigment colors. In other words, these are colors that can be created by mixing other colors. In this section, we will look at the commercially available colors that are used in some of the paintings shown in this book. We will see how to produce them easily by mixing, using colors that are not included in our basic palette here. This way, one can produce colors that are identical to the ones offered by the manufacturers. However, we also thought it would be useful to show how to get shades that are close to these colors just by using the basic palette. These colors will not be identical, but they will be similar to the non-monopigment colors shown in this book.

LUTEA BLUE INDIGO

SENNELIER BLUE INDIGO

WINSOR & NEWTON BLUE INDIGO

Indigo

Indigo blue is, originally, a very dark organic blue that was long used in the graphic arts and in dyes, before it was dethroned by modern blue pigments.

Today, the original pigment, made into a watercolor, can still be found, in particular, from the manufacturers Kremer and Lutea. On the other hand, it is no longer to be found in the ranges of the classic watercolors, because it is less permanent than modern blues.

Most often, indigo blue is a combination of a carbon black to which is added phtalo blue (PB15:3) or indanthrone blue (PB60). Some brands add to this mixture a quinacridone violet (PV19).

If you like granular colors, you will be able to get a very nice granular indigo by combining equal parts of ultramarine blue (PB29) with burnt umber (PBr7). This can then be used as a base and shaded with a touch of phtalo blue.

BURNT UMBER (PBR7)
+ ULTRAMARINE BLUE (PB29)
+ PHTALO BLUE (PB15:3)

USING YOUR PALETTE

The easiest way to do this is to work with one part phtalo blue (PB15:3) or Prussian blue (PB27) to one part pyrrole red deep (PR264). You can then adjust the blue to get a very deep blue that can act as an indigo.

You can also use equal parts of phtalo blue, pyrrole red deep, and ultramarine blue (PB29). If you want a brighter indigo, all you have to do is add a little more phtalo blue to this base.

PHTALO BLUE (PB15:3)
+ PYRROLE RED DEEP (PR264)

PRUSSIAN BLUE (PB27)
+ PYRROLE RED DEEP (PR264)

PHTALO BLUE (PB15:3)
+ PYRROLE RED DEEP (PR264)
+ ULTRAMARINE BLUE (PB29)

PHTALO BLUE (PB15:3)
(IN GREATER PROPORTIONS)
+ PYRROLE RED DEEP (PR264)
+ ULTRAMARINE BLUE (PB29)

WINSOR & NEWTON
PAYNE'S GRAY

REMBRANDT
PAYNE'S GRAY

Payne's Gray

Payne's gray is a deep, bluish gray. The bluish note is more or less pronounced depending on the brand.

Payne's gray can be obtained by combining a carbon black (PBk6) or an iron oxide black (PBk11) with an organic blue, such as phtalo blue (PB15:3) or indanthrone blue (PB60), which is already naturally very dark. This base can then be given some nuance using a little bit of quinacridone violet (PV19).

If you like granular colors, you can also create this gray by combining ultramarine blue (PB29) with your iron oxide black or carbon black, and then adding a hint of phtalo blue or quinacridone violet.

IRON OXIDE BLACK
+ ULTRAMARINE BLUE (PB29)
+ PHTALO BLUE (PB15:3)

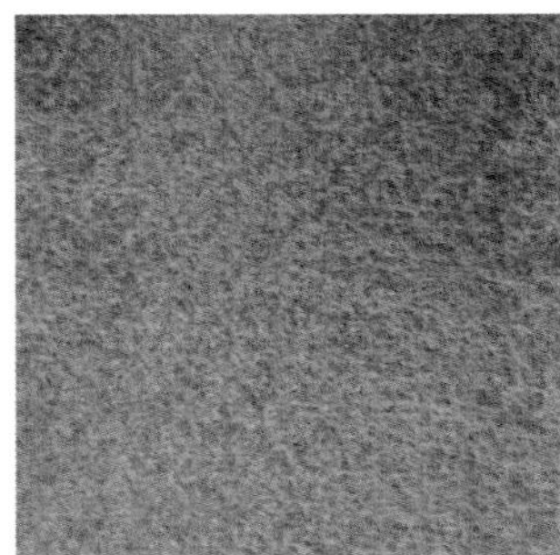

CARBON BLACK (PBK6)
+ ULTRAMARINE BLUE (PB29)
+ QUINACRIDONE VIOLET (PV19)

USING YOUR PALETTE

You can create a bluish gray by combining one part Prussian blue (PB27) with one half part scarlet red (PR255). Then, you can shade this base by adding ultramarine blue (PB29).

William Payne, a 19th-century watercolorist, used a formula for gray made up of Prussian blue, yellow ocher (PY42), and madder lacquer. We can take our inspiration from his formula, replacing madder red with pyrrole red deep (PR264). Start with equal parts Prussian blue and pyrrole red deep. Then, gradually add yellow ocher. This shade, in heavily diluted form, will allow you to create an interesting light gray that can be used for neutral backgrounds.

SCARLET RED (PR255)
+ PRUSSIAN BLUE (PB27)
+ ULTRAMARINE BLUE (PB29)

SCARLET RED (PR255)
+ PRUSSIAN BLUE (PB27)
+ ULTRAMARINE BLUE (PB29)
(IN GREATER PROPORTIONS)

PYRROLE RED DEEP (PR264)
+ PRUSSIAN BLUE (PB27),
SHADED WITH YELLOW OCHER
(PY42)

PYRROLE RED DEEP (PR264)
+ PRUSSIAN BLUE (PB27), SHADED
WITH YELLOW OCHER (PY42), AND
ALL OF THAT THEN DILUTED

SENNELIER VAN DYKE BROWN

ISARO VAN DYKE BROWN

Van Dyke Brown

Van Dyke brown was originally a Cassel earth color, an oxocarbon that was collected from peat or lignite deposits. However, it was not stable when exposed to light, so it is no longer used as a pigment in the arts.

Van Dyke brown is a deep brown that tends lightly toward violet. It is made up of a black pigment, such as iron oxide black (PBk11) or carbon black (PBk6), to which a synthetic iron oxide is added, such as Venetian red (PR101) or Indian red (also known as red oxide, PR101).

USING YOUR PALETTE

It is possible to create a slightly violet deep brown by combining one part Prussian blue (PB27), one part chartreuse yellow (PY129), and two parts pyrrole red deep (PR264). First, you need to mix together the blue and the yellow in order to create a green. Then add to this base the pyrrole red deep in order to break up the shade and draw the mixture toward brown. This color can be darkened using ultramarine blue (PB29). These shades are very useful as a brown contrast or as a way to deepen a color.

PRUSSIAN BLUE (PB27)
+ CHARTREUSE YELLOW (PY129)
+ PYRROLE RED DEEP (PR264)

PRUSSIAN BLUE (PB27)
+ CHARTREUSE YELLOW (PY129)
+ PYRROLE RED DEEP (PR264)
+ ULTRAMARINE BLUE (PB29)

SENNELIER SEPIA

SCHMINCKE SEPIA

Sepia

Sepia is a warm brown. It was originally an organic pigment obtained from squid ink. Like many organic natural pigments, it is not stable when exposed to light. But for the purists, this pigment is still available from Kremer.

This warm brown is made from the same base as Van Dyke brown, using a yellow iron oxide or a natural earth color.

USING YOUR PALETTE

You can just use the same base as you did for Van Dyke brown and then add some yellow ocher (PY42) to your mixture in order to warm it up and make it a little lighter.

PRUSSIAN BLUE (PB27)
+ CHARTREUSE YELLOW (PY129)
+ PYRROLE RED DEEP (PR264)
+ ULTRAMARINE BLUE (PB29)
+ YELLOW OCHER (PY42)

WINSOR & NEWTON
OLIVE GREEN

ISARO OLIVE GREEN

Olive Green

Olive green is a relatively subdued green. Like many compound greens, it is based on phthalocyanine green (PG7).

A lovely olive green can be obtained by combining phtalo green with a mineral yellow, such as light cadmium yellow (PY35), or an organic yellow, such is Isaro yellow light (PY154). The shade is then broken up with a hint of Isaro violet (PV19) and Isaro rose (PR122).

USING YOUR PALETTE

You can get a lovely olive green by combining two parts chartreuse yellow (PY129) with one part ultramarine blue (PB29). The shade is then broken up with a touch of Isaro rose (PR122). If you want the color to be a little brighter, you can add a touch of yellow ocher (PY42).

CHARTREUSE YELLOW (PY129)
+ ULTRAMARINE BLUE (PB29)
+ ISARO ROSE (PR122)

CHARTREUSE YELLOW (PY129)
+ ULTRAMARINE BLUE (PB29)
+ ISARO ROSE (PR122),
ALL LIGHTENED WITH
YELLOW OCHER (PY42)

SENNELIER CHINESE ORANGE

Chinese Orange

Sennelier's Chinese orange is a subtle mixture of three organic pigments: azo yellow (PY150), quinacridone red (PR206), and azo brown (PBr23).

USING YOUR PALETTE

First, you need to create a bright orange by combining equal parts of saffron yellow (PY110) and scarlet red (PR255). Then, add a hint of dark brown (either Van Dyke brown or sepia) or else Isaro rose (PR122). The brown will break up the brightness of the mixture, while the rose will break it up but in a less forceful way. Even if the orange that you create is not identical to the one that Sennelier offers, the shade will be close and will be a perfect replacement for most purposes.

SAFFRON YELLOW (PY110)
+ SCARLET RED (PR255)
+ SEPIA

SAFFRON YELLOW (PY110)
+ SCARLET RED (PR255)
+ ISARO ROSE (PR122)

3 / Creating Thematic Palettes

Targeted Practice

In this chapter, four watercolor artists will guide you through the choice of colors to focus on, depending on the subject matter. As we look at the artworks shown here, our analysis will address only the mix of colors.

The goal is to lead you to understand color mixing better through practical examples.

In this way, you will be in a position to build your own thematic palette in harmony with the subject that you want to paint. We think that before beginning to add color to a watercolor painting, the most important thing is to carefully choose your colors and visualize the mixtures that they will make possible.

Painting a Floral Composition

The two floral compositions that we study below provide a perfect illustration of Marie Boudon's mastery and very personal style. Marie's watercolors, which are always pleasantly fresh and possessed of a lovely tonal harmony, are also excellent exercises for understanding color mixtures. This artist's graphic elegance and very didactic work, which she shares enthusiastically, will allow you, with a little bit of practice and no discouragement, to create artworks with beautiful effects. This watercolor artist, who does not go in for hyperrealism at all, invites us to explore the world of flowers with a freer gaze and without many technical constraints. Roses, anemones, peonies, and foliage are painted simply, because it is the assembly of the bouquet, and thus the composition as a whole, that makes up the charm of Marie's paintings.

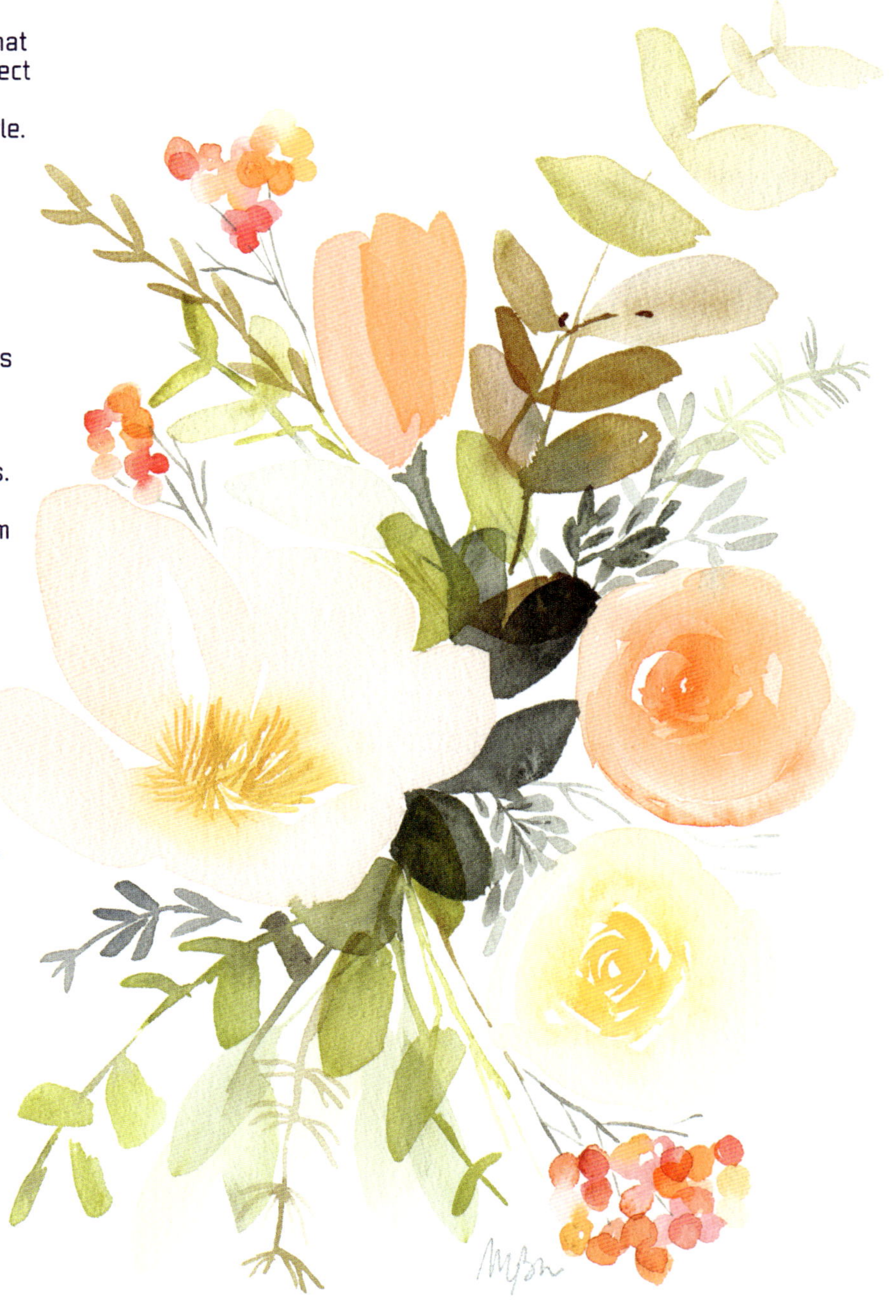

In Harmonious Warm Colors

> Marie Boudon

For this composition, Marie created a lovely range of greens and oranges.

Because this bouquet is a composition of warm tones, it makes sense that yellows would make themselves known. With saffron yellow (PY110), chartreuse yellow (PY129), and yellow ocher (PY42) as the foundation, Prussian blue (PB27) for the greens and scarlet red (PR255) for the oranges complete the assortment.

However, instead of choosing Isaro rose (PR122), Marie decided on two pigments in the same family, a violet and a magenta (PV19). The violet is cooler and bluer than Isaro rose, while the magenta is slightly warmer.

We will see that Isaro rose could also work in putting together Marie's mixtures. Thus, it is a personal choice whether or not to add these two colors to your palette. Nevertheless, if floral subjects are your favorite subject, as they are for Marie, then rounding out your selection with a few violets is fully justified.

Marie Boudon is the creator of Les tribulations de Marie (Marie's trials and tribulations), a platform for modern watercolor video classes where she teaches simple, universally accessible methods. Marie, who is an engineer by training, has also written several books on watercolors. In *Dare to Create!* (Rocky Nook, 2021), Marie shares her advice for boosting your creative process.

Marie's publications:
Fleurs à l'aquarelle (Watercolor flowers), Mango, Paris, 2018
J'ose créer, éditions Eyrolles, Paris, 2019 (published in English as *Dare to Create!,* Rocky Nook, 2021)
Jungle à l'aquarelle (Watercolor jungle), Mango, Paris, 2019

Follow Marie online:
Website – tribulationsdemarie.com
Instagram – @tribulationsdemarie
Email – contact@tribulationsdemarie

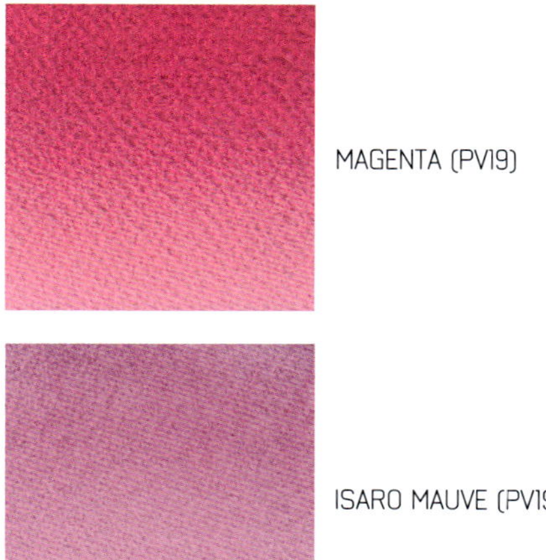

MAGENTA (PV19)

ISARO MAUVE (PV19)

SAFFRON
YELLOW (PY110)
+ MAGENTA
HEAVILY DILUTED
MIXTURE

SAFFRON
YELLOW (PY110)
+ ISARO ROSE (PR122)
HEAVILY DILUTED
MIXTURE

CHARTREUSE
YELLOW (PY129)
+ ISARO MAUVE (PV19)

CHARTREUSE
YELLOW (PY129)
+ ISARO ROSE (PR122)

SAFFRON
YELLOW (PY110)
+ PRUSSIAN
BLUE (PB27)
+ ISARO MAUVE (PV19)

SAFFRON
YELLOW (PY110)
+ PRUSSIAN
BLUE (PB27)
+ ISARO ROSE (PR122

ANALYSIS

> *For the yellow rose,* Marie works by expanding her range of primary colors (see "Expanding the Range of Primary Colors," page 38) and shades her saffron yellow (PY110) with a hint of yellow ocher (PY42).

> *For the orange rose,* a hint of scarlet red (PR255) reinforces the orangeish note of the saffron yellow (PY110) and allows her to easily obtain a lovely range of oranges (see page 58). The salmony hue of the peony is obtained by combining magenta with saffron yellow and heavily diluting the mixture. A similar color can be obtained by using Isaro rose (PR122) instead of the magenta.

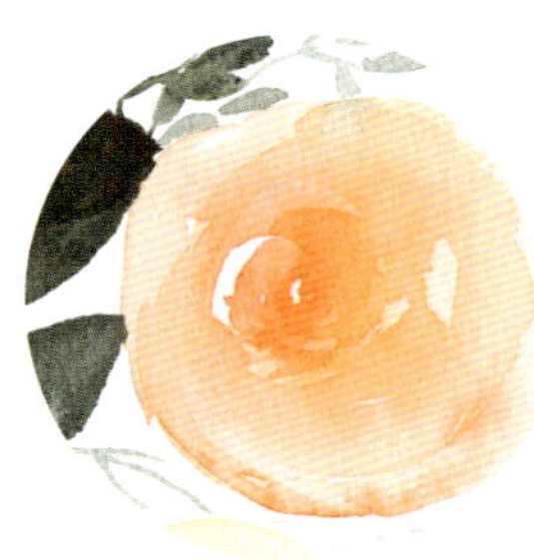

> *For the foliage,* Marie plays with the chartreuse yellow (PY129), which she uses to paint the most vibrant leaves at the base of her bouquet. This same yellow is then broken up using a hint of Isaro mauve (PV19), which pushes the mixture toward a greenish brown in the top part of the composition.

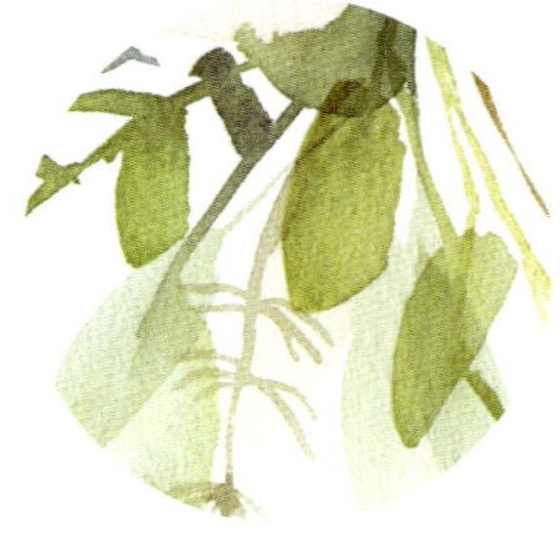
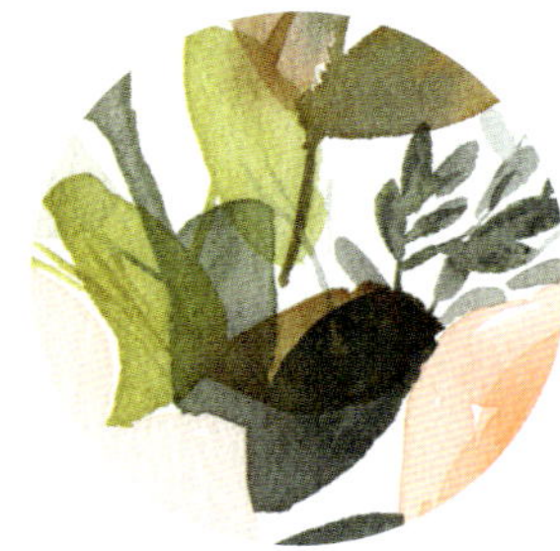

> *For the leaves in gray-green tones,* in the center of the floral arrangement, the watercolorist has combined saffron yellow (PY110) with Prussian blue (PB27), augmented with a hint of Isaro mauve (PV19). The different shades can be obtained by diluting the mixture to greater or lesser degrees. For this combination, Prussian blue has to be the dominant color. The Isaro mauve could be replaced by a rose, because even though the resulting shades will be slightly different, they will still be equally interesting.

In Harmonious Cool Colors

> Marie Boudon

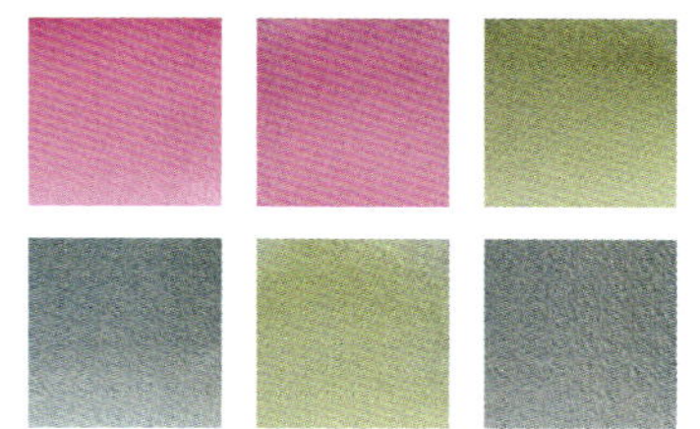

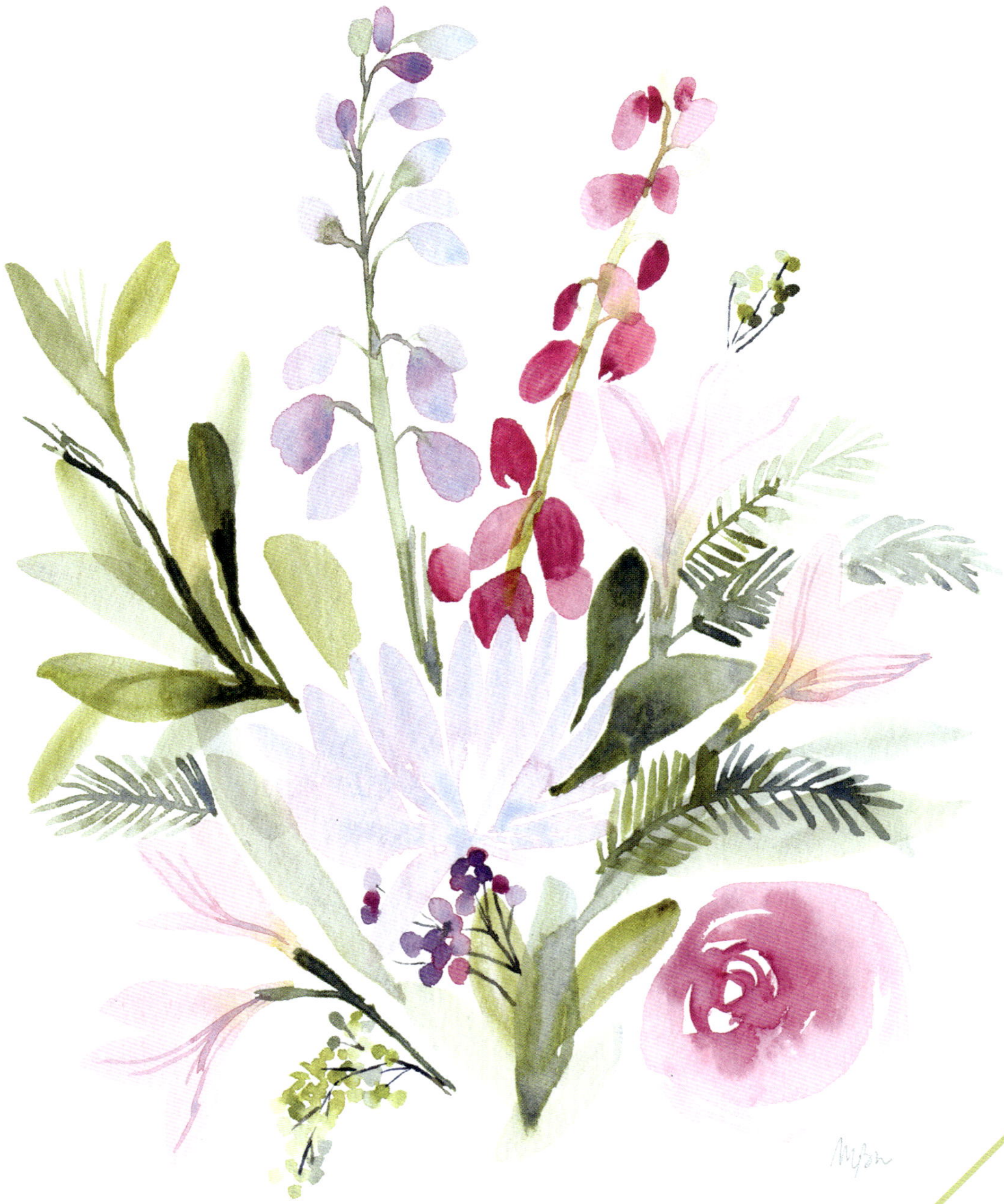

ISARO ROSE (PR122)
DEEPENED WITH
ISARO MAUVE (PV19)

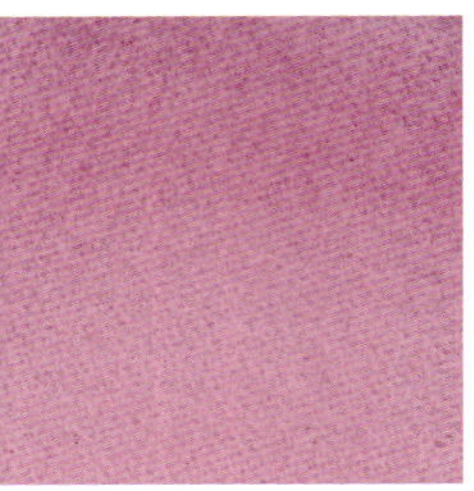

ISARO ROSE (PR122)
DEEPENED WITH
PYRROLE RED DEEP
(PR264), SOFTENED
WITH A HINT OF ULTRA-
MARINE BLUE (PB29)

ULTRAMARINE
BLUE (PB29)
+ CHARTREUSE
YELLOW (PY129)
+ ISARO MAUVE (PV19)

ULTRAMARINE
BLUE (PB29) IN
LARGER QUANTITIES
+ CHARTREUSE
YELLOW (PY129)
+ ISARO MAUVE (PV19)

ULTRAMARINE
BLUE (PB29)
+ CHARTREUSE
YELLOW (PY129)
+ ISARO ROSE (PR122)

ULTRAMARINE
BLUE (PB29) IN
LARGER QUANTITIES
+ CHARTREUSE
YELLOW (PY129)
+ ISARO ROSE (PR122)

The palette of this watercolor painting is structured around three colors that are essential for creating a beautiful range of complementary violets: ultramarine blue (PB29), cerulean blue (PB35), and Isaro rose (PR122) (see "Violets," page 51).

Chartreuse yellow (PY129) and Isaro yellow light (PY154) will be used for the creation of the foliage arrangements that organize this bouquet. Isaro mauve (PV19) completes the assortment.

ANALYSIS

> *The rose* is made using Isaro rose (PR122), darkened with a hint of Isaro mauve (PV19). In place of the Isaro mauve, a touch of pyrrole red deep (PR264), softened with a hint of ultramarine blue (PB29), could do as well.

> *The pale pink and violet shades of the dahlia,* as well as of the delphiniums and of the alstroemeria, are all obtained from cerulean blue (PB35) and Isaro rose (PR122), mixed together in different proportions (see "Isaro rose (PR122) + cerulean blue (PB35)," page 57).

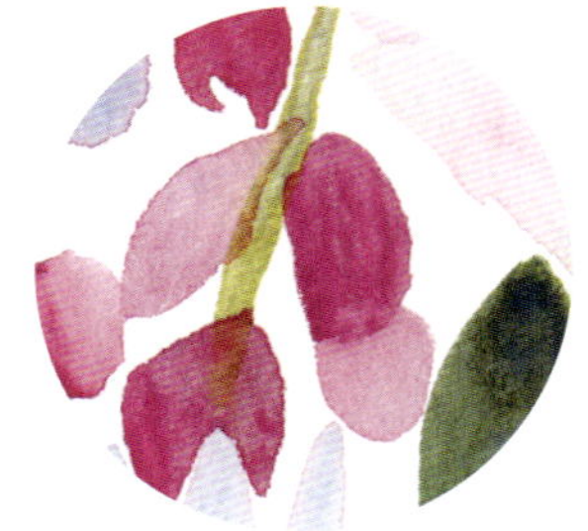

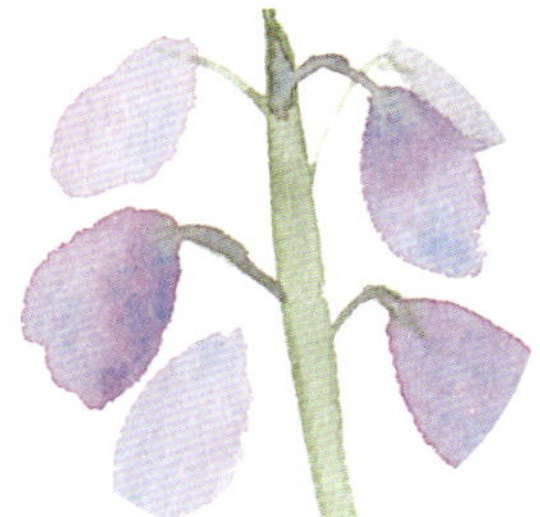

> *The light greens of the foliage arrangements* are created by combining ultramarine blue (PB29) and Isaro yellow light in different proportions (see "Isaro yellow light (PY154) + ultramarine blue (PB29)," page 43). The darker greens are the product of a combination of ultramarine blue with chartreuse yellow (PY129), which the artist has darkened with a hint of Isaro mauve (PV19) or Isaro rose (PR122).

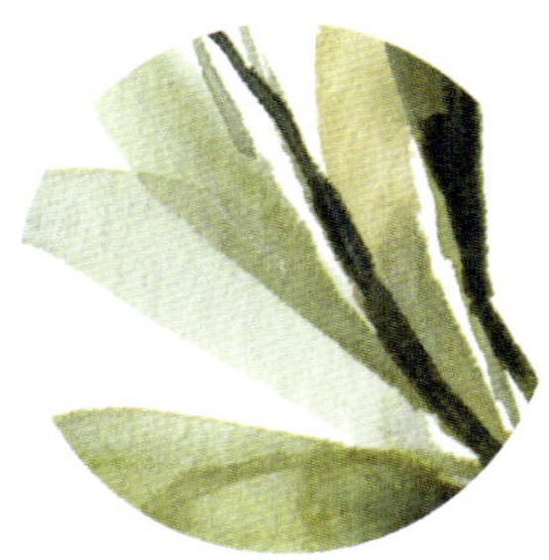

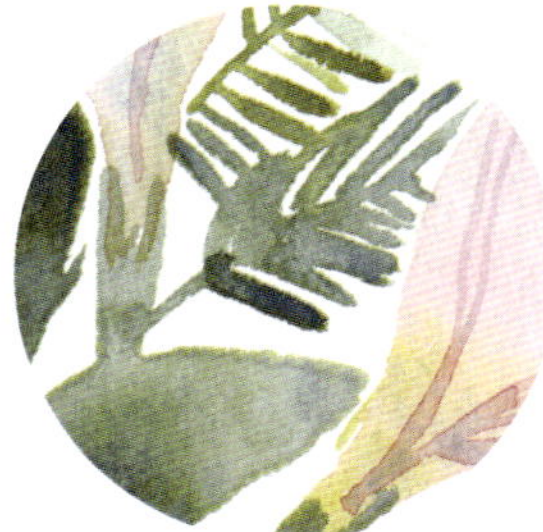

Why not phtalo green?

Phtalo green (PG7) is also very useful for easily creating a very large range of greens. And this pigment is also often present in the compound greens offered by color manufacturers.

RANGE OF WARM GREENS

50% PHTALO GREEN + 50% ISARO YELLOW LIGHT (PY154)	50% PHTALO GREEN + 50% SAFFRON YELLOW (PY110)	50% PHTALO GREEN + 50% CHARTREUSE YELLOW (PY129)	50% PHTALO GREEN + 50% YELLOW OCHER (PY42)

RANGE OF COOL GREENS

80% PHTALO GREEN + 20% PYRROLE RED DEEP (PR264)	65% PHTALO GREEN + 35% PYRROLE RED DEEP (PR264)	80% PHTALO GREEN + 20% ISARO ROSE (PR122)	50% PHTALO GREEN + 50% ULTRAMARINE BLUE (PB29)

50% PHTALO GREEN + 50% PRUSSIAN BLUE (PB27)	50% PHTALO GREEN + 50% PHTALO BLUE (PB15:3)	50% PHTALO GREEN + 50% CERULEAN BLUE (PB35)

Painting a Landscape

In studying these different kinds of landscapes, it is mainly the artist Manù who will serve as our guide. This watercolor artist is especially fond of painting landscapes. Sometimes, Manù likes to work with compound colors, such as Van Dyke brown or indigo blue. As he himself says cheerfully, it is mostly for the sake of convenience that these two colors have a place on his palette. Nevertheless, he creates most of his blends himself and is eloquent in sharing his love of watercolors, pigments, and color mixtures. He also offers classes and has put together many step-by-step sets of instructions that he shares on his website.

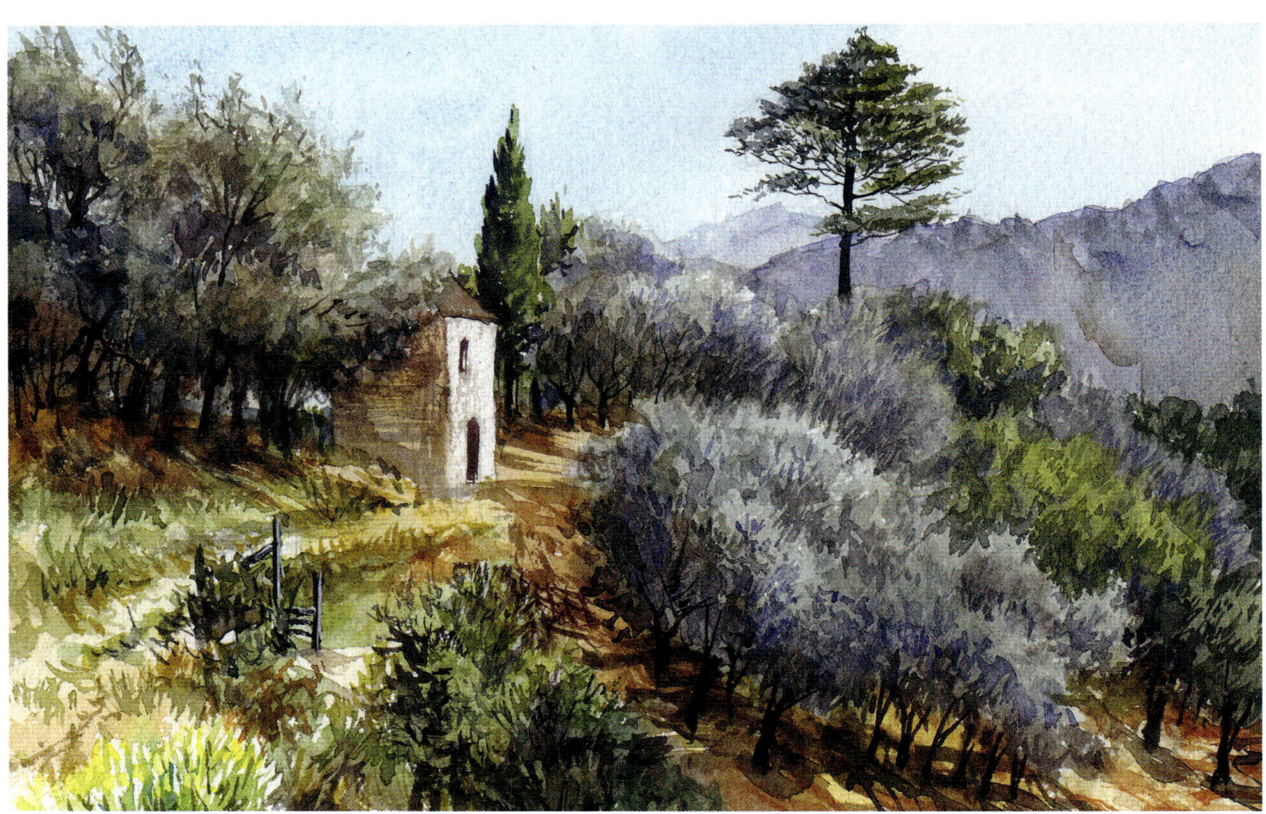

In Green Tones

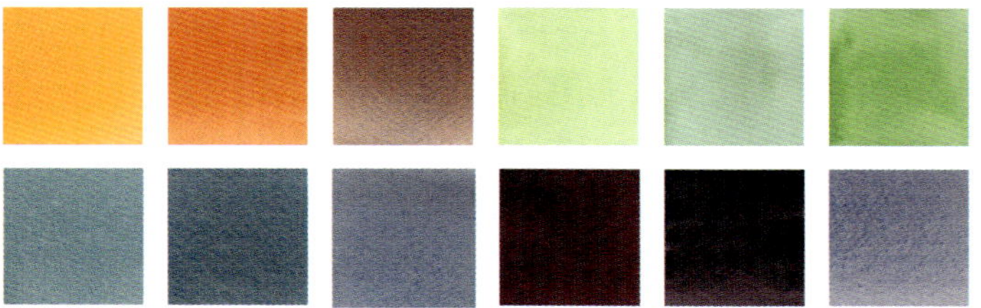

For this landscape, what is usually seen as the primary challenge is creating a broad palette of greens. And yet, one can create an infinite number of greens without much difficulty. In fact, the more interesting challenge is to respect the concept of an attractive chromatic harmony, rather than trying to stay faithful to reality at all costs. This will free up your intuition and allow the composition to be better balanced.

The colors to emphasize in order to produce natural greens are Prussian blue (PB27), along with the four yellows, namely Isaro (PY154), chartreuse yellow (PY129), saffron yellow (PY110), and yellow ocher (PY42). Prussian blue can be supplemented by ultramarine blue (PB29), or even replaced by it if you want to create cool greens. Manù's palette is rounded out with cerulean blue (PB35) and pyrrole red deep (PR264). You could also add Van Dyke brown, but, as we shall see, that color can also be obtained by doing your own mixing.

Manù studied watercolor painting at the Académie Kieffer. He then rounded out his artistic training by joining the Angoulême comics workshop. As he studied the works of William Turner, his vision of comic books and graphic novels evolved. He recognized himself less and less in the world of comics and, from then on, concentrated his artistic research on narrative art. He started to work on reportage collections, in which he mixed texts with traditional watercolors. His collection *La Corse en Aquarelles (Corsica in Watercolors)*, published by the éditions du Coprin, is a lovely overview of his work. Manù teaches watercolor painting and is also the founder of the YouTube channel Pilutu, where he tests and reviews art supplies and offers step-by-step how-to videos.

Follow Manù at:
Website – mesaquarelles.com
Instagram – @manu_aquarelle
Facebook – Les Aquarelles de Manu
Email – contact@mesaquarelles.com
YouTube – Pilutu
Twitter – manu_aquarelle

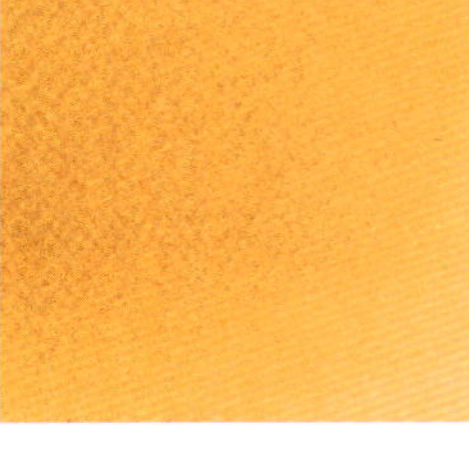

YELLOW OCHER (PY42) + SAFFRON YELLOW (PY110)

YELLOW OCHER (PY42) + SAFFRON YELLOW (PY110) + PYRROLE RED DEEP (PR264)

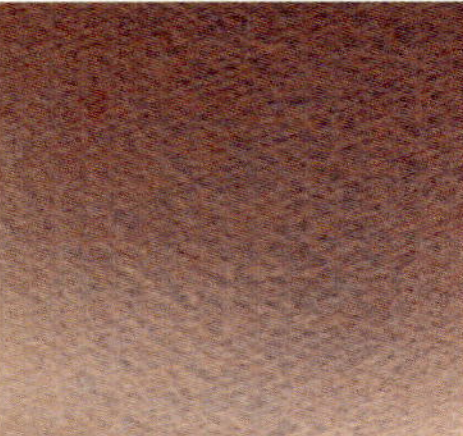

YELLOW OCHER (PY42) + SAFFRON YELLOW (PY110) + PYRROLE RED DEEP (PR264) + ULTRAMARINE BLUE (PB29)

YELLOW OCHER (PY42) + SAFFRON YELLOW (PY110) + CHARTREUSE YELLOW (PY129) IN EQUAL PARTS, THEN SHADED WITH PRUSSIAN BLUE (PB27)

YELLOW OCHER (PY42) + SAFFRON YELLOW (PY110) + PRUSSIAN BLUE (PB27)

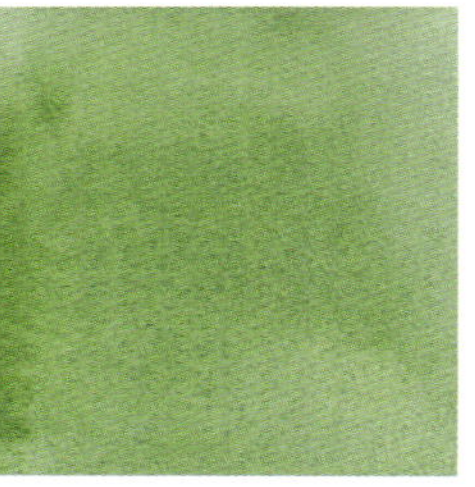

YELLOW OCHER (PY42) + CHARTREUSE YELLOW (PY129) + PRUSSIAN BLUE (PB27)

ANALYSIS

> *The blue of the sky* is rendered using cerulean blue (PB35), enhanced with ultramarine blue (PB29). This mixture is well diluted before it is placed on the page.

> *The ground* is created using layering. Over a liquid base of yellow ocher (PY42), Manù places a mixture of yellow ocher and saffron yellow (PY110). This mixture is then reinforced with pyrrole red deep (PR264) in order to add relief, and a hint of ultramarine blue (PB29) to bring out the shadows.

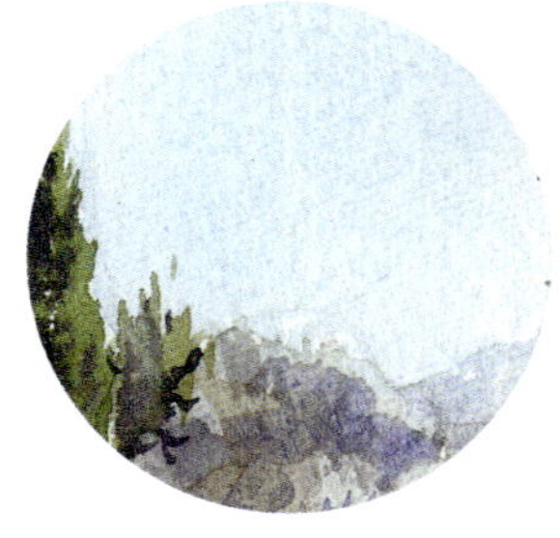 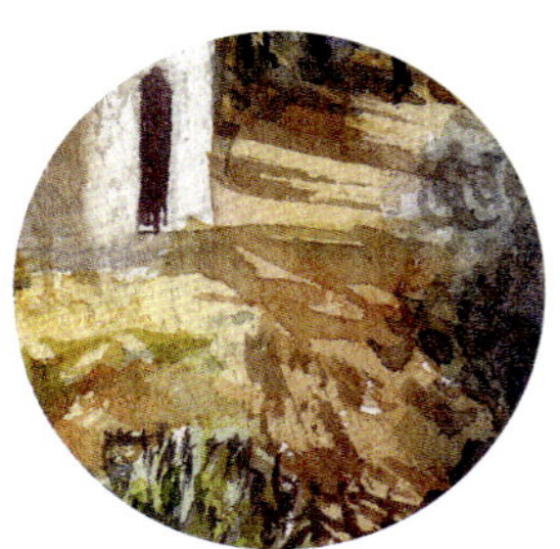

> *The house* remains within the same chromatic range as the mixtures used for the ground.

> *The greens in the foreground* are obtained by a variety of mixtures of yellow ocher (PY42), saffron yellow (PY110), chartreuse yellow (PY129), and Prussian blue (PB27). The color that dominates each mixture makes it possible to nuance the various greens, while respecting an overall tonal harmony. A hint of Isaro yellow light (PY154) brings in the brightness and catches the eye in certain areas (see "Greens," page 42).

> *The bluish green of the olive trees* is formed from a base of ultramarine blue (PB29) and yellow ocher (PY42), deepened by the judicious addition of a little bit of Prussian blue (PB27). In order to give volume to the foliage, the artist breaks up this mixture using a hint of pyrrole red deep (PR264). A few touches of ultramarine blue are used as a finishing touch for the arrangement of olive trees.

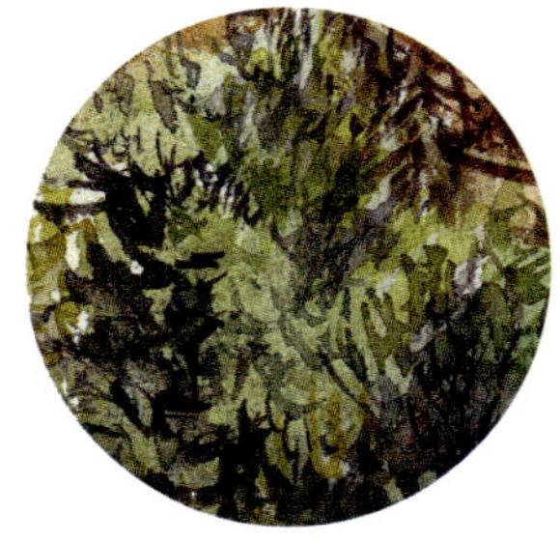 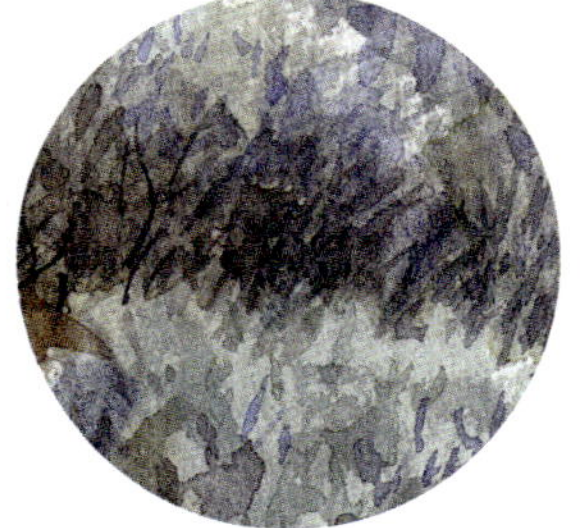

> **_The Mediterranean pine_** and the cypress tree are painted using a green made up of yellow ocher (PY42) and Prussian blue (PB27). The side that is most exposed to the light has a hint of chartreuse yellow (PY129), while the part in the shade has a touch of ultramarine blue (PB29).

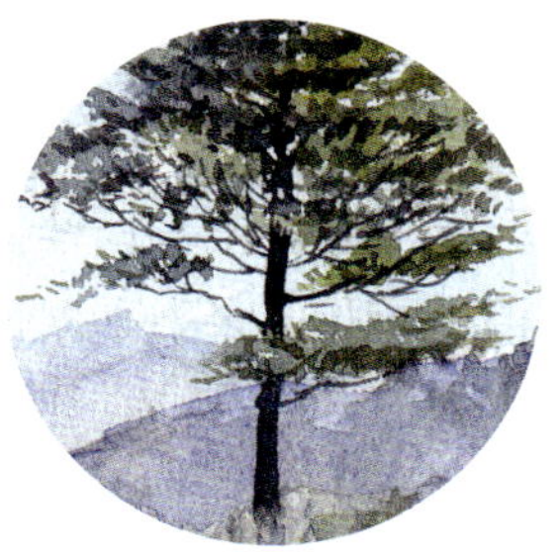 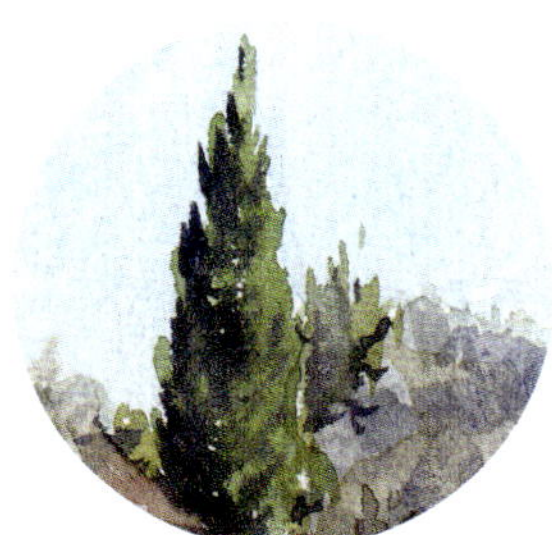

> **_The trees_** that abut the house are painted using a mixture of yellow ocher (PY42) and Prussian blue (PB27). The shade is broken up with the addition of a little bit of dark brown. Manù is in fact a big fan of Van Dyke brown, which is always to be found on his palette. This brown allows him to deepen his colors. It's what he uses to paint the tree trunks and to reinforce some of the shadows. As a substitute for Van Dyke brown (see page 70), you can create a similar dark brown using pyrrole red deep (PR264) with Prussian blue and chartreuse yellow (PY129) added to it. The addition of ultramarine blue (PB29) will allow you to deepen the tone and to use it for your final touches.

> **_The mountains_**, in the background, have to be cool in order to bring depth to the composition. This cool gray shade can be obtained by mixing a hint of pyrrole red deep (PR264) into ultramarine blue (PB29). The color is then further shaded by adding yellow ocher (PY42); be sure to dilute the mixture. A fine dark brown wash adds the finishing touch.

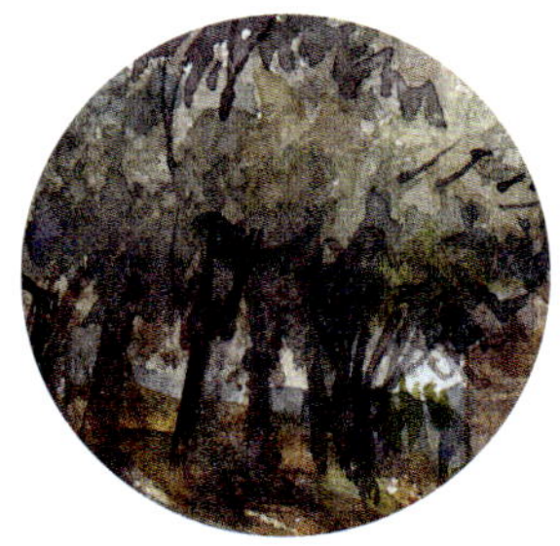 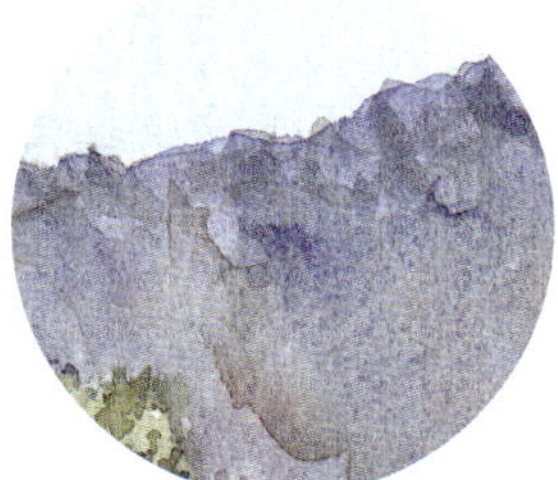

ULTRAMARINE BLUE (PB29) + YELLOW OCHER (PY42), PROGRESSIVELY DEEPENED WITH A HINT OF PRUSSIAN BLUE (PB27)

ULTRAMARINE BLUE (PB29) + YELLOW OCHER (PY42), PROGRESSIVELY DEEPENED WITH A HINT OF PRUSSIAN BLUE (PB27)

ULTRAMARINE BLUE (PB29) + YELLOW OCHER (PY42) + PRUSSIAN BLUE (PB27) + A HINT OF PYRROLE RED DEEP (PR264)

PRUSSIAN BLUE (PB27) + CHARTREUSE YELLOW (PY129) + PYRROLE RED DEEP (PR264)

SAME BASE, DEEPENED WITH ULTRAMARINE BLUE (PB29)

ULTRAMARINE BLUE (PB29) + PYRROLE RED DEEP (PR264) + YELLOW OCHER (PY42) TO BREAK UP THE SHADE

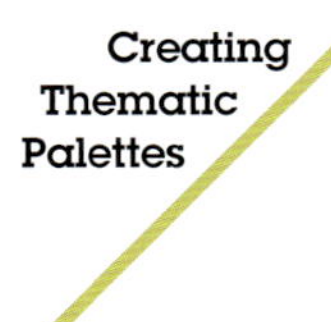

In Autumnal Tones

> Manù

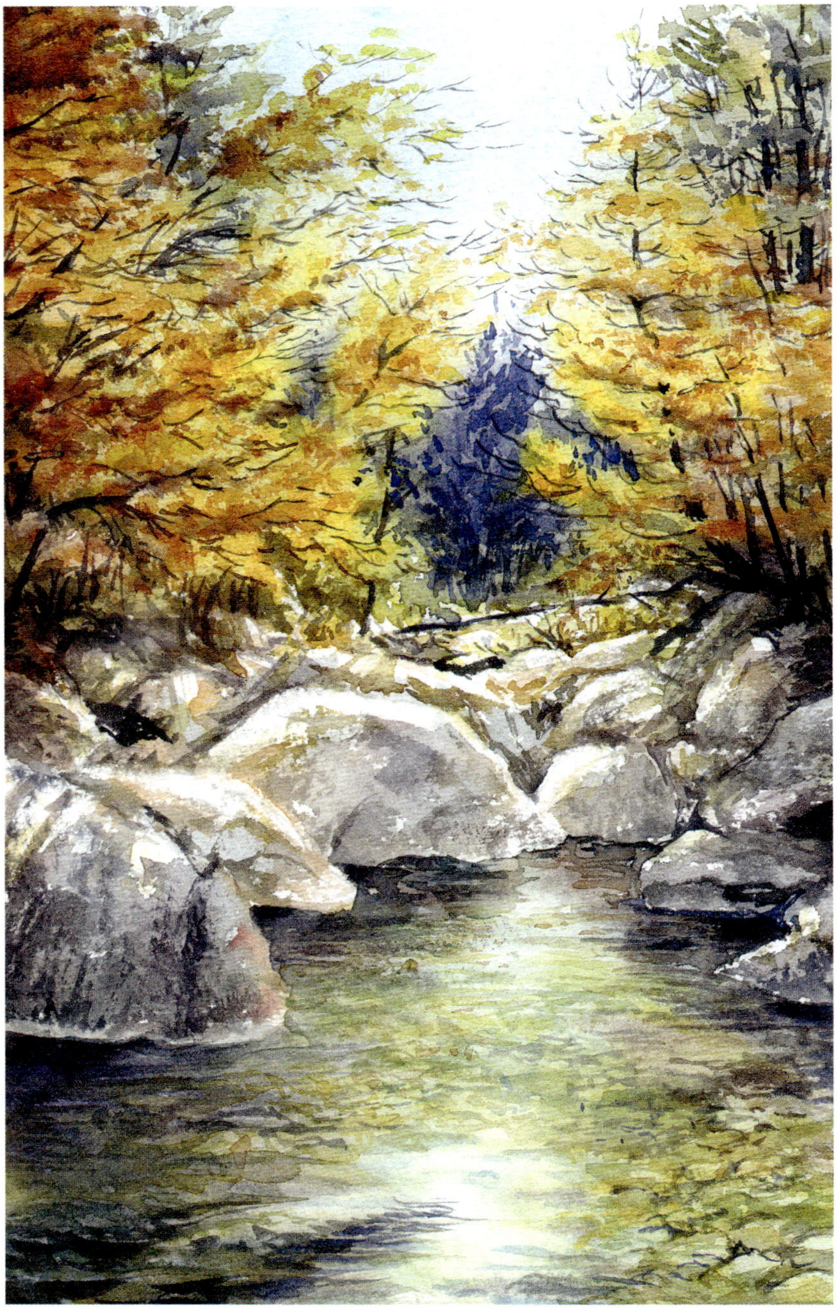

In order to paint a lovely autumnal atmosphere, the secret is to get the orange colors just right. Thus, in this analysis, we will concentrate mostly on these.

Autumnal oranges can be achieved by anchoring your color choices around pyrrole red deep (PR264) and three yellows: saffron yellow (PY110), chartreuse yellow (PY129), and yellow ocher (PY42).

For this watercolor painting, Manù's palette also included the following colors: phtalo blue (PB15:3), ultramine blue (PB29), and, in smaller quantities, cerulean blue (PB35), Prussian blue (PB27), scarlet red (PR255), and Isaro yellow light (PY154). Working with Van Dyke brown is optional.

ANALYSIS

> *For the sky*, Manu worked using cerulean blue (PB35), reinforced, in places, with phtalo blue (PB15:3).

> *The outline of the river* is built using cerulean blue along with Prussian blue (PB27) and chartreuse yellow (PY129). Thus, the cerulean blue of the sky is echoed in the water of the river, and the harmony between sky and earth is respected. A few touches of yellow ocher (PY42) outline the stones underneath the water.

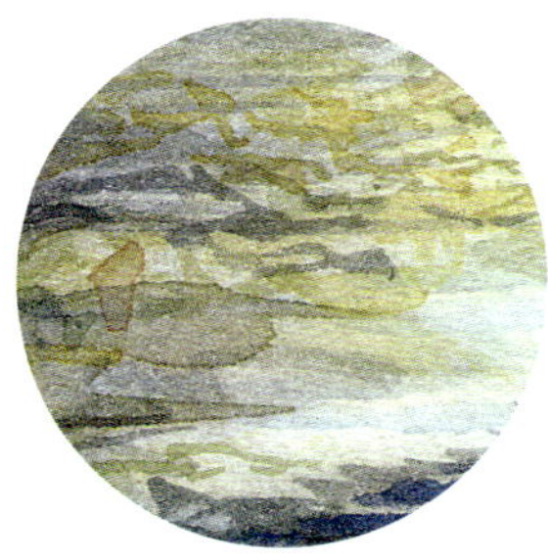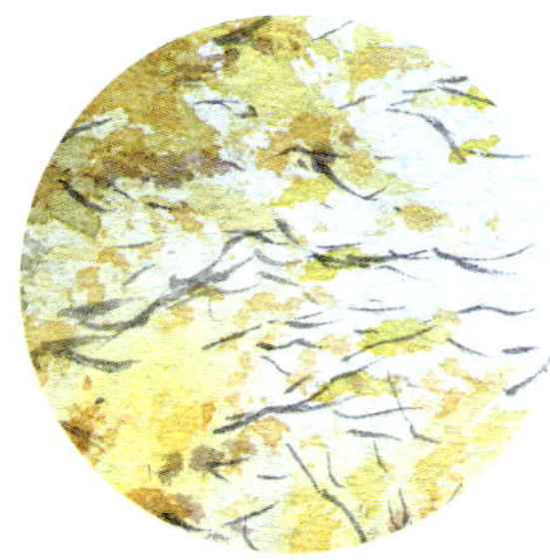

> *The foliage of the trees* is bounded by a first layer of yellow ocher (PY42) and saffron yellow (PY110). These yellows then melt into the blue of the sky while it is still damp, creating light greens by diffusion.

Once this first outline has been established, Manù accentuates the nuances using blues, browns, and dark greens that are present throughout the composition. In order to do the same, you could either use "ready-made" colors such as indigo blue, Van Dyke brown, and Payne's gray, or you could have the pleasure of finding these shades through mixtures created on your palette.

For dark blue, the combination of pyrrole red deep (PR264) and phtalo blue (PB15:3) is excellent. Blue and red are mixed in equal parts; you can then make light corrections if necessary.

CERULEAN BLUE (PB35) + CHARTREUSE YELLOW (PY129) + PRUSSIAN BLUE (PB27)

PHTALO BLUE (PB15:3) + PYRROLE RED DEEP (PR264)

ONE PART PHTALO BLUE (PB15:3) + ONE PART CHARTREUSE YELLOW (PY129) + TWO PARTS PYRROLE RED DEEP (PR264)

ONE PART PHTALO BLUE (PB15:3) + ONE PART SAFFRON YELLOW (PY110) + TWO PARTS PYRROLE RED DEEP (PR264)

BROWN BASED ON CHARTREUSE YELLOW (PY129), SHADED WITH A LITTLE BIT OF OCHER (PY42)

BROWN BASED ON SAFFRON YELLOW (PY110), SHADED WITH A LITTLE BIT OF OCHER (PY42)

DARK BROWN BASED ON CHARTREUSE YELLOW (PY129) + DARK BLUE, IN VARYING QUANTITIES

DARK BROWN BASED ON SAFFRON YELLOW (PY110) + DARK BLUE, IN VARYING QUANTITIES

For the dark brown, you can refer to the one that was chosen for the execution of the green landscape (see page 83). However, in order to stay within the same chromatic harmony, you can replace Prussian blue (PB27) with phtalo blue (PB15:3). You can also choose to use saffron yellow (PY110) instead of chartreuse yellow (PY129). In both cases, you will first want to put together a green by combining blue and yellow. Then, break up that mixture using red. For softening the browns, a little bit of yellow ocher (PY42) is perfect.

To finish up, the dark grays can be created by combining the brown and blue that we analyzed previously. In general, these grays can be warmed up with the addition of yellow ocher (PY42) or cooled down with ultramarine blue (PB29).

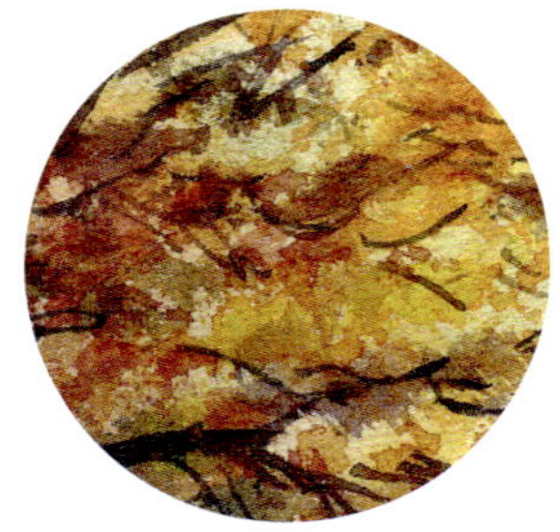 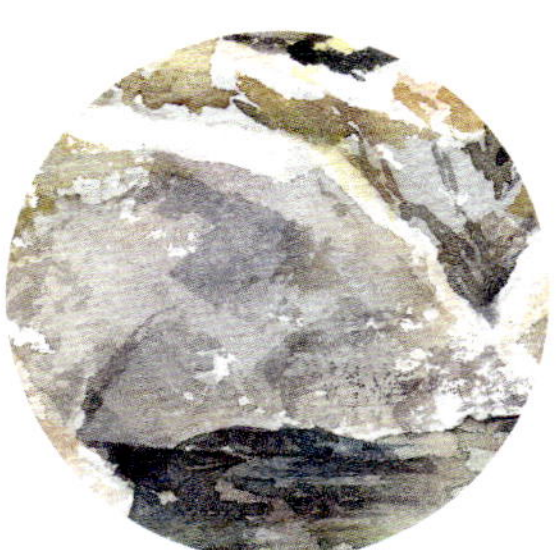

Manù uses this array of dark colors, concentrated to varying degrees in different spots, in order to create the trees in the background, the rocks and their reflections in the water, and the tree branches and tree trunks. Elsewhere, the dark brown associated with the green of the water allows the painter to show the shimmering on top of the river. A hint of pyrrole red deep (PR264) helps to suggest the reflections of the trees on the rocks.

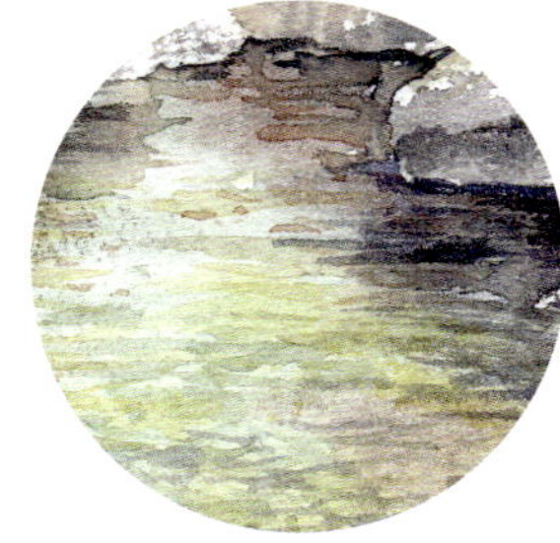 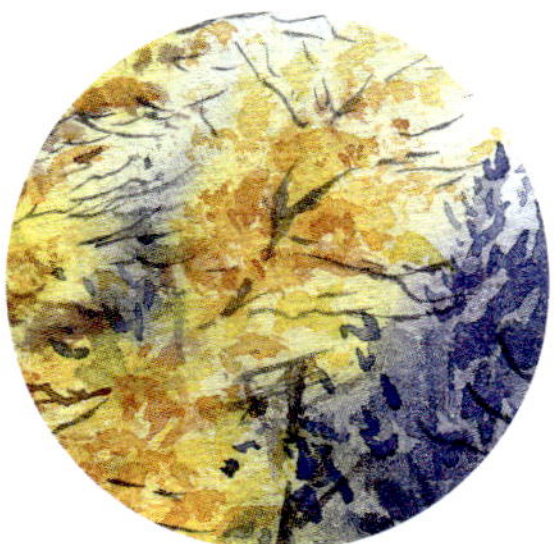

It is interesting to take the time to discover the nuances that the combinations described above will allow you to achieve. Some of these colors are simply magnificent.

Expanding Your Autumnal Range

For painting foliage, we recommend that you start looking for your orange colors by concentrating on the combination of three colors: pyrrole red deep (PR264), yellow ocher (PY42), and saffron yellow (PY110). Then, some areas can be brightened by incorporating some chartreuse yellow (PY129) into the pyrrole red deep and, in places, adding a little bit of yellow ocher. You can make yourself a small personal color chart, which is always helpful as a reminder. That way, you will have the pleasure of discovering that it is easy to master a very broad range of oranges, going from brightly shimmering to not at all, depending on which color is dominant. Here are a few examples.

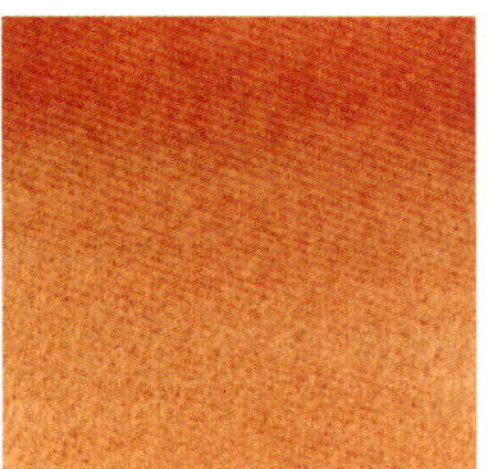

SAFFRON YELLOW (PY110) + PYRROLE RED DEEP (PR264)

CHARTREUSE YELLOW (PY129) + PYRROLE RED DEEP (PR264)

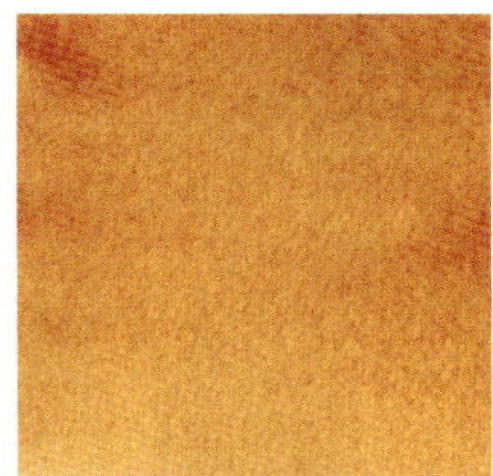

SAFFRON YELLOW (PY110) + PYRROLE RED DEEP (PR264) + CHARTREUSE YELLOW (PY129)

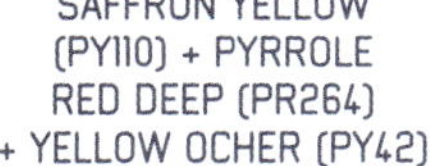

SAFFRON YELLOW (PY110) + PYRROLE RED DEEP (PR264) + YELLOW OCHER (PY42)

CHARTREUSE YELLOW (PY129) + PYRROLE RED DEEP (PR264) + YELLOW OCHER (PY42)

This range of oranges can be cooled down by adding ultramarine blue (PB29), in order to create deep, warm browns, which are useful for shadows and volumes.

SAFFRON YELLOW (PY110) + PYRROLE RED DEEP (PR264) + ULTRAMARINE BLUE (PB29)

CHARTREUSE YELLOW (PY129) + PYRROLE RED DEEP (PR264) + ULTRAMARINE BLUE (PB29)

A few last notes of a luminous orange, using a base of saffron yellow (PY110) and scarlet red (PR255), put the finishing touches on the coloring of the foliage.

The Mediterranean Coast

> Manù

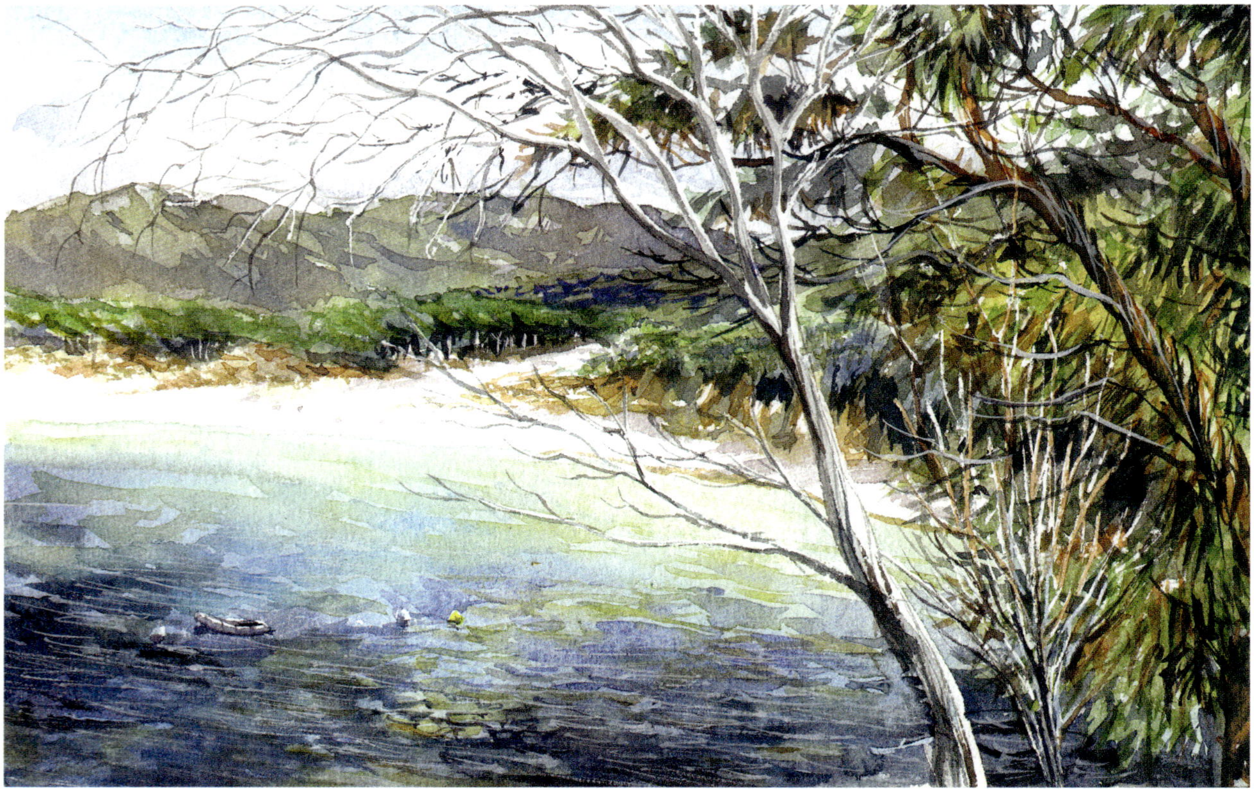

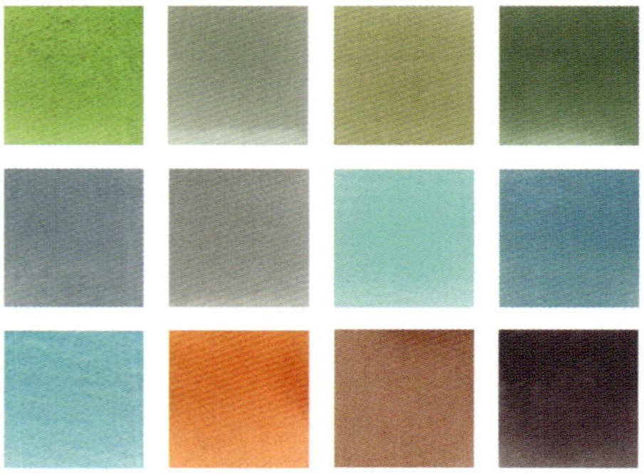

For a coastal landscape, the painting of the water is often seen as the main difficulty. On closer inspection, however, it turns out to be simply an exercise in patience, a matter of taking the time to paint in successive layers. You have to pay attention, as Manù has done, to keeping the same chromatic range and concentrating the touches of color.

The greens are developed in the same general way as those we have already looked at. The artist put them together beginning with a blue, in this case phtalo blue (PB15:3), and four yellows, namely Isaro yellow light (PY154), chartreuse yellow (PY129), saffron yellow (PY110), and yellow ocher (PY42). His palette is rounded out with cerulean blue (PB35) for the sky, ultramarine blue (PB29), and pyrrole red deep (PR264) for contrasts.

ANALYSIS

> *In order to paint the sea,* you first have to create a beautiful light turquoise green. It can be achieved by mixing Isaro yellow light (PY154) and phtalo blue (PB15:3) in equal parts. Then add this green, small touches at a time, to cerulean blue (PB35).

This basic color serves as a first coat on which are then laid various nuances of blue, all of them created from this light turquoise.

Turquoise Waters

Manù nuances his basic color with Isaro yellow light (PY154) or phtalo blue (PB15:3) in order to obtain turquoise colors that lean more toward either green or blue. He deepens them by adding varying quantities of ultramarine blue (PB29) and pyrrole red deep (PR264). It's an interesting exercise to make oneself a little color chart based on these five colors in order to study all the different nuances that you can obtain from them. Here are a few examples.

| BASIC COLOR: PHTALO BLUE (PB15:3) + ISARO (PY154), THEN ADDED TO CERULEAN BLUE (PB35) | BASIC COLOR WITH MORE PHTALO BLUE (PB15:3) ADDED | BASIC COLOR WITH A HINT OF ULTRAMARINE BLUE (PB29) AND PYRROLE RED DEEP (PR264) | BASIC COLOR WITH A LARGER AMOUNT OF ULTRAMARINE BLUE (PB29) AND PYRROLE RED DEEP (PR264) |

Note that the various layers of colors influence each other thanks to the play of transparency between them. The examples above are just general guidelines because in practice, these shades will be influenced by the color that is underneath them. This is the whole point and the beauty of this process!

PHTALO BLUE (PB15:3)
+ CHARTREUSE
YELLOW (PY129)
+ YELLOW OCHER
(PY42) (MORE
STRONGLY PRESENT)

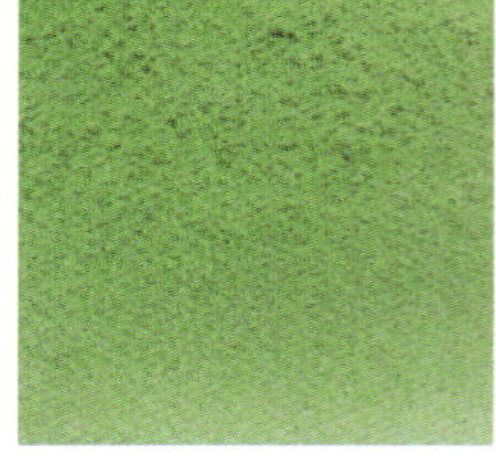

PHTALO BLUE (PB15:3)
+ CHARTREUSE
YELLOW (PY129)

PHTALO BLUE (PB15:3)
+ CHARTREUSE
YELLOW (PY129)
+ YELLOW OCHER
(PY42)

PHTALO BLUE (PB15:3)
+ CHARTREUSE
YELLOW (PY129)
+ YELLOW OCHER
(PY42)
+ PYRROLE RED DEEP
(PR264)

COOLED DOWN USING
ULTRAMARINE BLUE
(PB29)

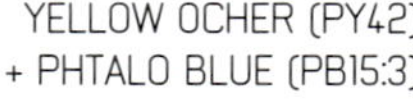

YELLOW OCHER (PY42)
+ PHTALO BLUE (PB15:3)

The greens in this watercolor painting can all be obtained
starting with a mixture of phtalo blue (PB15:3) and chartreuse
yellow (PY129). This vibrant green is then modulated with varying
proportions of yellow ocher (PY42). Pyrrole red deep (PR264)
helps to darken the greens, while ultramarine blue (PB29) cools
them down.

> *The mountains*, in the background, are created using cool,
restrained greens. These can be obtained by combining yellow
ocher (PY42) and a little bit of phtalo blue, augmented with
ultramarine blue (PB29), to cool the color down, and pyrrole red
deep (PR264) to bring out the volumes.

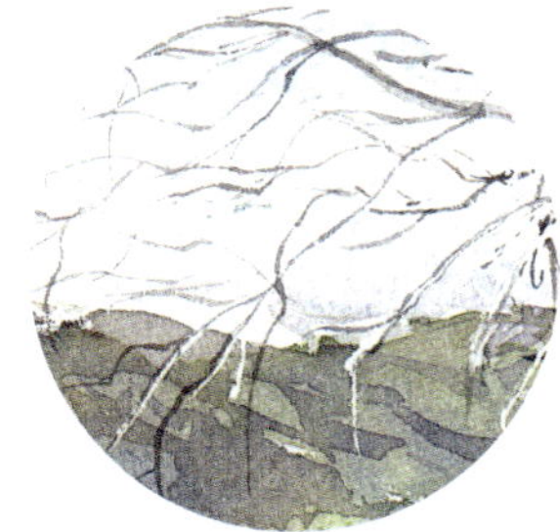
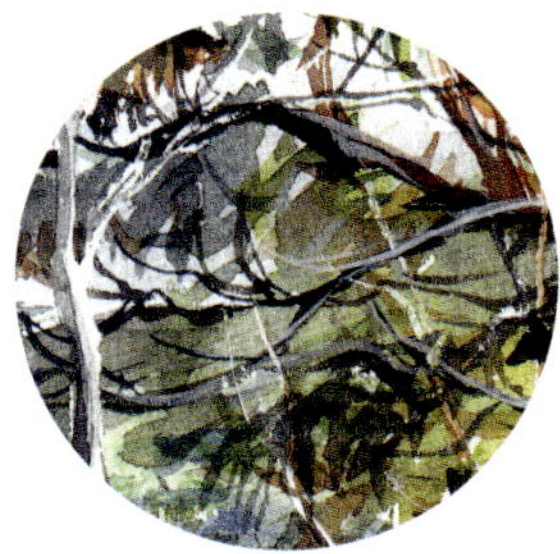

YELLOW OCHER (PY42)
+ PHTALO BLUE (PB15:3)
+ ULTRAMARINE BLUE
(PB29)

YELLOW OCHER (PY42)
+ PHTALO BLUE (PB15:3)
+ ULTRAMARINE BLUE
(PB29), ALL OF THAT
THEN CONTRASTED
WITH PYRROLE RED
DEEP (PR264)

> *The ground, the branches, and the tree trunks* are all painted in shades of deep red and reddish brown. This palette of colors is created using a base of saffron yellow (PY110) and yellow ocher (PY42). In order to draw the mixture more toward reddish ochers, simply add more pyrrole red deep (PR264). The color can be darkened using phtalo blue (PB15:3) in order to obtain a medium brown.

YELLOW OCHER (PY42) + SAFFRON YELLOW (PY110) + PYRROLE RED DEEP (PR264)

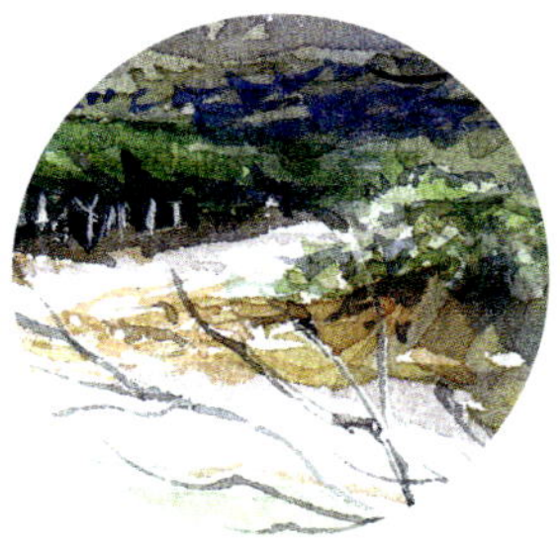

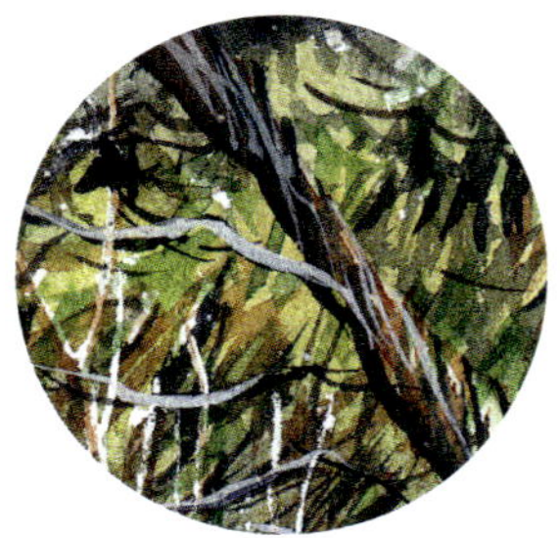

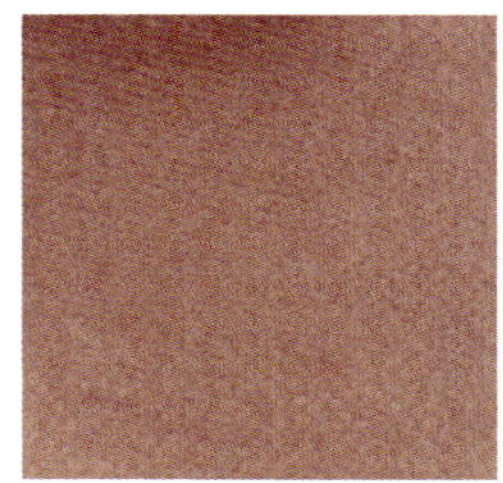

YELLOW OCHER (PY42) + SAFFRON YELLOW (PY110) + PYRROLE RED DEEP (PR264), ALL REINFORCED WITH PHTALO BLUE (PB15:3)

> *The details of the branches and tree trunks* can be created using the dark green discussed above. This green, touched up with a hint of ultramarine, reinforces your medium brown and creates a contrasting color that is very useful for the final touches.

EXAMPLE OF A CONTRASTING

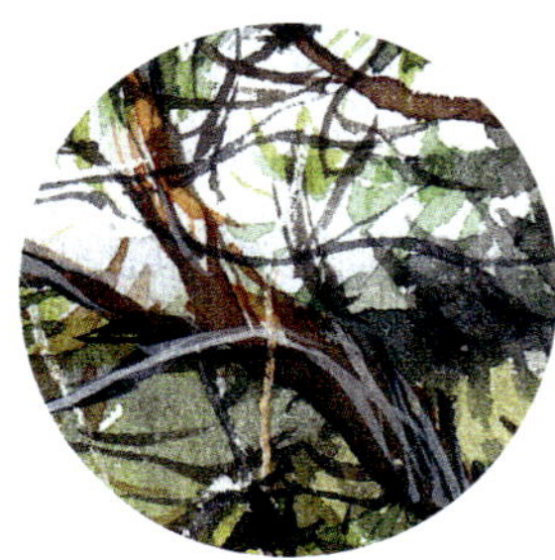

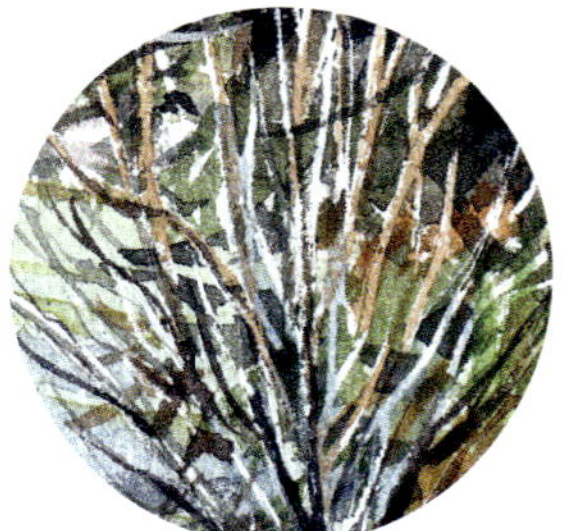

Tip

A very dark green can be created by mixing chartreuse yellow (PY129), pyrrole red deep (PR264), and phtalo blue (PB15:3). Start by mixing the yellow and the blue, in equal parts. Then deepen the color using pyrrole red deep. This color is very useful by itself, or used sparingly to darken your greens.

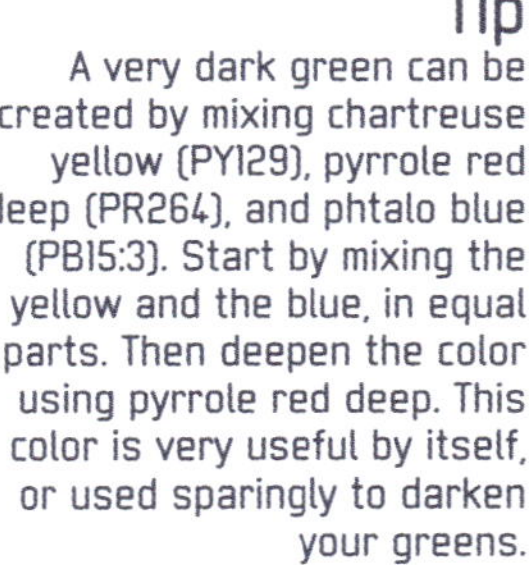

DARK GREEN: CHARTREUSE YELLOW (PY129) + PHTALO BLUE (PB15:3) + PYRROLE RED DEEP (PR264)

The Atlantic Coast

> Manù

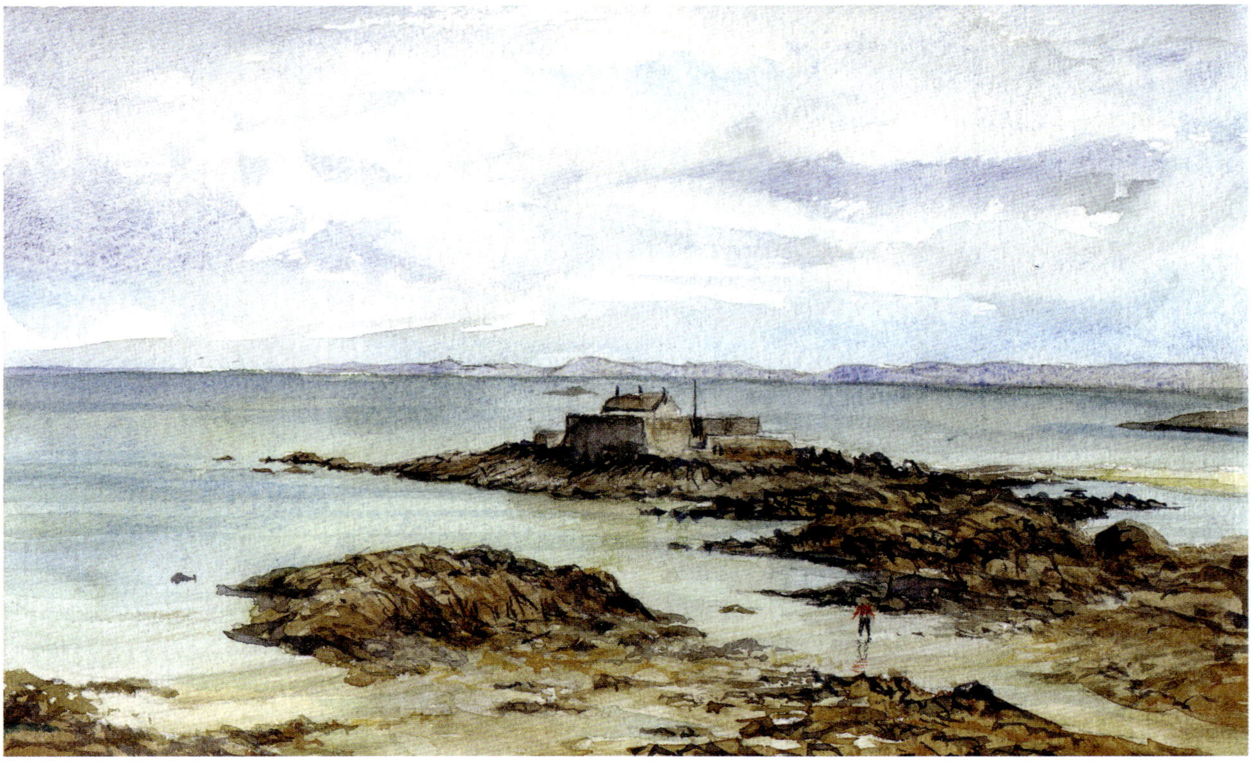

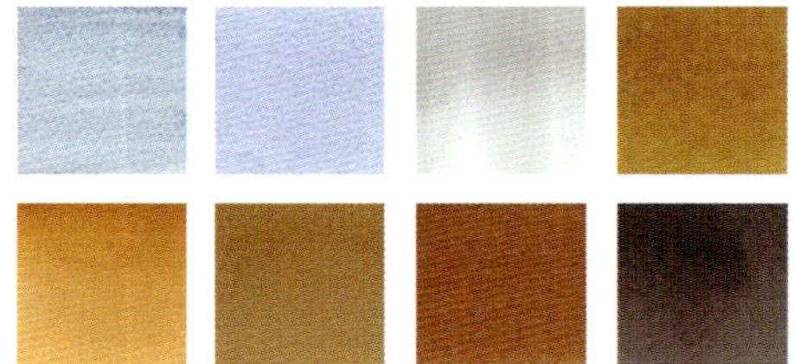

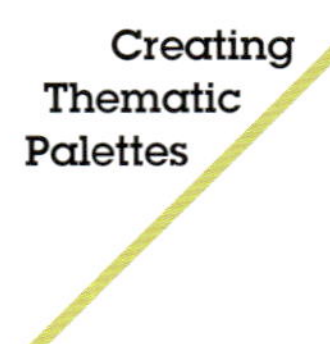

In this maritime watercolor, the work on the sky is very interesting. One of the peculiarities of Manù's palette is the presence of lapis lazuli from Daniel Smith. This mineral pigment is the forerunner of our modern ultramarine blue (PB29). Less vibrant and more restrained than the modern color, this lapis lazuli is also very granular. Manù finds these three characteristics particularly appealing for painting his skies.

For this painting, Manù's palette includes the following three blues: lapis lazuli, Prussian blue (PB27), and cerulean blue (PB35); in addition, there are saffron yellow (PY110), pyrrole red deep (PR264), and yellow ocher (PY42). As we shall see, ultramarine blue (PB29) can replace the lapis lazuli, and the use of Van Dyke brown is optional.

ANALYSIS

> *The coastline* is painted using shades of light, medium, and dark brown. As we have seen, these browns can easily be created using a dark brown obtained by mixing equal parts of saffron yellow (PY110) and Prussian blue (PB27). To that, we can add up two parts of pyrrole red deep (PR264). Or, as Manù does, we could replace this mixture with a ready-made Van Dyke brown or any other dark brown. Then, using a hint of dark brown, he breaks up the color of the saffron yellow (PY110). This color can be shaded, as desired, using either pyrrole red deep (PR264), yellow ocher (PY42), or a combination of the two.

Starting with a yellow ocher wash, and then using these various shades of brown, Manù outlines the shapes of the coastline. For the details, a hint of Prussian blue or ultramarine blue (PB29) makes it possible to deepen the base brown, if necessary.

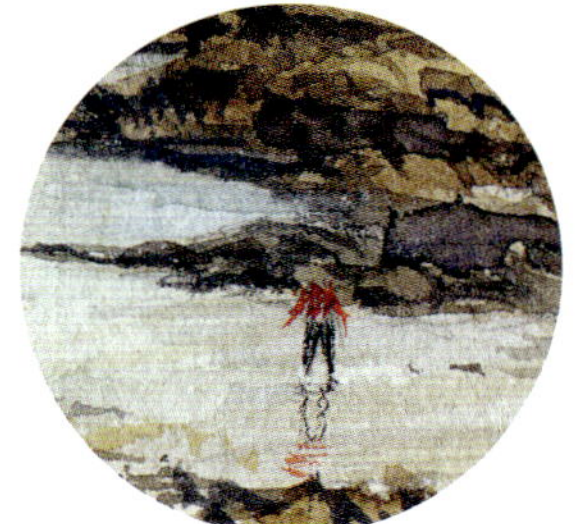

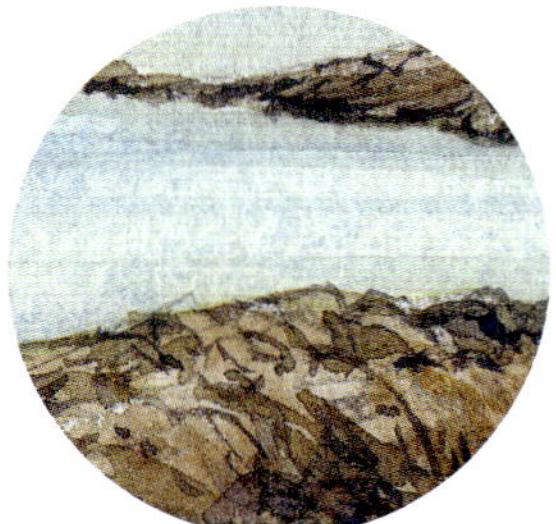

DARK BROWN BASE

SAFFRON YELLOW (PY110) BROKEN UP WITH DARK BROWN

SAFFRON YELLOW (PY110) BROKEN UP WITH DARK BROWN + YELLOW OCHER (PY42)

SAFFRON YELLOW (PY110) BROKEN UP WITH DARK BROWN (IN GREATER QUANTITIES) + YELLOW OCHER (PY42)

SAFFRON YELLOW (PY110) BROKEN UP + YELLOW OCHER (PY42) + PYRROLE RED DEEP (PR264) (IN VARYING QUANTITIES)

DARK BROWN BASE WITH PRUSSIAN BLUE (PB27)

SAFFRON YELLOW
(PY110)

DANIEL SMITH
LAPIS LAZULI

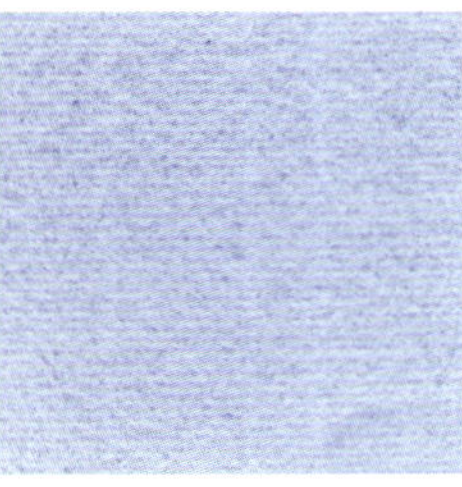

ULTRAMARINE
BLUE (PB29) BROKEN
UP WITH SCARLET
RED (PR255)—TO
BE HEAVILY DILUTED
BEFORE ADDING IT
TO THE PAGE

CERULEAN BLUE
(PB35) BROKEN UP
WITH DARK BROWN

> **The sea** is painted using saffron yellow (PY110) and cerulean blue (PB35). Using layering, a little bit of Prussian blue (PB27) then accentuates the darker areas. Manù also added some touches of lapis lazuli in order to echo the sky. If you are not using lapis lazuli, you can work with ultramarine blue (PB29) with a touch of scarlet red (PR255) or pyrrole red deep (PR264) worked into it. If you want to accentuate the mixture's granular effect, you can add a few drops of a granular medium. Then, this color is laid down using small, well-diluted touches.

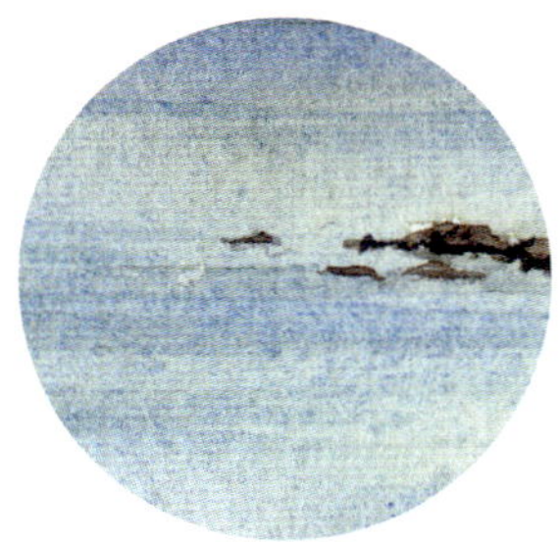
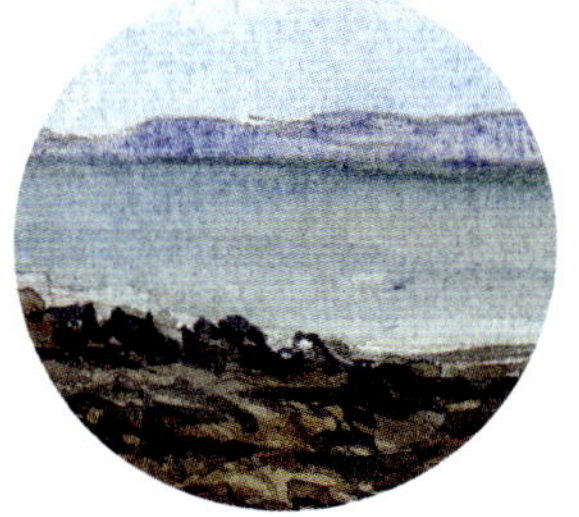

> **At the edge of the water**, saffron yellow (PY110) is more strongly present, to render the effect of the waves breaking on the sand.

> **The sky** is painted using cerulean blue (PB35), nuanced with lapis lazuli and a few small touches of Prussian blue (PB27). Thus, we find there the same shades of blue as were used to paint the sea. This is a way to respect a pleasant visual harmony.

The shades of gray are achieved by adding a little bit of dark brown to the cerulean blue. Of course, as with the sea, a modified ultramarine blue (PB29) can take the place of the lapis lazuli.

A Cityscape

> Manù

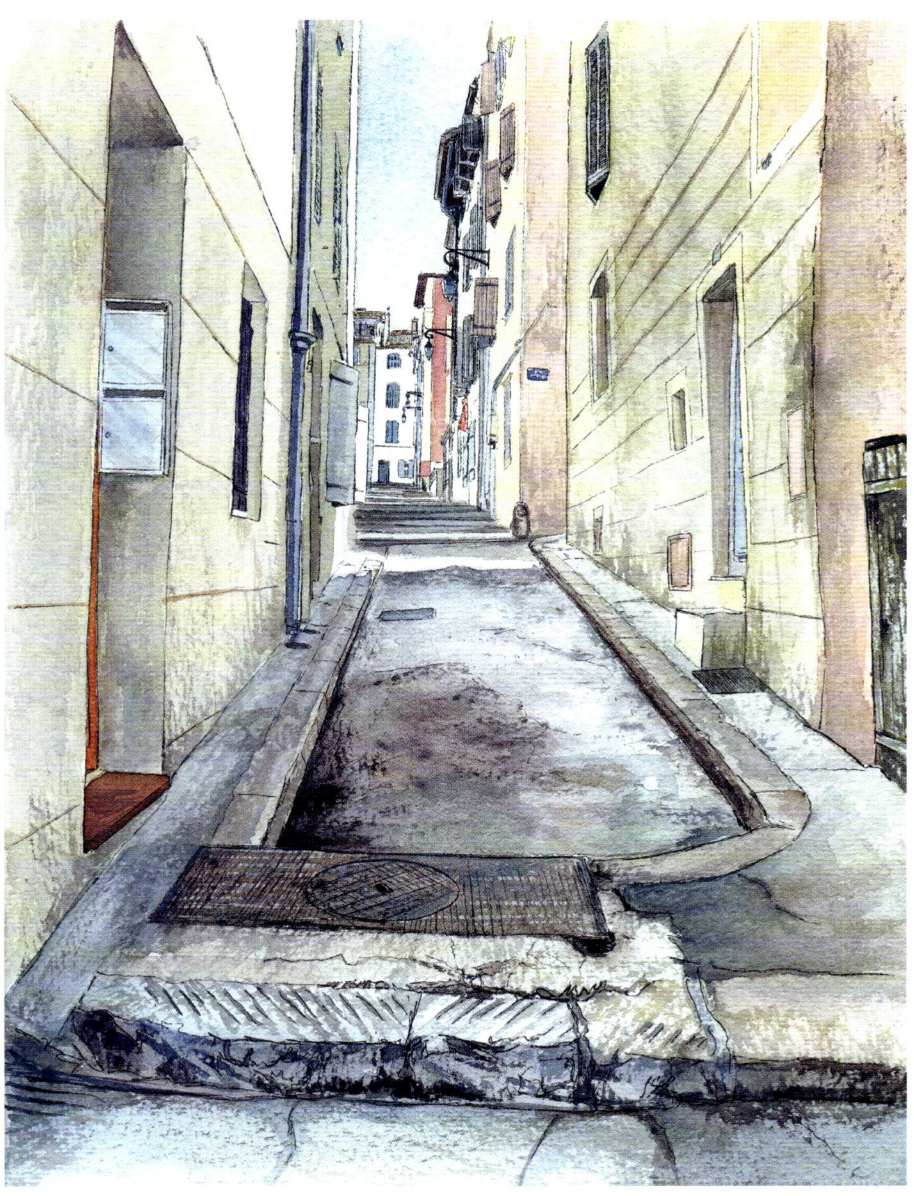

For this little alleyway, Manù works in a relatively restrained harmony of colors centered around yellow ocher (PY42), which is then complemented by Prussian blue (PB27), phtalo blue (PB15:3), and pyrrole red deep (PR264). Saffron yellow (PY110) brings a little bit of warmth to the composition, and cerulean blue (PB35) is useful for the sky.

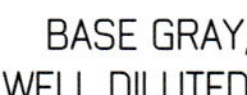
BASE GRAY,
WELL DILUTED

BASE GRAY WITH
AN EXTRA TOUCH OF
PRUSSIAN BLUE (PB27)

BASE GRAY
+ YELLOW OCHER
(PY42) IN VARYING
PROPORTIONS

ANALYSIS

> **The sky,** as is often the case in Manù's work, is painted using cerulean blue (PB35) augmented with a touch of yellow ocher (PY42) in order to echo the shades used to paint all of his buildings.

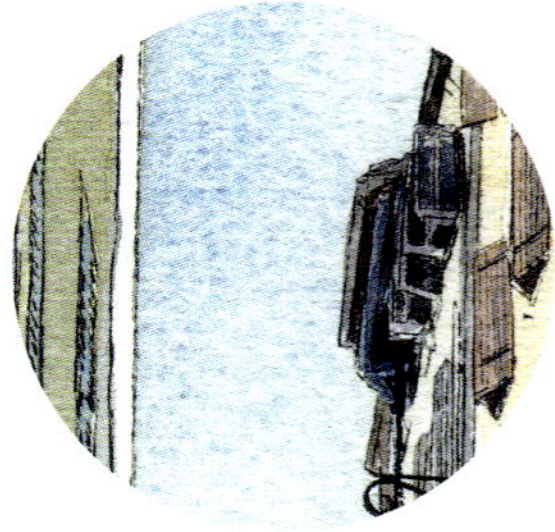
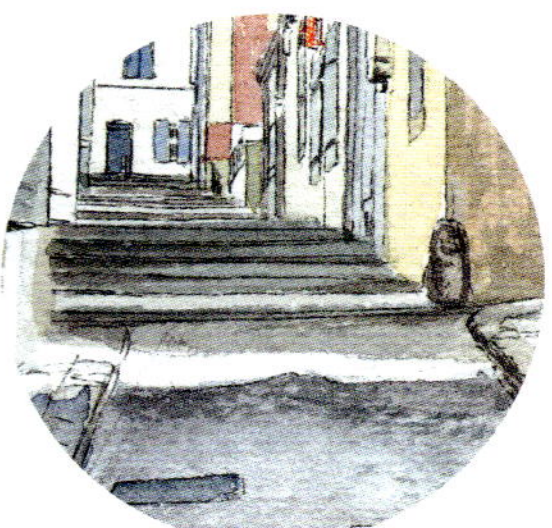

> **The alleyway and its sidewalk** are painted in shades of gray, some more and some less diluted. We have already addressed the process of creating grays at various points in this book. However, in order to respect the colors chosen for the execution of this painting, the most prudent approach is to use the original formula for Payne's Gray (see page 68), which we will call base gray here. Thus, we mix one part Prussian blue (PB27) with one part pyrrole red deep (PR264) and then shade it using yellow ocher (PY42).

At this point, it is easy to draw the color more toward brown, by letting the yellow ocher dominate, or else more toward a bluish gray, by letting the Prussian blue take the upper hand. A few complementary touches of red pyrrole deep nuance the gray of the ground and keep it from becoming too uniform and flat.

> **The details of the manhole cover and of the edges of the sidewalks** are drawn using a very dark brown, like Van Dyke brown, which you can make yourself (see page 70).

> **The pink building** in the foreground, as well as the one farther back, are painted using a mixture of yellow ocher (PY42) adjusted with pyrrole red deep (PR264) and a touch of Isaro rose (PR122). The color is heavily diluted before being laid down. Manù has chosen to replace the Isaro rose with titanium white (PW6).

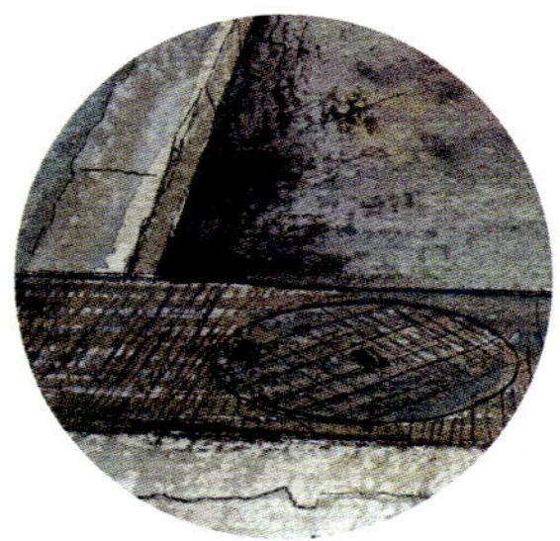
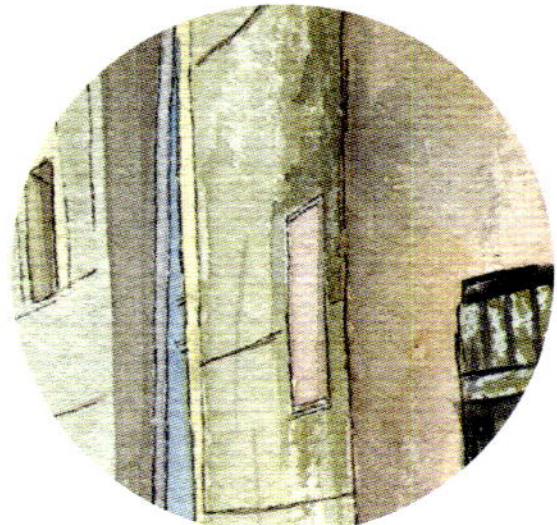

Using White in Watercolors?

It is the rare watercolor artist who dares to incorporate white into their mixtures.

In watercolors, it is customary to believe that white should be avoided, because only the lightness of the paper should count. Using white sometimes even results in penalties for those who want to enter watercolor contests.

Technically, indeed, it is really not acceptable to paint a detail in white in a watercolor painting, because you ought to have just kept that space free for the white of the paper to show through. For example, Manù shows the white of the building at the end of the alleyway by just keeping the white page clear in that spot.

On the other hand, knowing that a watercolor white contains the exact same ingredients as a colored watercolor, there is no need to reject the white when creating a shade. And in fact, if you look at the components more closely, you will see that watercolor manufacturers do use white in the composition of several of their colors.

The choice of whether or not to introduce white into your mixtures is your own. Adding white to a color will always take it in the direction of a pastel shade. There are two watercolor whites: titanium white (PW6) and zinc white (PW4). The first is very opaque, the second more transparent.

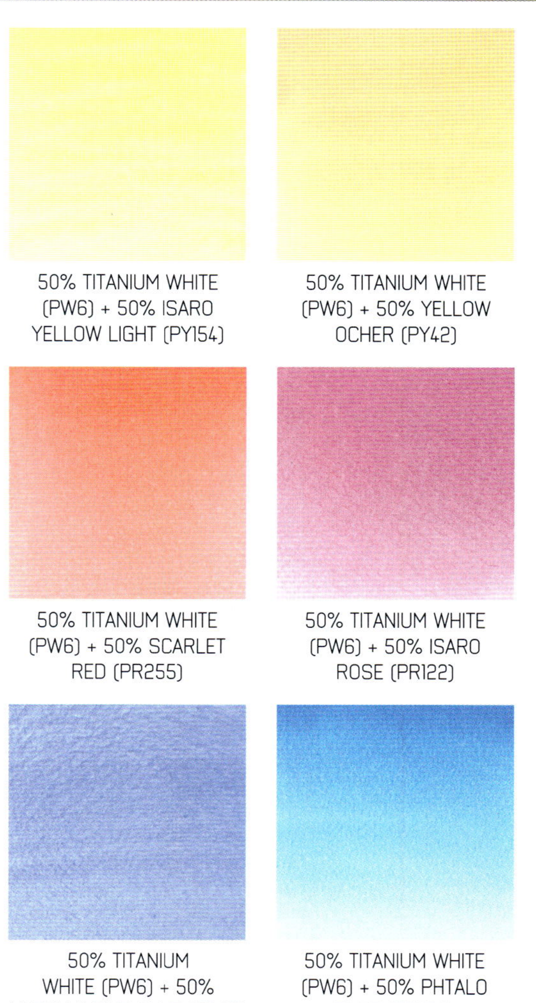

50% TITANIUM WHITE (PW6) + 50% ISARO YELLOW LIGHT (PY154)

50% TITANIUM WHITE (PW6) + 50% YELLOW OCHER (PY42)

50% TITANIUM WHITE (PW6) + 50% SCARLET RED (PR255)

50% TITANIUM WHITE (PW6) + 50% ISARO ROSE (PR122)

50% TITANIUM WHITE (PW6) + 50% ULTRAMARINE BLUE (PB29)

50% TITANIUM WHITE (PW6) + 50% PHTALO BLUE (PB15:3)

> **The yellow houses** are colored with a mixture of yellow ocher (PY42) and phtalo blue (PB15:3). The shade is broken up with a touch of pyrrole red deep (PR264) in order to avoid letting the mixture go too far toward green. The presence of the phtalo blue is stronger in the shaded areas, and a few touches of saffron yellow (PY110) emphasize the sunlit buildings.

As a finishing touch, Manù adds a gray-brown wash over all of his shapes.

YELLOW OCHER (PY42) + PHTALO BLUE (PB15:3) + WELL-DILUTED PYRROLE RED DEEP (PR264)

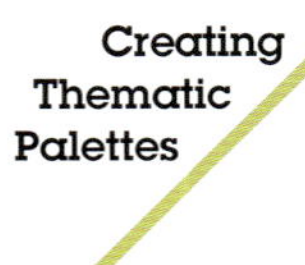

In the Snow

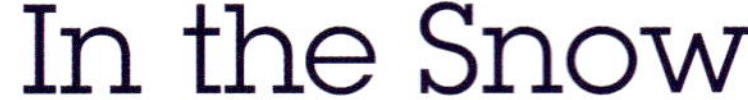

> Fabien Petillion

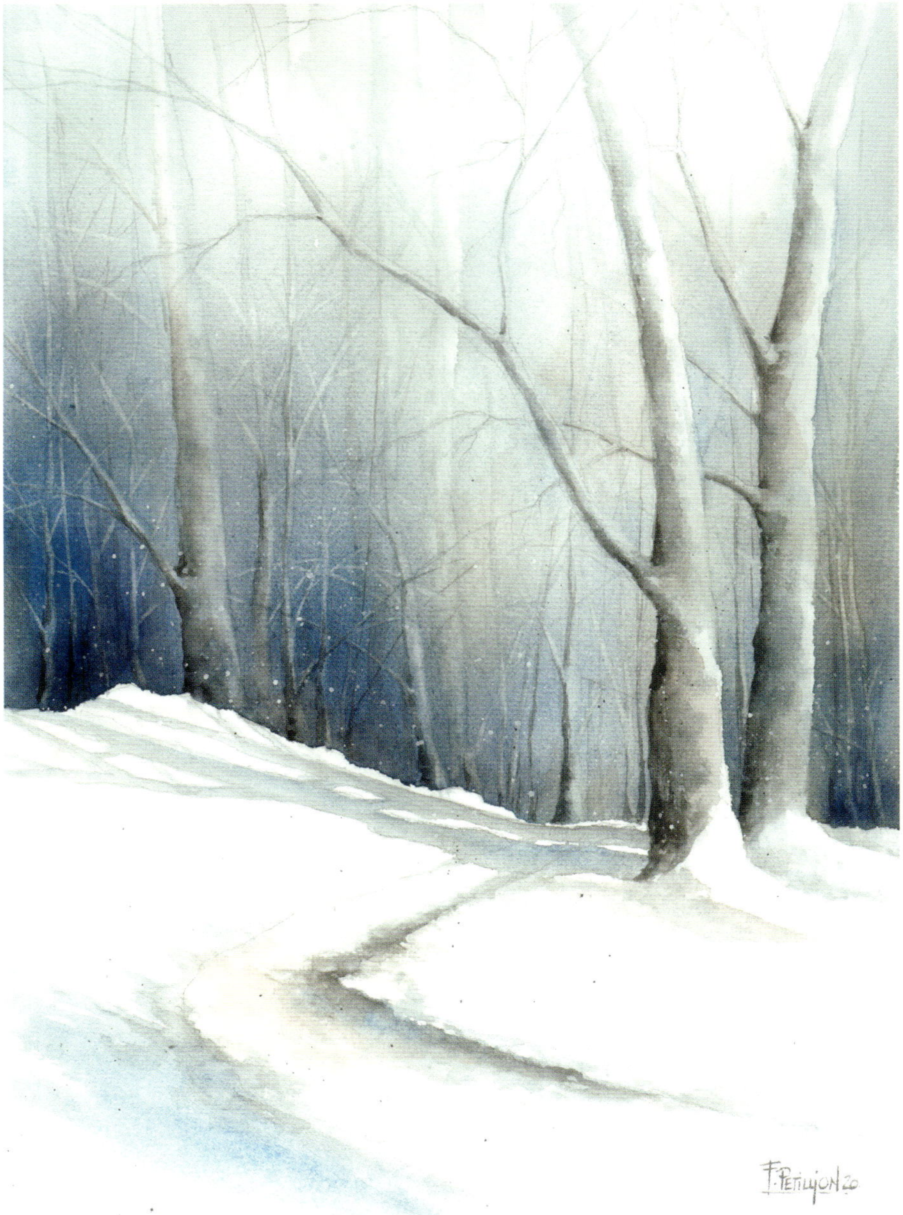

Very few colors were used in the painting of this snow-filled landscape. Cerulean blue (PB35), Prussian blue (PB27), and, for contrast, indigo blue, Payne's Gray, and sepia are the colors that organize Fabien's palette.

ANALYSIS

On a page moistened with clear water, the artist colors his entire background using a mixture of cerulean blue (PB35) deepened with Prussian blue (PB27). Unlike other watercolor artists, Fabien likes to create his mixtures right on the paper, rather than on his palette. This technique allows him to let his colors melt into each other and to bring much more nuance into the execution of his paintings. Still working wet-on-wet here, he then added touches of indigo blue to indicate the contrasts, especially at the foot of the trees. He also could have used a dark blue based on Prussian blue with pyrrole red deep (PR264), but that combination would have drawn the background closer to violet. This is why Fabien ends up choosing a more neutral indigo based on burnt umber (PBr7) and ultramarine blue (PB29), in equal parts, enriched with a hint of Prussian blue. This mixture can be adjusted using a little bit of ultramarine if you want it to be more bluish.

> ***Only the three largest tree trunks*** have been kept white. The other trees are drawn by removing color using a dry brush while the paper is still lightly moist. This technique allows the artist to avoid pure whites, which would have been much too blunt.

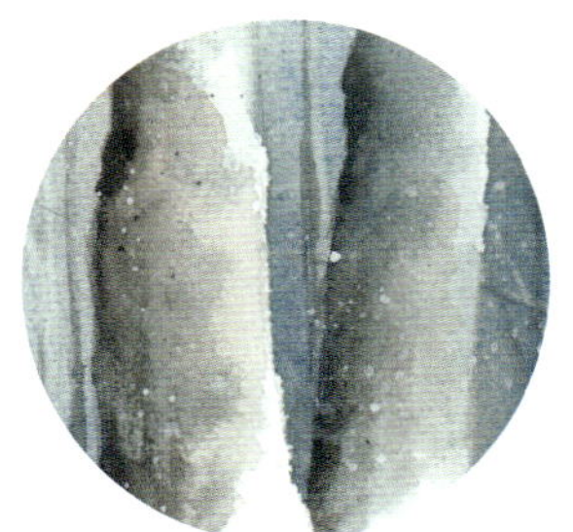 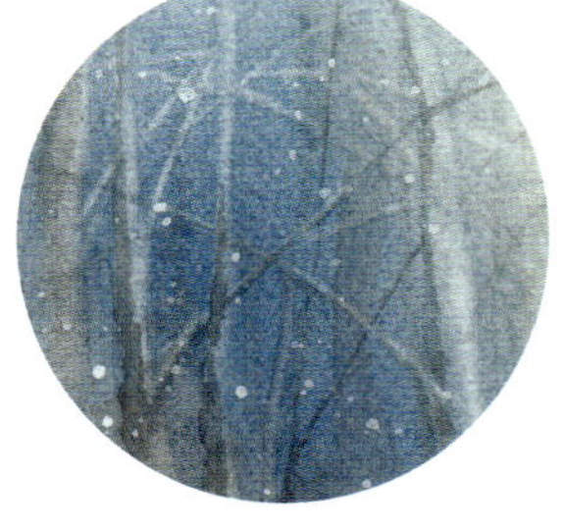

> ***The gray shades***, of the trees' shadows, of the road, and of the three trunks, are rendered using a bluish gray. Fabien particularly likes Payne's gray, which he lightly nuances with a hint of sepia. As in Manù's autumnal landscape (see "In Autumnal Tones," page 86), these nuances can be obtained through mixtures. But working with ready-made colors allows Fabien to more easily preserve a unified chromatic array of grays. This is even more justified if you, too, work in large formats.

The snow should reflect the color of the sky. Thus, Fabien gives a reminder of that color, at the level of the road, by adding a few touches of cerulean blue (PB35) colored with a hint of Prussian blue (PB27).

BURNT UMBER (PBR7) + ULTRAMARINE BLUE (PB29) + A HINT OF PRUSSIAN BLUE (PB27)

PAYNE'S GRAY + SEPIA (HEAVILY DILUTED)

PAYNE'S GRAY + SEPIA (LESS DILUTED)

Tip

To finish off, Fabien lays down, in spots, a wash with a burnt sienna base. The warm note of this brown softens the otherwise somewhat harsh contrasts between the white of the snow and the blue of the sky.

Painting a Portrait

One of the main difficulties presented by portrait painting is getting the skin tone right. Fabien Petillion, who has many years of experience in this subject, will take you through the creation of color mixtures for three kinds of skin tone: light, olive, and dark. Because he offers daily classes and internships, this artist is regularly confronted with the pitfalls that his watercolor students encounter. In order to help them better, Fabien has developed a method of constructive learning based on a good mastery of drawing and a perfect knowledge of how colors behave. We will see that, in order to paint these portraits, Fabien adds some colors that are not included in the basic palette. Reproducing skin color is, indeed, complex, and the precise choice of certain specific shades substantially simplifies the problem.

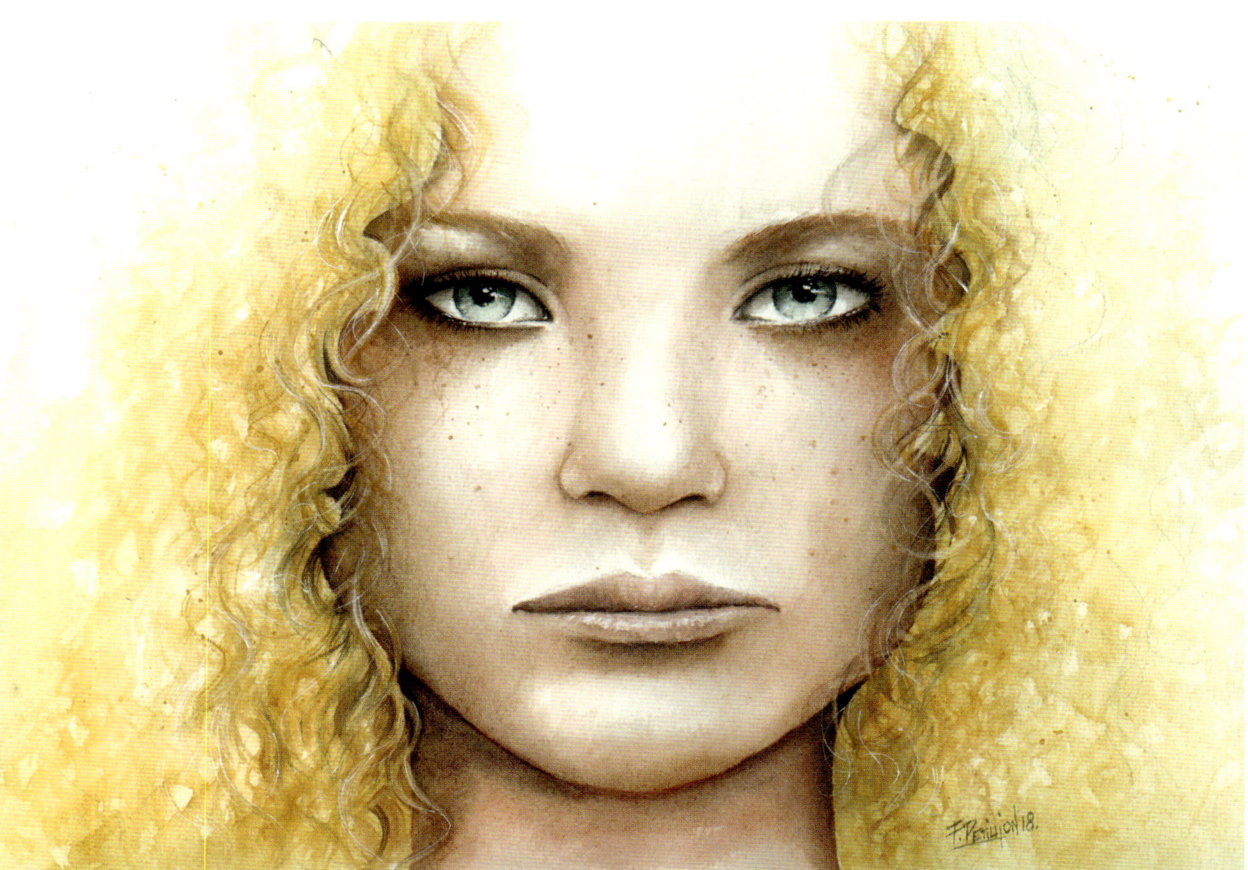

With Fair Skin Tones

> Fabien Petillion

For this portrait, Fabien uses a limited palette. The skin tone is painted using three colors: yellow ocher (PY42), Isaro rose (PR122), and pyrrole red deep (PR264). The shadows use a dark brown, and phtalo blue (PB15:3) is used for the green of the eyes.

ANALYSIS

In order to achieve this light skin color, Fabien works with a base made up of Isaro rose (PR122) and yellow ocher (PY42). Isaro rose is a powerful color. So we start with one part yellow ocher and very gradually, in small quantities, add the Isaro rose. We recommend that you test the mixture, after diluting it well, on a separate piece of paper in order to check the shade.

> **The whole face** is colored with this rosy shade, which Fabien dilutes to varying degrees in order to preserve the light areas. This step is carried out on moist paper. The most illuminated parts of the face, especially on the forehead, are painted using this same mixture, warmed up through the presence of a larger proportion of yellow ocher (PY42).

Then, Fabien strengthens certain areas of the face, adding a hint of pyrrole red deep (PR264) to his mixture. This is particularly the case at the young woman's neck, the base of her chin, and around her eyes.

> **The shadows of the neck** and of the brow bone and the shadows formed by the hair around the face are rendered using a dark brown that is well diluted and then placed on a dry page. This brown can be created by mixing colors, using sepia or Van Dyke brown, which we have already looked at (see pages 70–71). However, you could also choose to use a ready-made dark brown. That way you could be sure you would be able to keep the exact same shade of brown over the entire face.

> **The blond hair** is drawn using only yellow ocher (PY42), diluted to varying degrees. The few locks that are a little darker are painted with dark brown.

> **The green of the eyes** is a mixture of yellow ocher (PY42) and phtalo blue (PB15:3). Because the skin contains some red, which is the complementary color of green, it emphasizes the gaze of the green eyes.

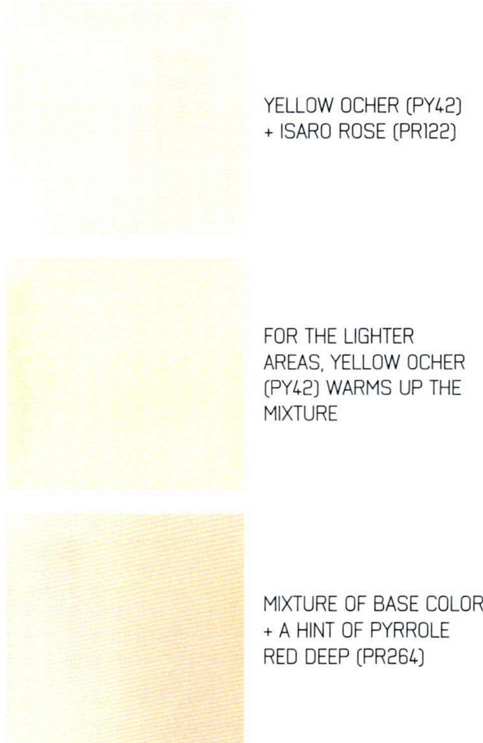

YELLOW OCHER (PY42)
+ ISARO ROSE (PR122)

FOR THE LIGHTER AREAS, YELLOW OCHER (PY42) WARMS UP THE MIXTURE

MIXTURE OF BASE COLOR + A HINT OF PYRROLE RED DEEP (PR264)

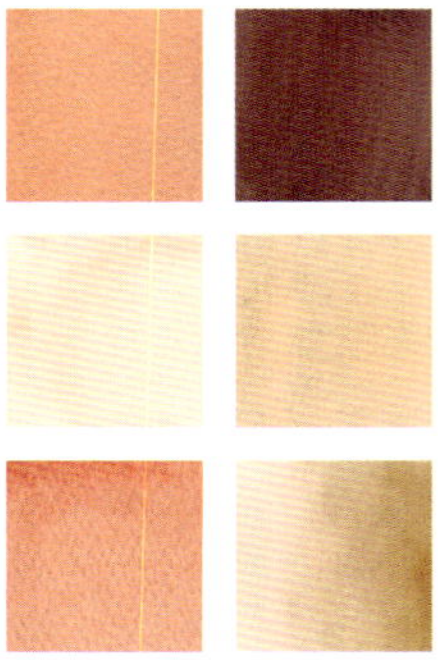

With Olive Skin Tones

> Fabien Petillion

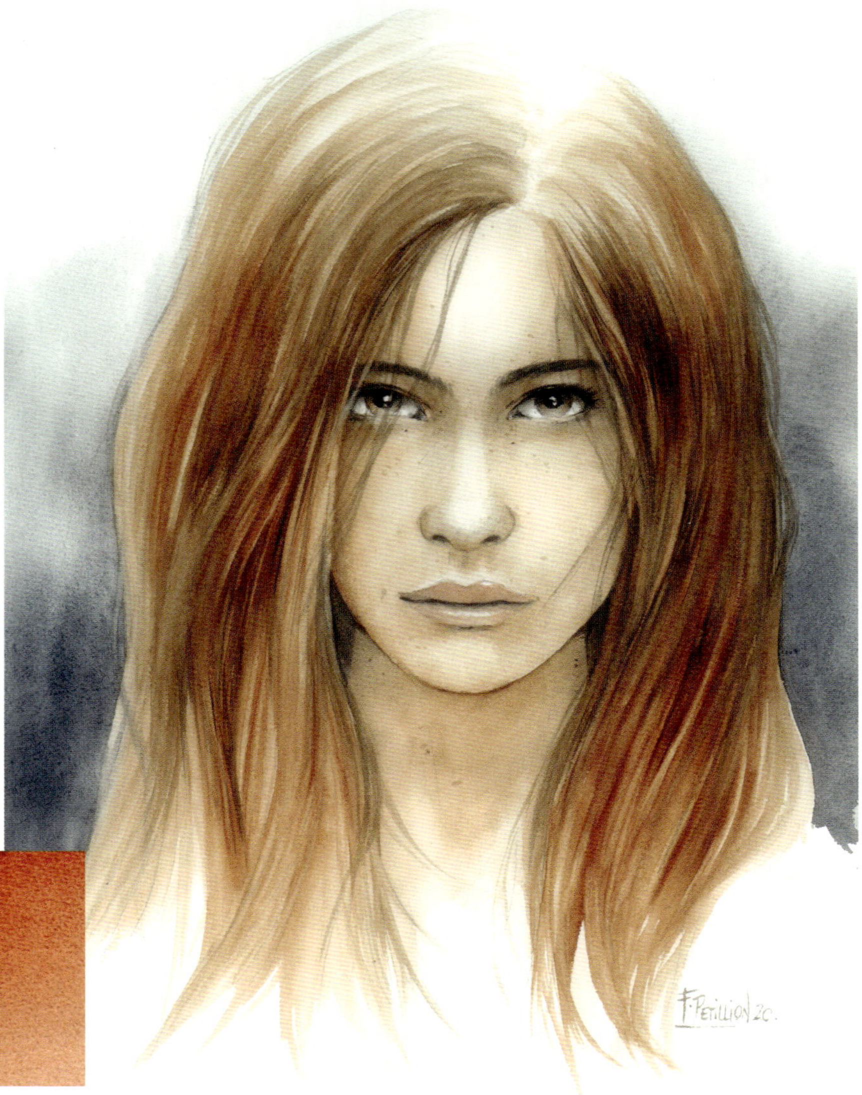

BURNT SIENNA

BURNT UMBER (PBR7)

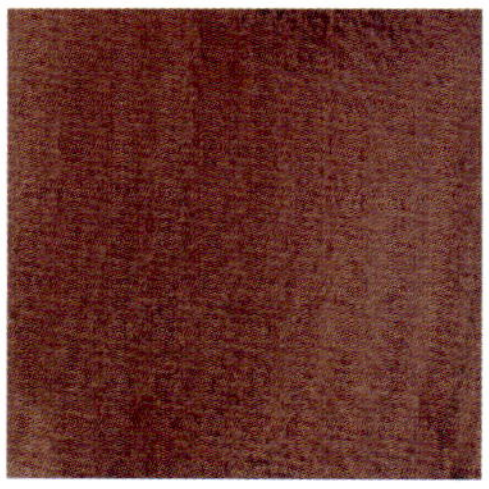

For this portrait, with an olive skin tone, Fabien uses two colors that are not included in the base palette: burnt sienna and burnt umber (PBr7). The first is a warm, reddish brown, the second a very dark brown. These two colors are monopigment colors and lightly granular.

Throughout this book, we have tried to work mainly with color mixtures. We have seen that a large number of colors can be created on the palette. These two earth colors are no exception. A reddish brown, similar to burnt sienna, can be obtained by combining yellow ocher (PY42), pyrrole red deep (PR264), and saffron yellow (PY110). As for burnt umber, we have already seen some formulas for dark browns (see page 89).

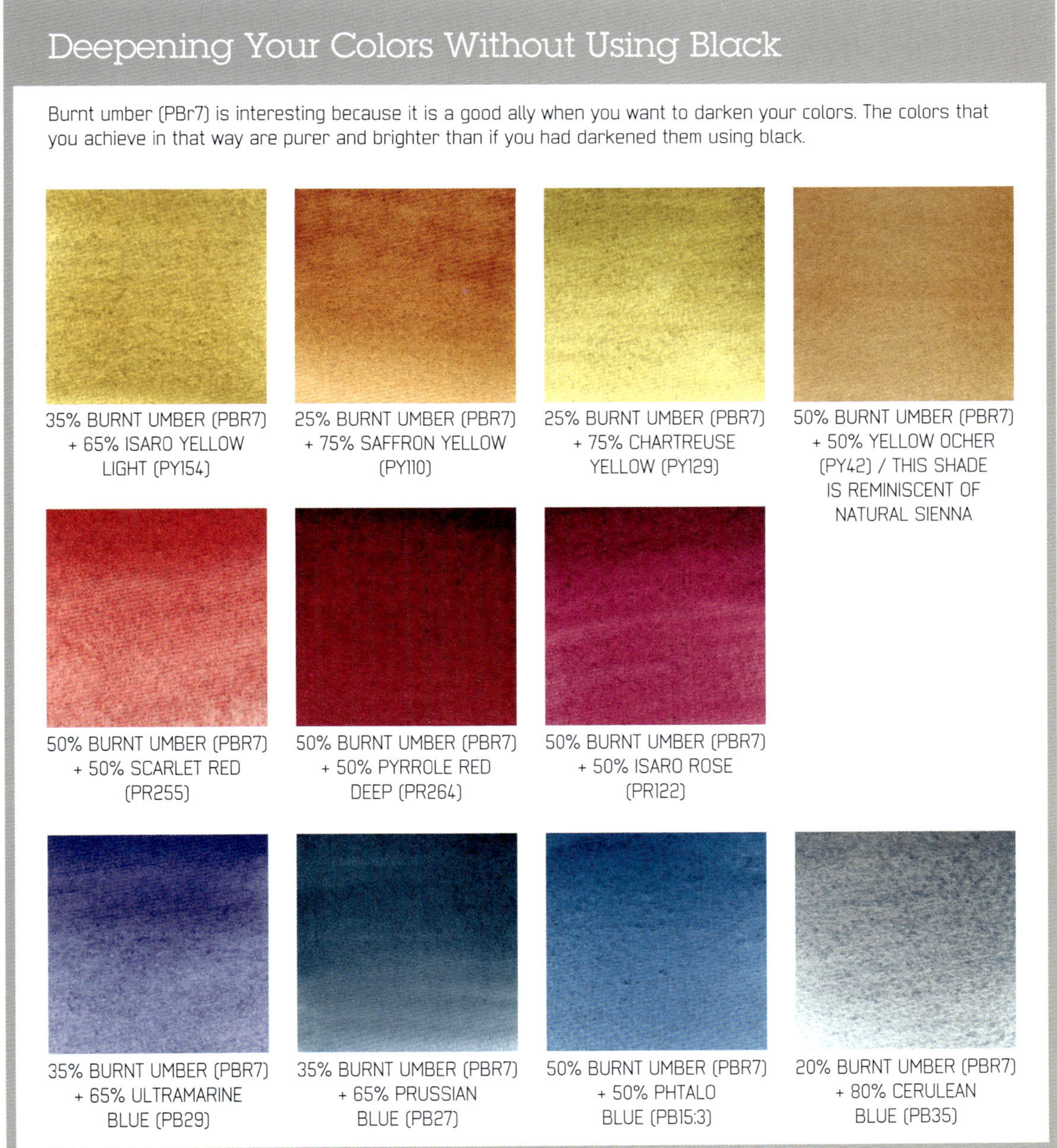

Deepening Your Colors Without Using Black

Burnt umber (PBr7) is interesting because it is a good ally when you want to darken your colors. The colors that you achieve in that way are purer and brighter than if you had darkened them using black.

YELLOW OCHER (PY42)
+ PYRROLE RED
DEEP (PR264)
+ SAFFRON
YELLOW (PY110)

YELLOW OCHER (PY42)
+ BURNT SIENNA
+ ISARO ROSE (PR122)

YELLOW OCHER (PY42)
+ BURNT SIENNA (IN
GREATER QUANTITIES)
+ ISARO ROSE (PR122)

SHADED WITH
BURNT UMBER (PBR7)

However, in the case of skin tones, getting the skin color just right does not allow for a variation in shade. If we work by mixing colors, and therefore with non-monopigment shades, the mixture can end up pushing toward an underlying note that is not what you want. And that would strongly compromise the accuracy of the portrait.

The two earth tones selected by Fabien provide the neutrality of color that is essential for the execution of this portrait.

ANALYSIS

To yellow ocher (PY42), the artist gradually adds burnt sienna and Isaro rose (PR122). This shade is then laid down over the whole face, which has been previously moistened with clear water. Fabien plays with the colored water, diluting the color to varying degrees in order to preserve light areas. He darkens the areas that are more in shadow by adding a little more burnt sienna to his base mixture.

Then, working on the dry page, Fabien strengthens the shadows at the eyes, nose, and neck. He adjusts his base color using burnt umber (PBr7). This adjustment must be made by working directly on the page, rather than by a mixture made on the palette. This will allow the shades to melt into each other in the first layer, and the shadows will blend into the rest of the face with no delineation.

> **_For the hair,_** working wet-on-wet, Fabien puts down layers of burnt sienna and burnt umber (PBr7), following the movement of the hair. He then starts withdrawing some of the color, using a dry brush, while the paper is still moist. The aim is to suggest the movement of the hair and to allow its different shades of brown to come out. Then, on a dry page and using a fine, wet brush, he finalizes the color withdrawals, which are now more precise. This technique adds dimensionality to the hair and keeps it from turning into a mass of brown, which would be less natural. Finally, touches of a very dark brown are added to indicate the movement of the hair.

With Dark Skin Tones

> Fabien Petillion

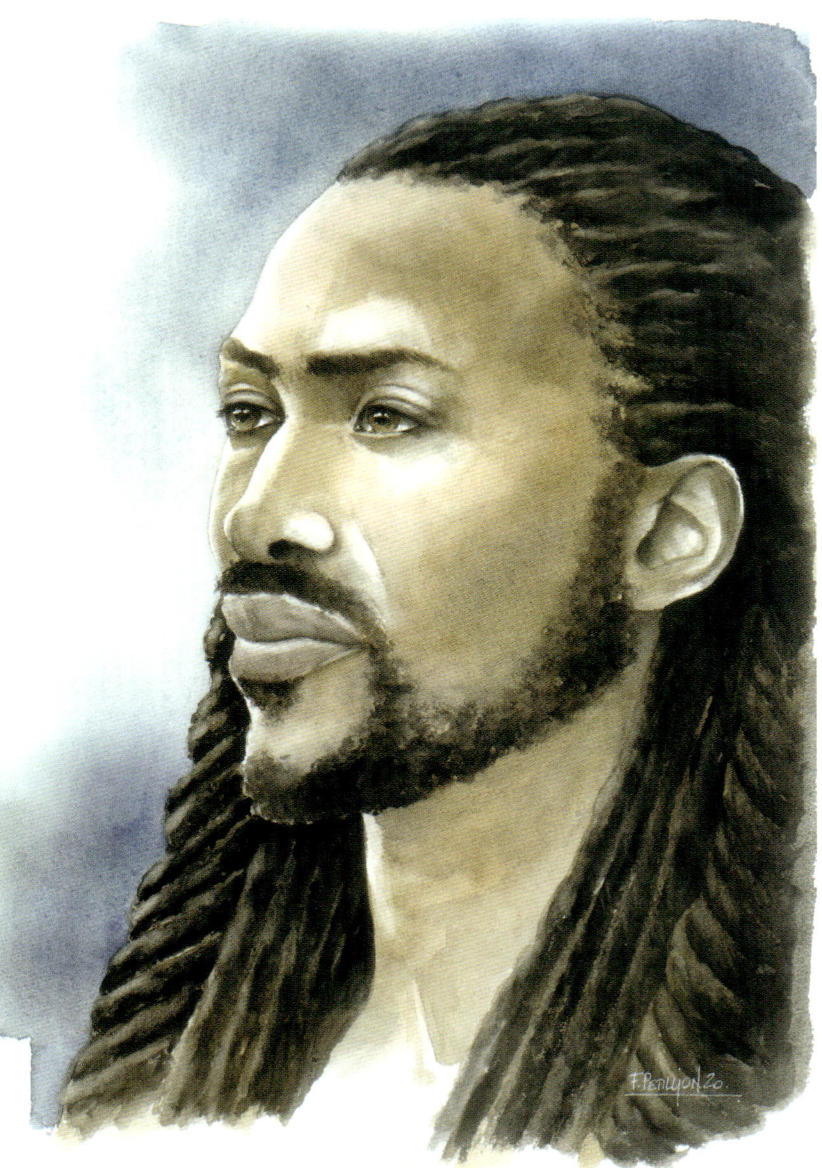

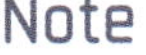

Note

We have seen that the exactitude of skin tones is very important. However, it is also entirely possible to decide to make portraits in shades that are absolutely non-realist. In such cases, it is essential to strengthen the facial expression and the expression of the eyes in order to communicate an emotion. This emotion should be the heart of the work, so that the skin color can then take a back seat.

For this portrait, with a dark complexion, Fabien has chosen four colors that allow him to get the color tones just right, in a way that is essential to the somewhat complex execution of this watercolor painting. His final choice included a light gray, a burnt sienna, a burnt umber (PBr7), and a carbon black (PBk6).

LIGHT GRAY
WASH

BURNT SIENNA
+ BURNT UMBER
(PBR7)

BURNT SIENNA
+ BURNT UMBER (PBR7)
(IN GREATER
PROPORTIONS)

CARBON BLACK
(PBK6) WASH

SHADED WITH
CARBON BLACK
(PBK6)

ANALYSIS

> *The entirety of the face and hair* is colored, to begin with, with a well-diluted light gray wash. Fabien leaves some white areas on the forehead, the nose, and the ear. After this step has fully dried, he starts to work on the skin tone of the face using burnt sienna and burnt umber (PBr7). In this combination, burnt umber is dominant so that the mixture will not be pushed too far toward red. Then, once the underlying layer is completely dry, the artist strengthens the contrasts at the neck, the forehead, and the cheek using burnt umber in varying degrees of dilution.

For the finishing touches, Fabien paints the shadows, using a very light wash based on carbon black (PBk6). In watercolors, people often avoid black, and rightly so, because it has a reputation for making mixtures muddy. You might be tempted to use it to darken a color very quickly, but it is wiser to avoid that. We have already seen that it is possible to deepen a shade without using black (see page 105) in order to make our mixtures more luminous.

In certain very specific cases, however, the addition of a hint of black as a finishing touch, as in this portrait, can help to reinforce shadows and dimensions. Its use is well considered, and justified, when you want to work with a very saturated neutral shade to strengthen a piece that was painted in a harmony of dark browns. Working with a mixture that includes carbon black is particularly delicate, and all we can suggest is that you practice ahead of time. If you haven't mastered it, you run the risk of muddying the whole face and of turning the white highlights gray. It is key not to overload the brush, so that it will be completely clear of black once you get to the lightest areas. In this portrait, the black is present at the hollow of the cheek, at the temple, and to structure the brow bone.

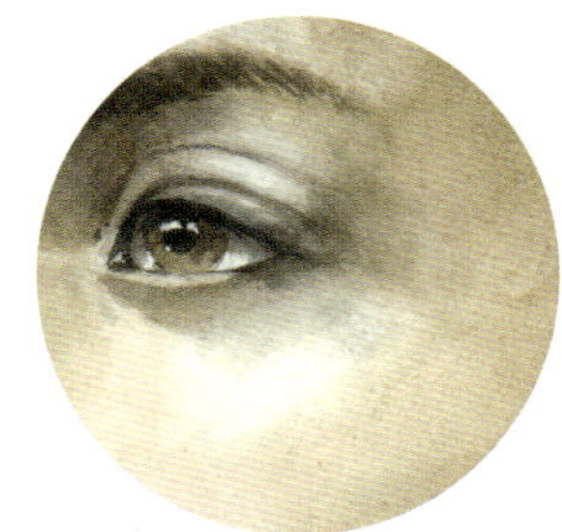

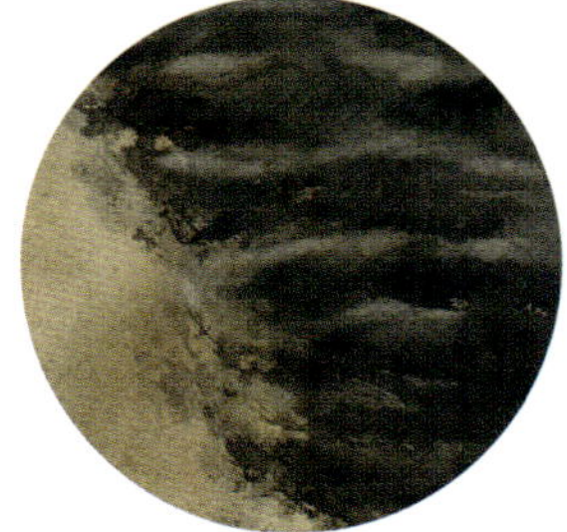

> *The hair* is painted by overlaying black on top of a first coat painted using burnt umber (PBr7). Fabien then draws off some of the paint while the paper is still wet in order to create movement in the hair, and then he draws off more when the paper is dry, to draw the dreadlocks more precisely.

Painting Animals

We will use Cindy Barillet's works as a way to study animal portraits. This is a very broad subject and therefore also involves an equally extensive array of colors. Therefore, we have settled on two very popular domestic animals, namely dogs and cats. In addition, Cindy illustrates her mastery of color mixtures in three portraits of more highly colored animals. Cindy is passionate about nature and the animal kingdom, and with equal passion, she shares her tips on her blog using video demonstrations and articles. From a travel notebook sketched on the fly to watercolors painted in minute detail and bursting with realism, Cindy's works radiate her positive state of mind. As such, there is no kind of experimentation that Cindy turns away from under the principle that in art no attempt is a mistake. They all enrich your creativity and, in the end, carry you toward a greater mastery of color.

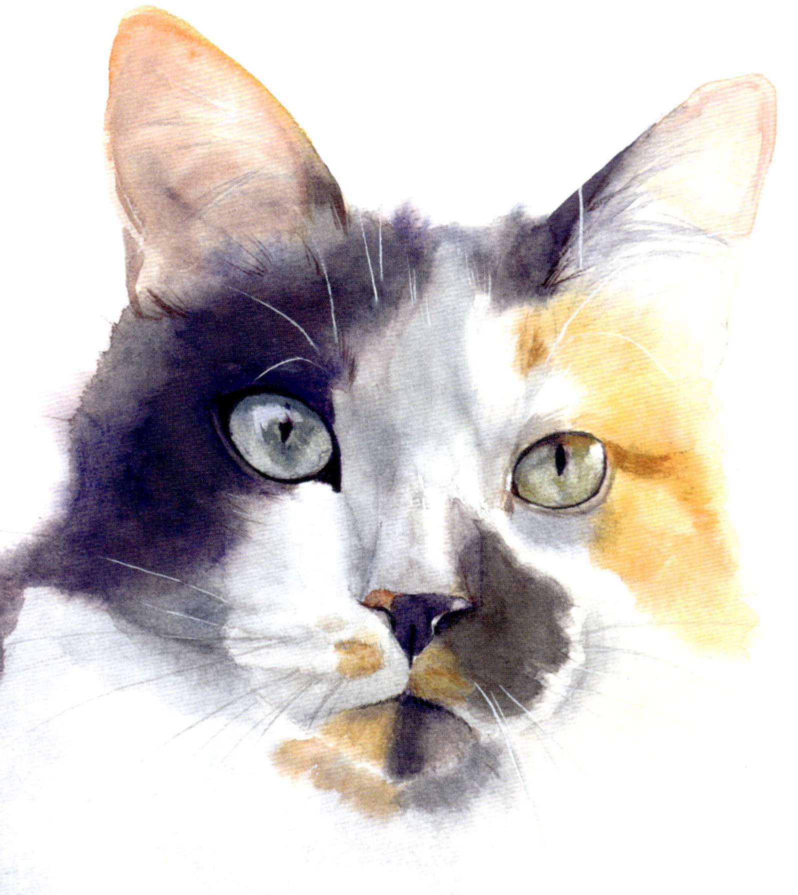

Cindy Barillet has been painting commissioned portraits of companion animals from photographs since 2011. She is a specialist in this subject matter. She began as a proponent of dry pastels but then began exploring all kinds of painting techniques, as well as other subjects, while still retaining her predilection for animal art. Since 2015, she has been sharing her experiences on her painting blog, with demonstrations that she films and annotates.

Follow Cindy at:
Website – artiste-animalier.com
YouTube – cindybarillet
Instagram – @cindybarillet
Facebook – Cindy Barillet - Art animalier

A Cat

> Cindy Barillet

In painting this cat, Cindy Barillet uses a very restrained palette, built mainly around ultramarine blue (PB29), Prussian blue (PB27), scarlet red (PR255), and yellow ocher (PY42). A small amount of Isaro yellow light (PY154) is then added. By limiting her palette and choosing her colors carefully, Cindy is able to keep a lovely tonal elegance throughout her composition.

The entirety of this painting falls delicately into place through a varying dilution of colors and a judicious layering of tones. Ultramarine blue is a regular feature of this artist's mixes, used to build the shadows of her subject.

It is interesting to note that Cindy's mixtures, for this watercolor painting, are made up of at the most three colors each. As a result, her colors are easy to re-create if you learn about the coloring power of scarlet red and Prussian blue.

As you practice working with this very reduced color palette, you will discover its full potential and how essential it will be to you when painting similar subjects.

ANALYSIS

> **The cat's black coat** is a layering game. For the first layer, the artist applies a dark color made up of scarlet red (PR255) and ultramarine blue (PB29). Because scarlet red is so powerful, it should be added to the ultramarine blue very gradually.

Cindy then strengthens this tone by applying a second wash made up of Prussian blue (PB27), scarlet red (PR255), and yellow ocher (PY42). For this mixture, start with an equal quantity of red and blue. If the color that you get is too red, add a little more blue. Then, incorporate the yellow ocher and try out the color on a piece of paper. What we are trying for here is a very dark, warm brown-black. For painting the parts that are most exposed to the light, the color needs to contain a larger proportion of yellow ocher. This dark brown will also be used to create the outline of the eye, which is the part that is least exposed to light.

SCARLET RED (PR255)
+ ULTRAMARINE
BLUE (PB29)

SCARLET RED (PR255)
+ PRUSSIAN
BLUE (PB27)
+ YELLOW
OCHER (PY42)

OVERLAY, ON TOP
OF THE SCARLET
RED (PR255)
+ ULTRAMARINE BLUE
(PB29) MIXTURE, OF
A MIXTURE OF
SCARLET RED
+ PRUSSIAN BLUE
(PB27)

YELLOW OCHER (PY42)
+ ULTRAMARINE
BLUE (PB29)

> **The white areas of the fur** are created by using a heavily diluted yellow ocher (PY42). The shaded areas are emphasized by reprising the mixture used for the black fur, but with a little more ultramarine.

> **The gray-white of the cat's eyes** uses a base of ultramarine and ocher (PY42), which Cindy then lightens using a hint of Isaro yellow light (PY154). This is used even more heavily in the mixture for the color of the eye, which is the lightest part.

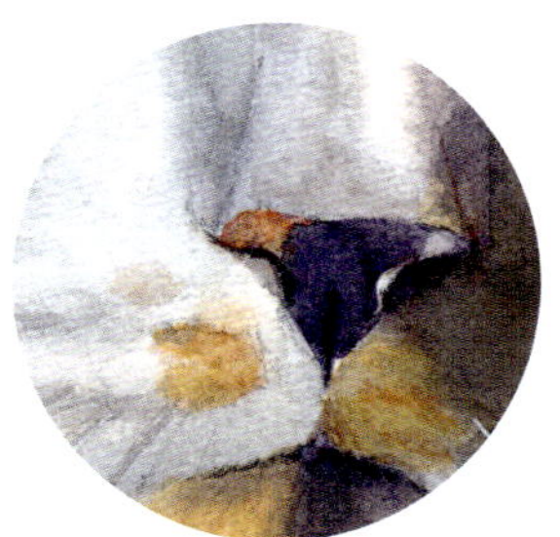
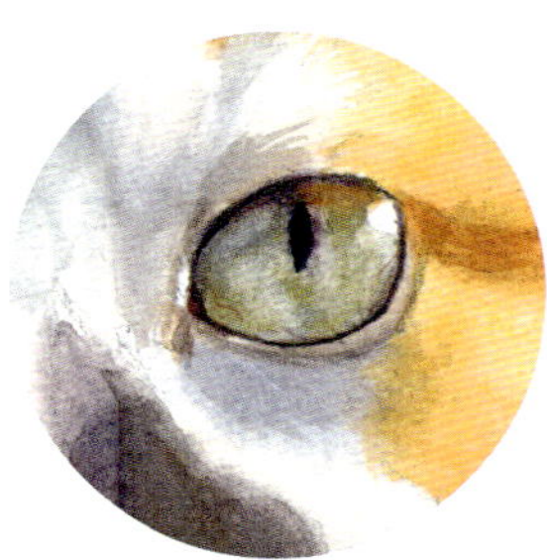

> **The red fur** is obtained by mixing the two warmest colors in this palette, namely scarlet red (PR255) and yellow ocher (see "yellow ocher (PY42) + scarlet red (PR255)," page 63). It is advisable to add the scarlet red to the yellow ocher only gradually, testing the color as you go. This orange is then also used to draw the outline of the eye that is most in the light. The shadows are made by adding a hint of ultramarine, which cools the mixture down.

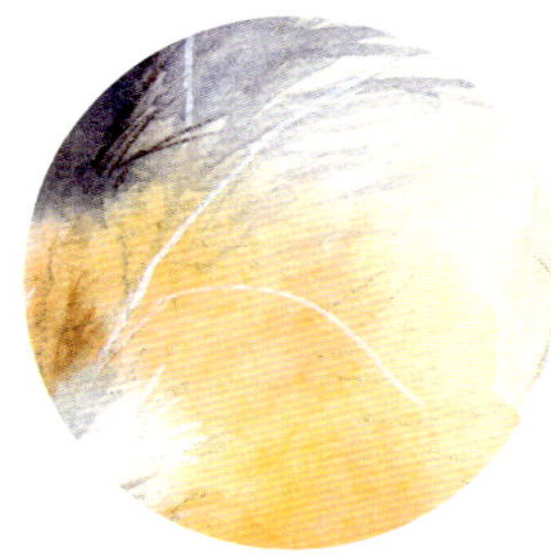
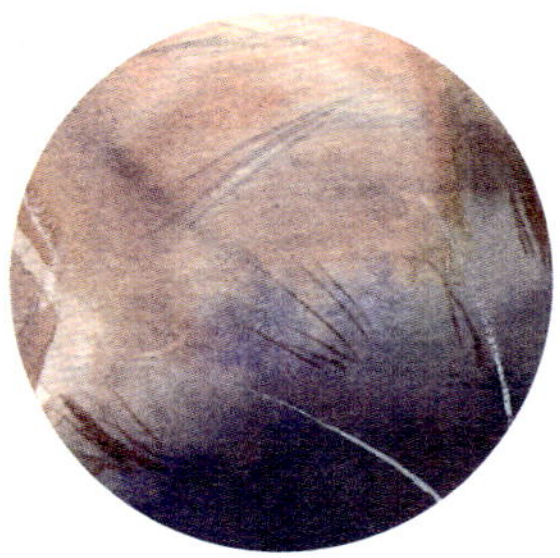

> **For the inside of the ears**, Cindy continues to use scarlet red (PR255) and yellow ocher (PY42), but she draws the mixture more toward red and dilutes the color to get it just right. The addition of ultramarine allows her here, as in the rest of this painting, to create the shadows.

YELLOW OCHER + ULTRAMARINE BLUE (PB29) + ISARO YELLOW LIGHT (PY154)

SCARLET RED (PR255) + YELLOW OCHER (PY42)

SCARLET RED (PR255) + YELLOW OCHER (PY42) + ULTRAMARINE BLUE (PB29)

SCARLET RED (PR255) + YELLOW OCHER (PY42), HEAVILY DILUTED

SCARLET RED (PR255) + YELLOW OCHER (PY42) + ULTRAMARINE BLUE (PB29), HEAVILY DILUTED

A Dog

> Cindy Barillet

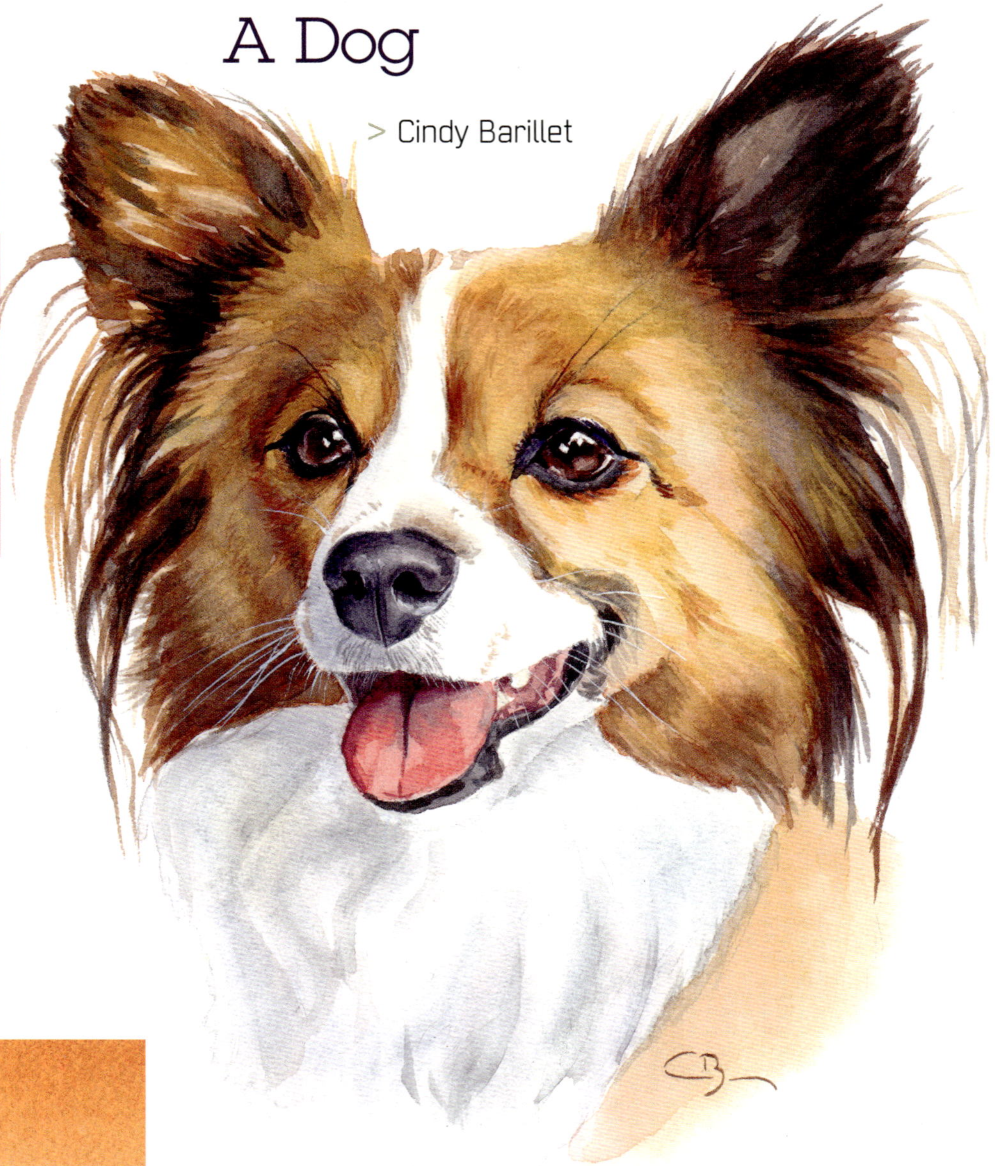

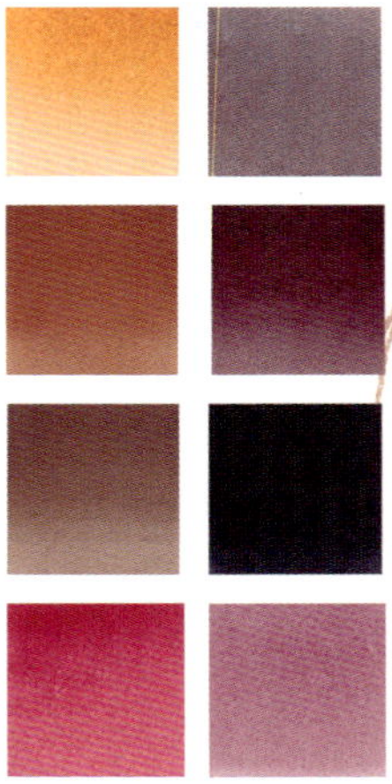

YELLOW OCHER (PY42)
+ SAFFRON YELLOW
(PY110)

YELLOW OCHER (PY42)
+ SCARLET RED (PR255)
+ ULTRAMARINE BLUE
(PB29) (IN EQUAL
PARTS)

For this subject, Cindy Barillet continues to use a restrained palette, in the same tones that she used for the cat.

Yellow ocher (PY42), scarlet red (PR255), saffron yellow (PY110), and blue ultramarine are the most important colors used here. Prussian blue (PB27) and Isaro rose (PR122) are brought in for certain details.

This painting is built on the logic of shadows, which Cindy has mastered perfectly. The shaded zones tend to be cool, using a range of blues and violets, while the light is rendered with warmer tones.

ANALYSIS

> *For the red coat*, yellow ocher (PY42) forms the base, reinforced by the addition of saffron yellow (PY110) in order to introduce light.

By contrast, the darker areas are created by starting with yellow ocher enriched with scarlet red (PR255). Ultramarine blue (PB29) cools the color down and helps to create the shadows. For the darker areas, the artist adds a hint of Prussian blue (PB27). These four colors allow her to obtain a broad chromatic range of browns, some warmer than others, depending on which color is dominant. It is an interesting exercise to take the time to discover what possibilities of mixtures these colors offer. Here are two examples.

> *The pupils, gums, and nostrils* are painted using a mixture of scarlet red (PR255) and Prussian blue (PB27), not very diluted at all.

> *The white fur* is structured thanks to the light gray that is made from an ultramarine blue (PB29) augmented with a hint of scarlet red (PR255) and yellow ocher (PY42). In composing these shaded areas, you must make sure to strongly dilute the mixture. As for the areas that are exposed to the light, they are made with a combination based on yellow ocher.

Isaro rose (PR122), shaded with scarlet red (PR255) and a subtle touch of Prussian blue, allows the artist to achieve an ideal color for painting the tongue. For the shadows, the Prussian blue is more strongly present.

YELLOW OCHER (PY42) + ULTRAMARINE BLUE (PB29) + ONE HALF PART SCARLET RED (PR255)

TWO PARTS YELLOW OCHER (PY42) + ONE PART SCARLET RED (PR255) + ONE HALF PART ULTRAMARINE BLUE (PB29) + A HINT OF PRUSSIAN BLUE (PB27)

TWO PARTS YELLOW OCHER (PY42) + ONE PART SCARLET RED (PR255) + ONE PART ULTRAMARINE BLUE (PB29) + ONE HALF PART PRUSSIAN BLUE (PB27)

PRUSSIAN BLUE (PB27) + SCARLET RED (PR255)

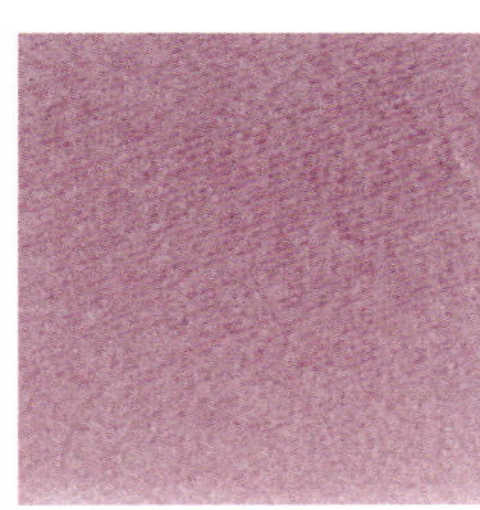

ONE PART ISARO ROSE (PR122) + ONE HALF PART SCARLET RED (PR255), BROKEN UP BY PROGRESSIVELY LARGER QUANTITIES OF PRUSSIAN BLUE (PB27)

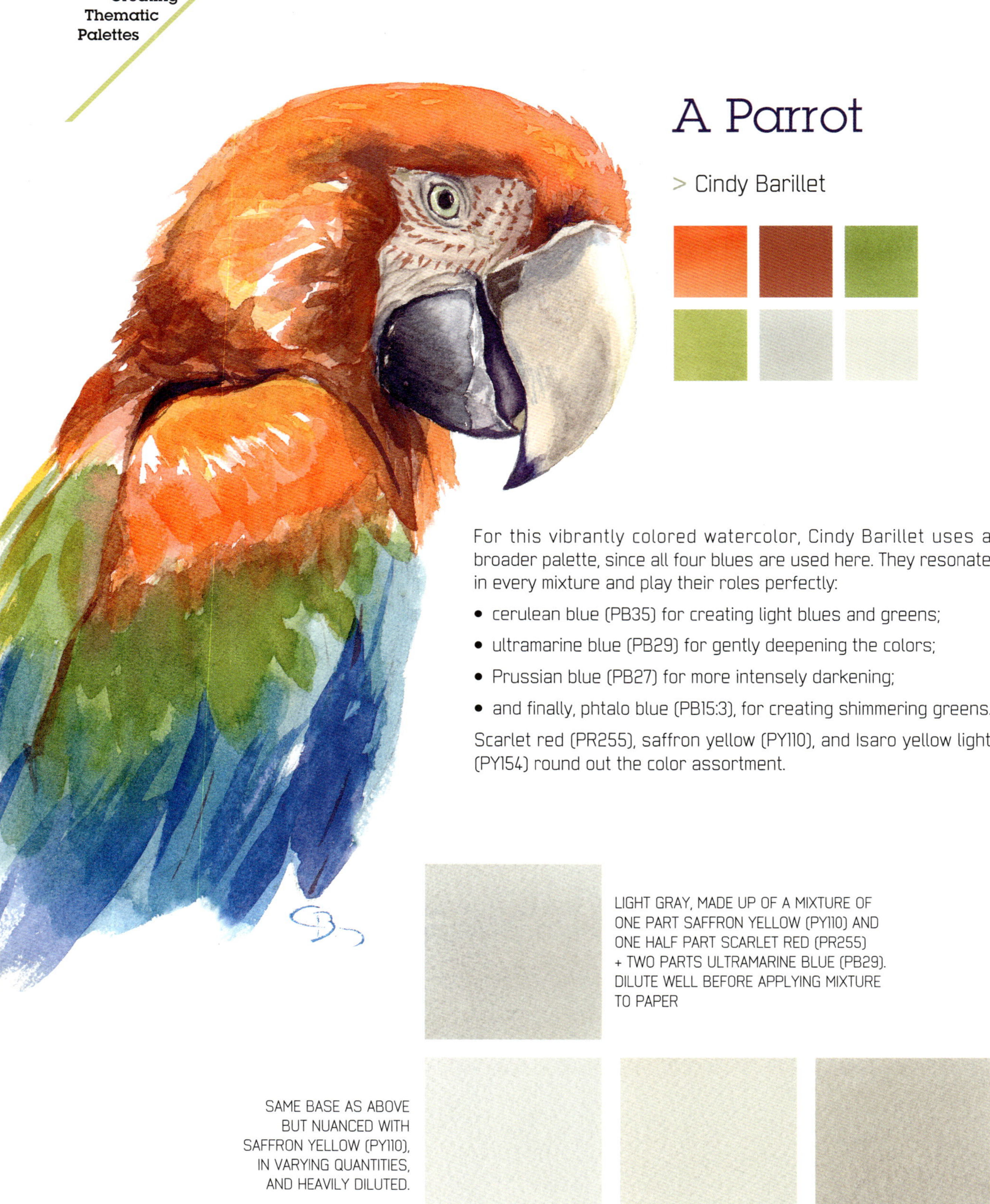

A Parrot

> Cindy Barillet

For this vibrantly colored watercolor, Cindy Barillet uses a broader palette, since all four blues are used here. They resonate in every mixture and play their roles perfectly:

- cerulean blue (PB35) for creating light blues and greens;
- ultramarine blue (PB29) for gently deepening the colors;
- Prussian blue (PB27) for more intensely darkening;
- and finally, phtalo blue (PB15:3), for creating shimmering greens.

Scarlet red (PR255), saffron yellow (PY110), and Isaro yellow light (PY154) round out the color assortment.

LIGHT GRAY, MADE UP OF A MIXTURE OF ONE PART SAFFRON YELLOW (PY110) AND ONE HALF PART SCARLET RED (PR255) + TWO PARTS ULTRAMARINE BLUE (PB29). DILUTE WELL BEFORE APPLYING MIXTURE TO PAPER

SAME BASE AS ABOVE BUT NUANCED WITH SAFFRON YELLOW (PY110), IN VARYING QUANTITIES, AND HEAVILY DILUTED.

ANALYSIS

> *The different shades of light gray in the bird's beak* are all made using a mixture of saffron yellow (PY110), scarlet red (PR255), and ultramarine blue (PB29). Depending on which color is dominant, the mixture can be either warm or cool. The easiest thing to do is to start with an orange created by combining one half part scarlet red and one part saffron yellow. Then add up to two parts of ultramarine blue, to create gray. You can vary the shade as you wish using saffron yellow to make it warmer. Cindy generously dilutes her mixture before applying it to the paper.

> *The black of the beak* is the result of a mixture of ultramarine blue (PB29), scarlet red (PR255), and Prussian blue (PB27). This dark tone, which is often essential when you want to create black, was already studied in our discussion of Cindy's dog portrait (see page 112).

> *The red feathers* are obtained using scarlet red (PR255). For the warmer nuances, the artist adds varying amounts of saffron yellow (PY110). This combination necessarily pushes the mixtures toward an extended range of bright oranges (see "Saffron yellow (PY110) + scarlet red (PR255)," page 60).

For the more shaded parts, Cindy simply shaded her scarlet red with some ultramarine blue (PB29) or Prussian blue (PB27).

> *The greens of the feathers* are made by creating a medium yellow, made up of saffron yellow (PY110) and Isaro yellow light (PY154), to which you still have to add a small quantity of phtalo blue (PB15:3).

> *The very light green of the parrot's eye* is a combination of Isaro yellow light (PY154) and cerulean blue (PB35).

> *The blue feathers* involve varying mixtures in which ultramarine blue (PB29), phtalo blue (PB15:3), and cerulean blue (PB35) work together to structure the wings.

SCARLET RED (PR255)
+ SAFFRON YELLOW
(PY110)

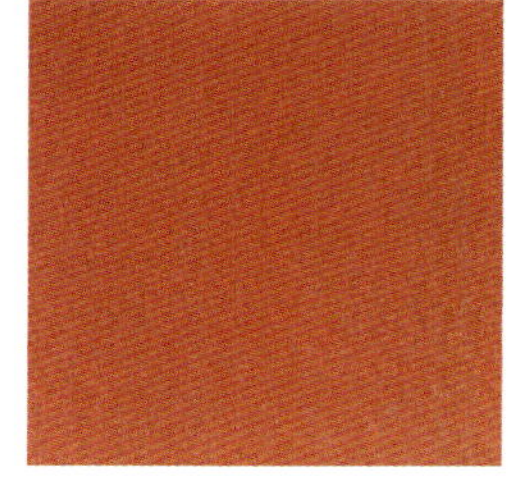

SCARLET RED (PR255)
+ ULTRAMARINE BLUE
(PB29)

SCARLET RED (PR255)
+ PRUSSIAN BLUE
(PB27)

ISARO YELLOW LIGHT
(PY154)
+ SAFFRON YELLOW
(PY110)
+ A HINT OF PHTALO
BLUE (PB15:3)

ISARO YELLOW LIGHT
(PY154)
+ SAFFRON YELLOW
(PY110)
+ A LARGER QUANTITY
OF PHTALO BLUE
(PB15:3)

ISARO YELLOW
LIGHT (PY154)
+ CERULEAN
BLUE (PB35)

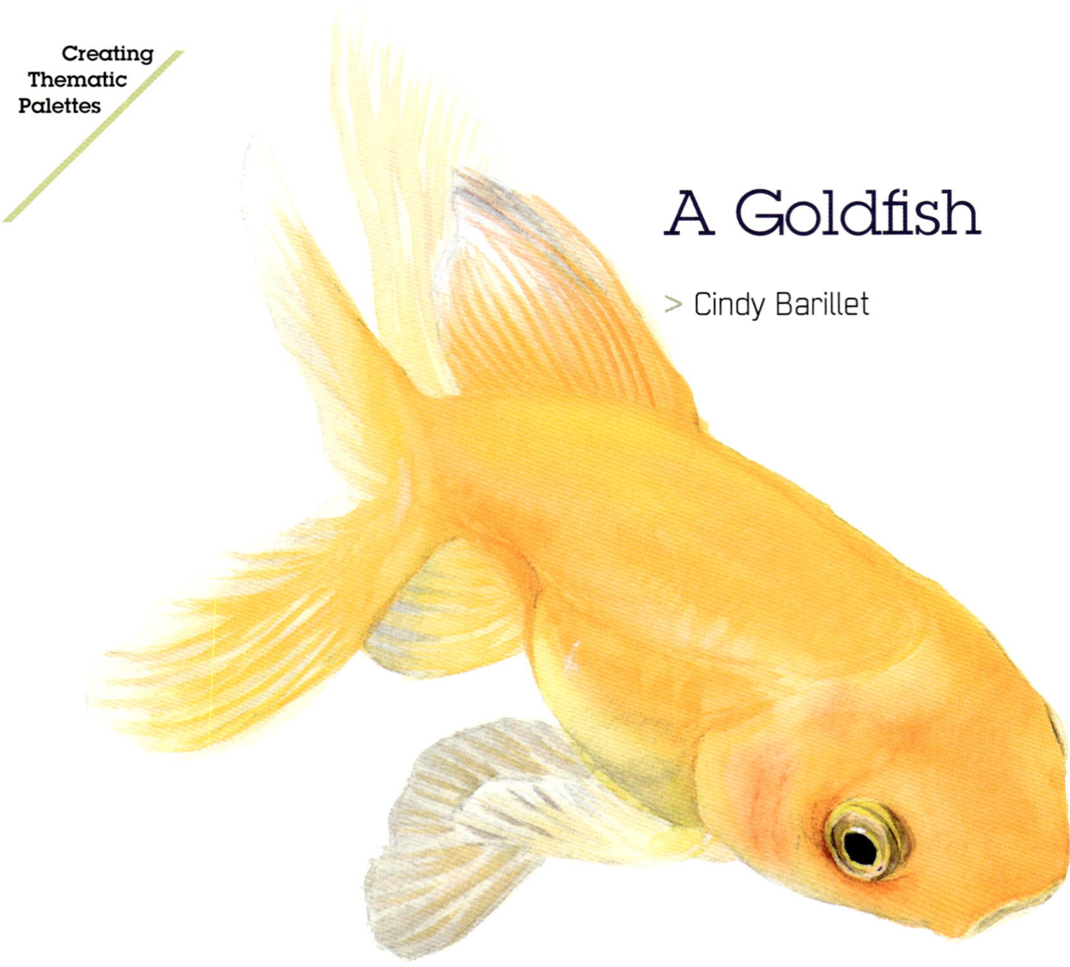

A Goldfish

> Cindy Barillet

This goldfish requires a restrained and carefully chosen palette that will make it possible to create bright, vibrant oranges.

Therefore, the colors that should be emphasized are saffron yellow (PY110), Isaro yellow light (PY154), and scarlet red (PR255). To complement them, ultramarine blue (PB29) is of interest for creating shadows and Prussian blue (PB27) for painting the pupil.

ANALYSIS

> **For the fish's body**, Cindy uses saffron yellow (PY110). For the more highly pigmented areas, like the outline of the eye, the gills, and the top of the head, she darkens her yellow using a touch of scarlet red (PR255) (see page 60).

> **The cooler reflections**, which can be seen at the lower end of the belly, the side, and the caudal fin, are painted using Isaro yellow light (PY154).

> **The transparency of the fins** is rendered thanks to a very diluted light gray that Cindy composes by combining saffron yellow (PY110) with scarlet red (PR255) and ultramarine blue (PB29) (see light gray, page 114).

An Aquatic Environment

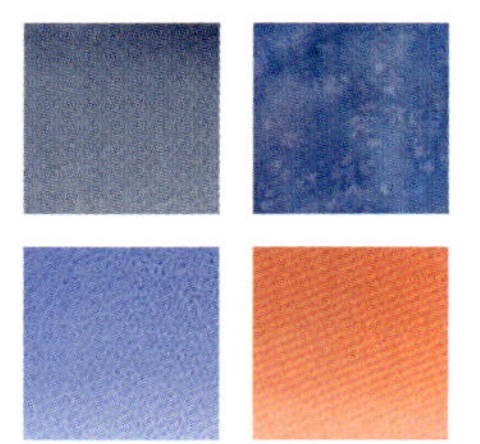

> Cindy Barillet

The background work of this watercolor, in a very different style, is particularly interesting. In addition, this highly colored fish, inspired by the ornate wrasse, is a perfect exercise for familiarizing yourself with color mixtures without burdening yourself with an overly complex drawing.

Three blues, namely Prussian blue (PB27), ultramarine blue (PB29), and phtalo blue (PB15:3), along with three reds, namely Isaro rose (PR122), pyrrole red deep (PR264), and scarlet red (PR255), as well as, finally, Isaro yellow light (PY154) and saffron yellow (PY110), form Cindy's palette.

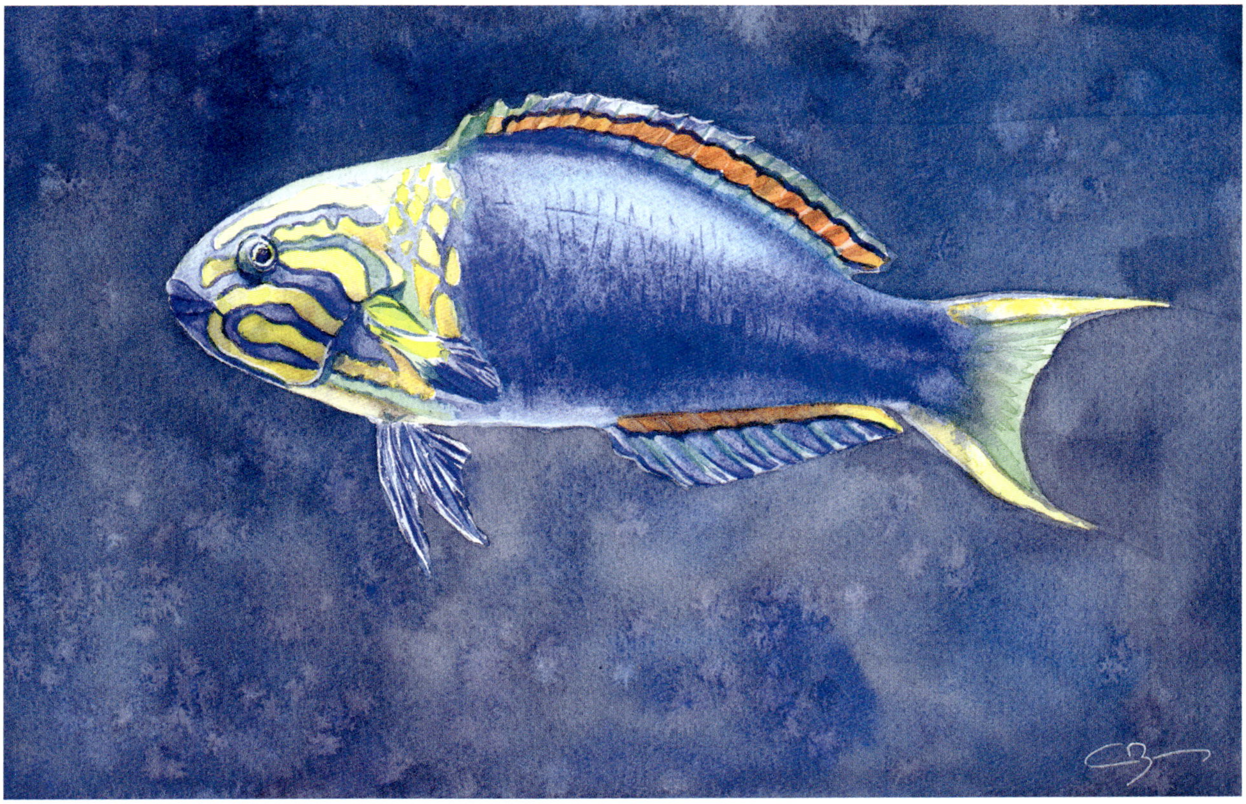

PRUSSIAN BLUE (PB27) + PYRROLE RED DEEP (PR264)

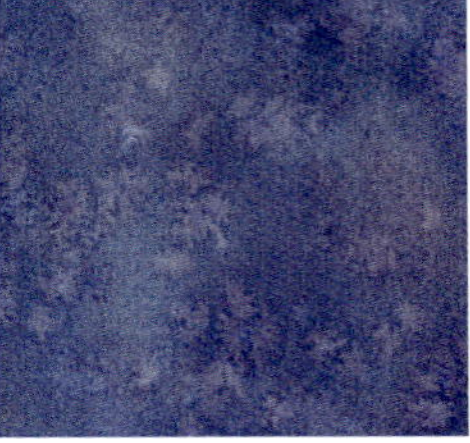

CLOSE-UP OF THE BACKGROUND

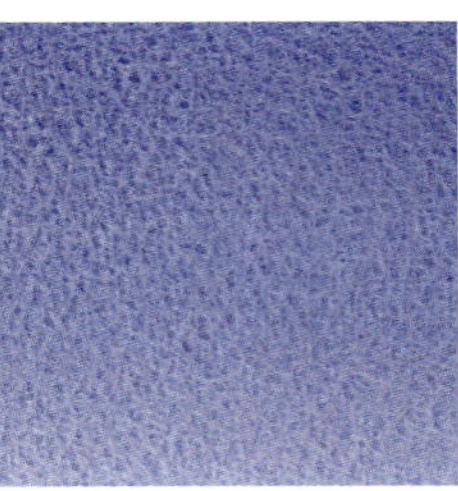

ULTRAMARINE BLUE (PB29) DEEPENED WITH PRUSSIAN BLUE (PB27) AND BROKEN UP WITH A HINT OF PYRROLE RED DEEP (PR264)

ANALYSIS

To avoid having her background become too uniform and flat, Cindy paints it using layers of different shades of blue. First, she applies Prussian blue (PB27), darkened with pyrrole red deep (PR264). Then she shades her background by adding some phtalo blue (PB15:3), and then ultramarine blue (PB29), to her mixture. Finally, while the paper is still wet, Cindy sprinkles salt on it in varying amounts and achieves an astonishing, random constellated effect.

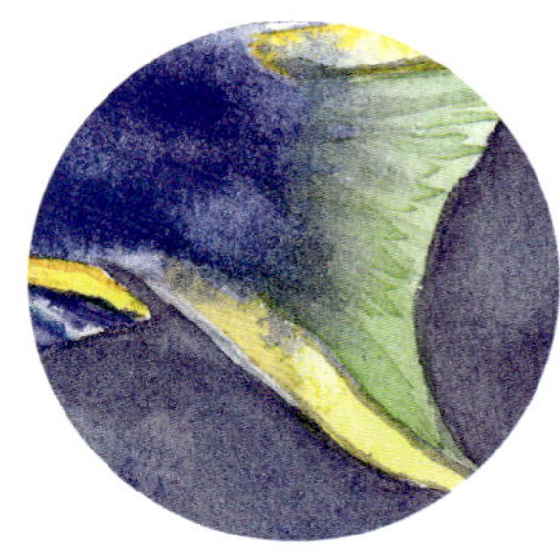
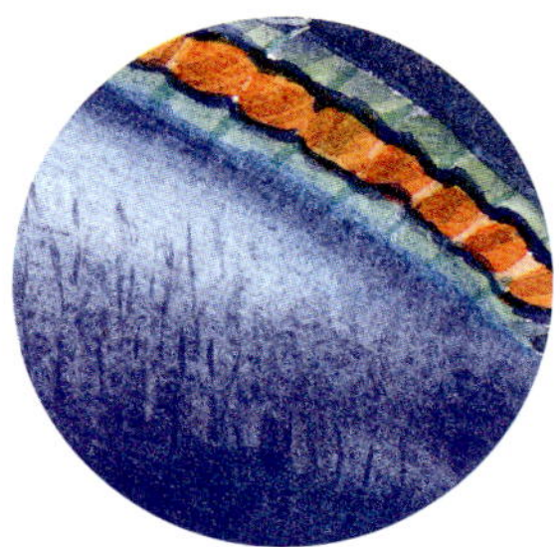

> **The fish's body** is painted with ultramarine blue (PB29), intensified with a hint of phtalo blue (PB15:3) (see "Blues," page 38). The darker areas are suggested using ultramarine blue deepened with Prussian blue (PB27) and broken up with a hint of pyrrole red deep (PR264).

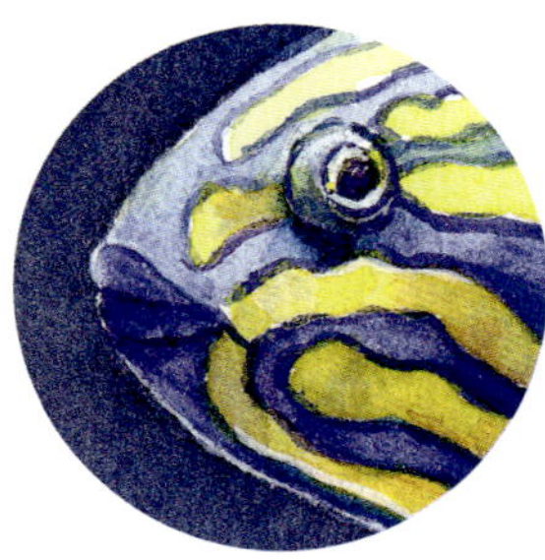
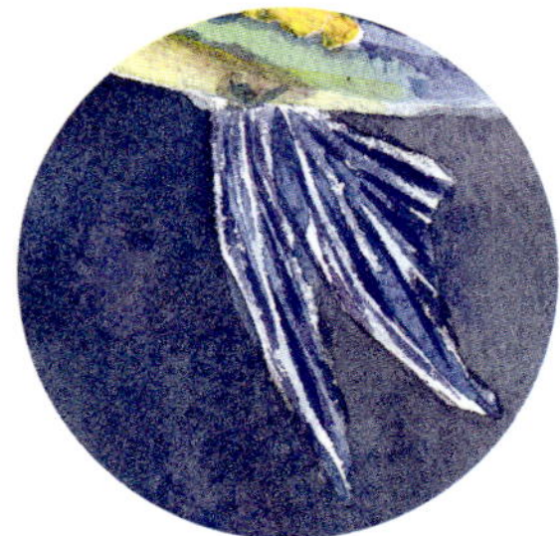

> **The fish's head** is painted using Isaro yellow light (PY154) shaded with a hint of saffron yellow (PY110) (see "Yellows," page 40). For the shadows, Cindy created a violet using Isaro rose (PR122) and ultramarine blue (PB29), and used it to adjust her yellow.

> *On the dorsal fin*, the orange used is a combination of scarlet red (PR255) and saffron yellow (PY110), darkened with a hint of Prussian blue (PB27).

The vibrant green is a result of combining Isaro yellow light (PY154) with phtalo blue (PB15:3) (see page 44).

> *For the eye*, in particular, the black can be achieved, as detailed below, by combining Prussian blue (PB27) with scarlet red (PR255).

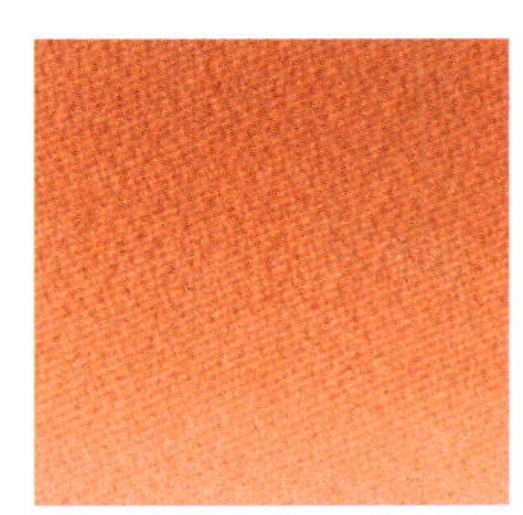

SCARLET RED (PR255) + SAFFRON YELLOW (PY110) DARKENED WITH A HINT OF PRUSSIAN BLUE (PB27)

Black without Black?

It is possible to obtain very dark colors that, if applied with high saturation, will give the illusion of black. This is particularly appropriate for small details. However, when they are more diluted, these colors are not as neutral as true black, such as carbon black, for example.

35% SCARLET RED (PR255) + 65% PHTALO BLUE (PB15:3)

35% SCARLET RED (PR255) + 65% PRUSSIAN BLUE (PB27)

50% PRUSSIAN BLUE (PB27) + 25% CHARTREUSE YELLOW (PY129) + 25% SCARLET RED (PR255)

35% PYRROLE RED DEEP (PR264) + 65% PRUSSIAN BLUE (PB27)

CARBON BLACK. NOTE THAT, EVEN WHEN DILUTED, THIS COLOR IS NEUTRAL.

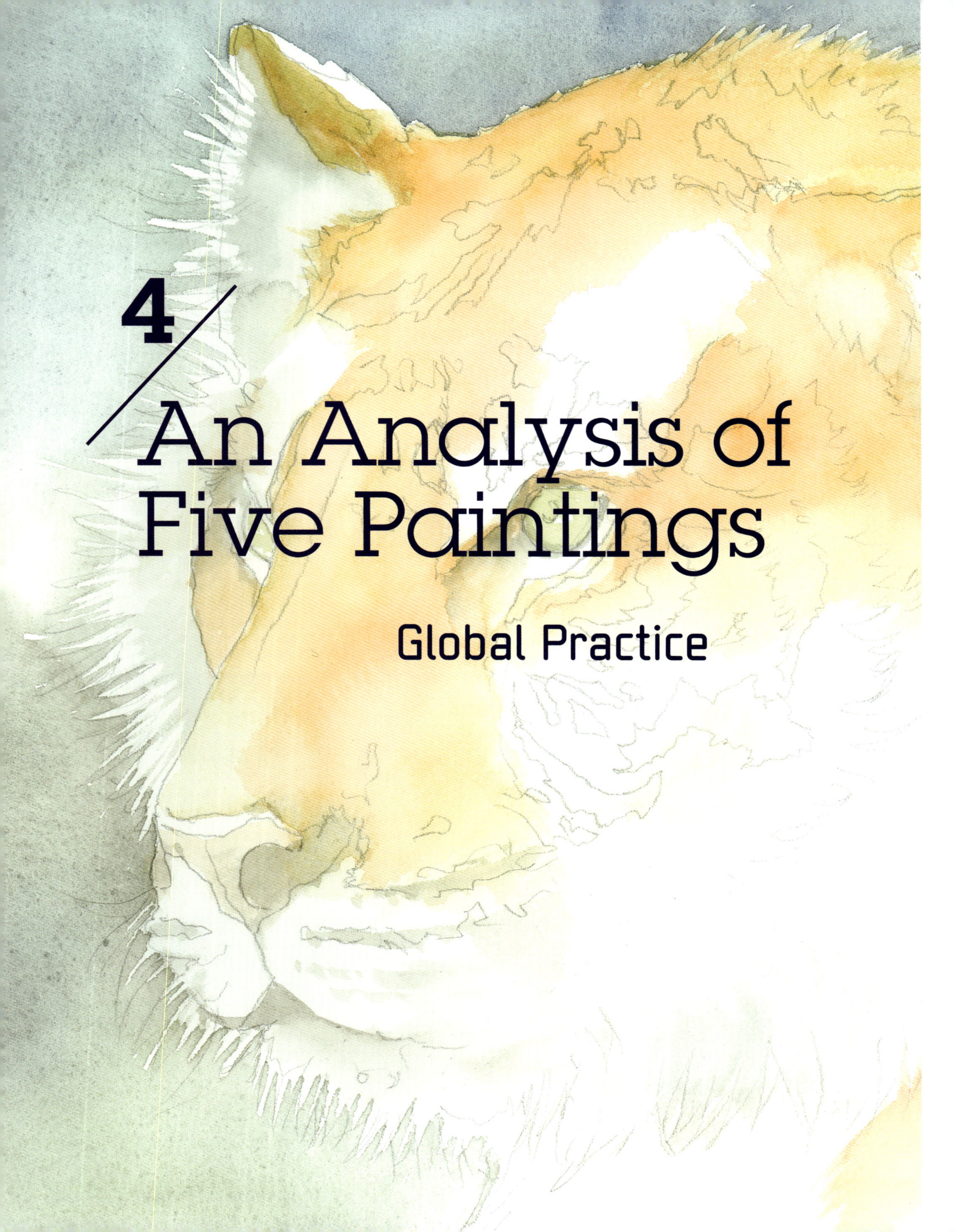

4
An Analysis of
Five Paintings
Global Practice

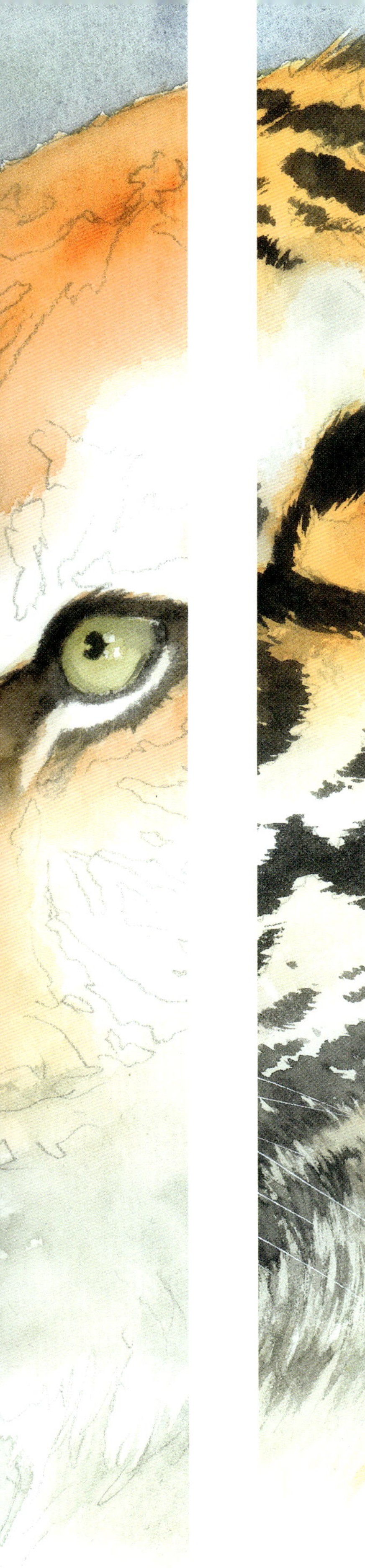

The mastery of color mixing does not by itself guarantee the perfect execution of a creation. There are other elements that can disrupt the harmony of your painting and deeply disturb the spectator.

In this chapter, with Fabien Petillion's help, we will analyze the steps required to complete five different watercolor paintings. Here we will study color mixing within the context of a global practice, drawing your attention to the coloring of the piece but also to other specific features in order to help you avoid certain obvious pitfalls.

A Floral Composition

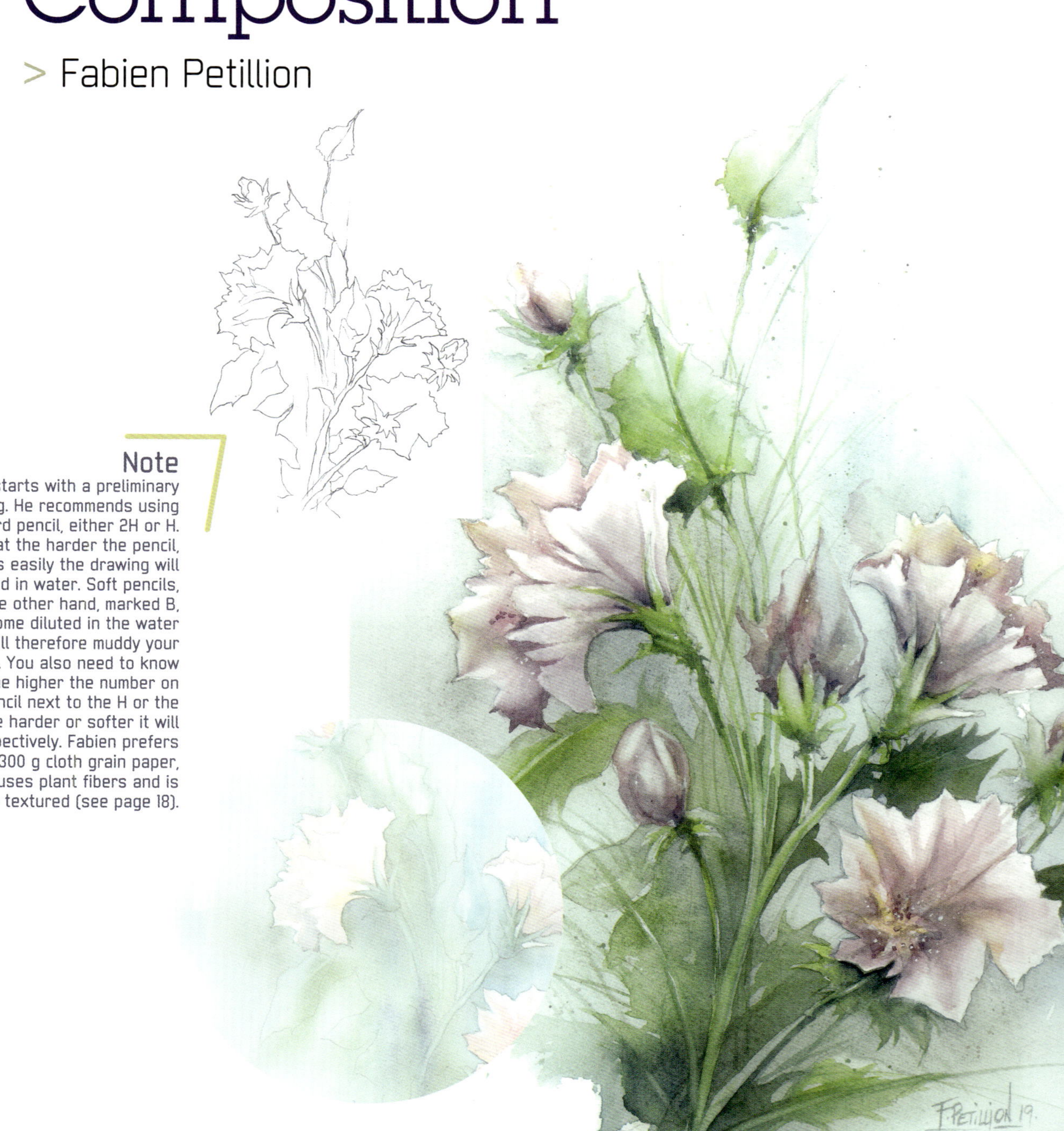

Note

Fabien starts with a preliminary drawing. He recommends using a hard pencil, either 2H or H. Note that the harder the pencil, the less easily the drawing will be diluted in water. Soft pencils, on the other hand, marked B, will become diluted in the water and will therefore muddy your page. You also need to know that the higher the number on your pencil next to the H or the B, the harder or softer it will be, respectively. Fabien prefers Arches 300 g cloth grain paper, which uses plant fibers and is highly textured (see page 18).

DRAFTING AND COMPOSITION

In this composition, the floral bouquet moves vertically. Its relatively massive base becomes narrower and lighter as it moves upward, suggesting that the flowers are soaring toward the light source.

In watercolors, light plays an essential role, and it is important to take the time to figure out where it is coming from, and what direction it is pointing, in order to represent it correctly. The person viewing the painting has to understand instantly where the light is coming from. This will also determine how to build the volumes and the shadows.

For this painting, Fabien has the light coming down from above. Thus, his colors will have to be the lightest at the top of the painting, sometimes even using the white of the paper itself. The base of the bouquet, on the other hand, is darker, because it is receiving less light.

COLORING

Step 1

Fabien paints his background using cool tones to add depth. On a moistened page, he lays down a few very light touches of phtalo blue (PB15:3), reinforced with olive green (see page 72). All of this is done working wet-on-wet so that the shades can fuse and meld. The background has to remain subdued so that it will not visually upstage the bouquet. Nevertheless, by playing with the light and the color, the artist does manage to give life to his background and keep it from becoming too unified and monotonous. He also takes care to make sure the color values stay lighter at the top of his composition than at the bottom.

Then Fabien colors his flowers, which he has saved for now, using a wash made up of Isaro rose (PR122) and yellow ocher (PY42).

1.1/BACKGROUND AND COLORING FLOWERS

1.2/CLOSE-UP OF THE BACKGROUND

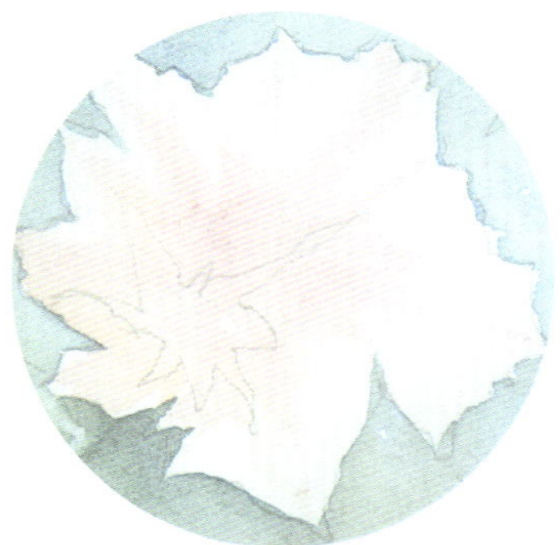

1.3/CLOSE-UP OF THE COLORING OF THE FLOWER

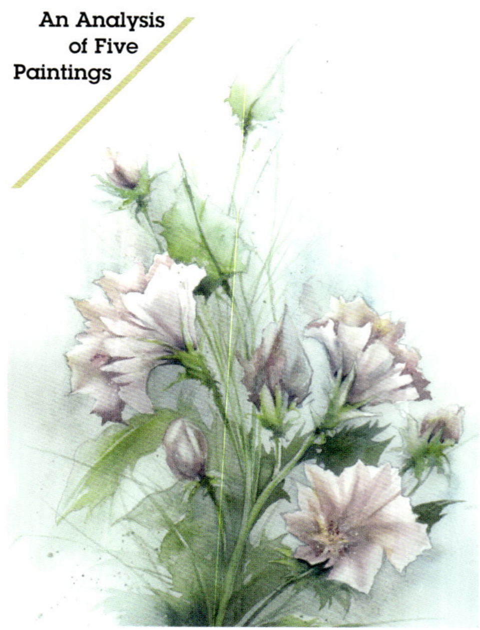

2.1/CONTRASTS AND DETAILS

Step 2

On a piece of dry paper, Fabien reinforces some of the areas of his painting, creating contrasts using olive green, which he shades with chartreuse yellow (PY129) and indigo blue (see "Indigo," page 66). Because watercolors tend to become lighter as they dry, you should not hesitate to change the shades and accentuate the colors.

Once this step has dried, Fabien takes the time to detail the leaves and the stems of his bouquet. In watercolors, in order to make an element stand out, you have to paint it in a lighter and warmer shade than the background. This is why Fabien warms up his greens using a hint of chartreuse yellow (PY129).

He also adds a touch of Isaro yellow light (PY154) in his flowers, which allows the bouquet to stand out clearly from the background.

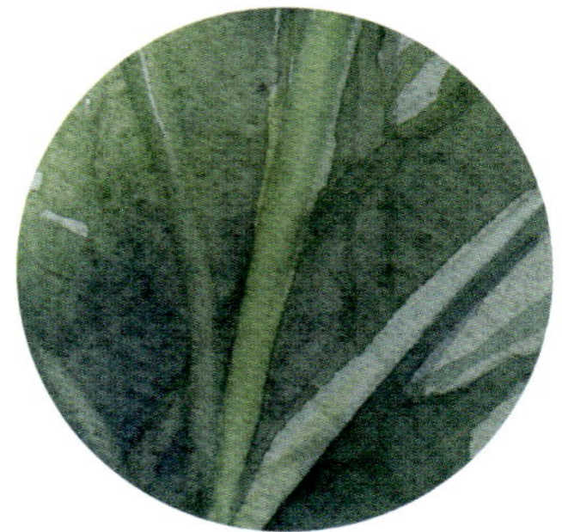

2.2/CLOSE-UP OF THE WORK ON A STEM

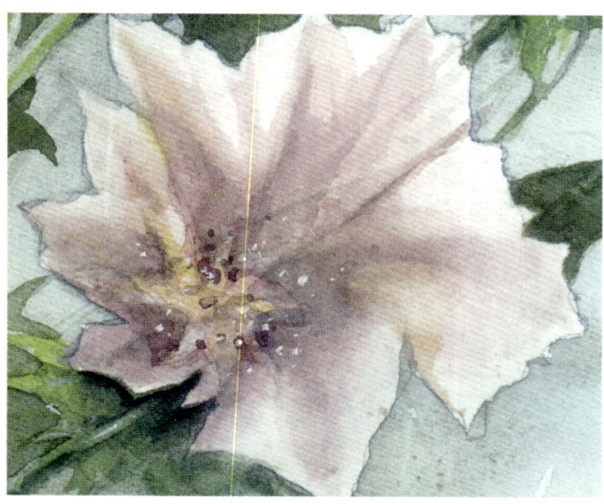

2.3/CLOSE-UP OF THE WORK ON THE FLOWERS

Finally, a few bursts of light are created by drawing paint away from the leaves at the top of the bouquet. This technique allows you to let the light play on certain elements of the composition. Using a dry paintbrush, Fabien withdraws some of the wet color and reveals once again the white of the paper. This same technique is used on the petals to lightly shade the border between the white edge of the petal and the background. In this way, Fabien creates a gentle union between his subject and his background.

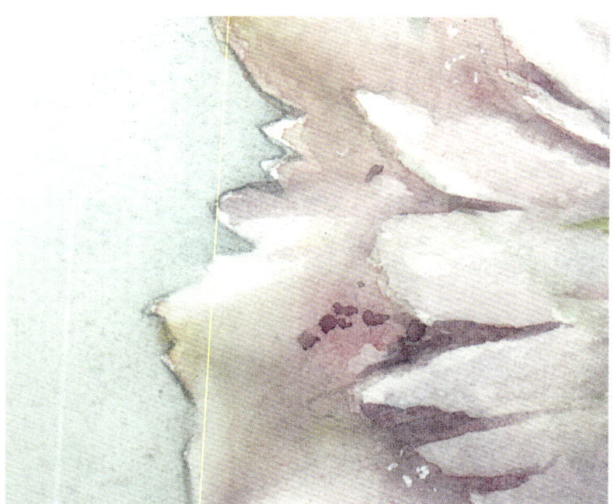

2.5/SHADING USING COLOR WITHDRAWAL BETWEEN THE EDGE OF THE PETAL AND THE BACKGROUND

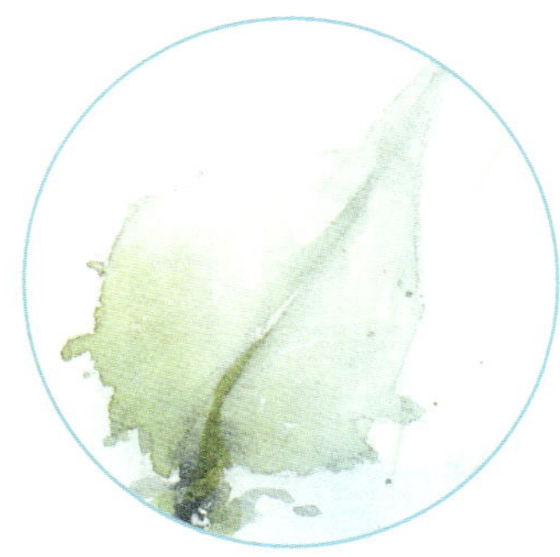

2.4/CLOSE-UP OF THE WITHDRAWAL OF PAINT TO ALLOW LIGHT TO COME INTO A LEAF

A Rural Landscape

> Fabien Petillion

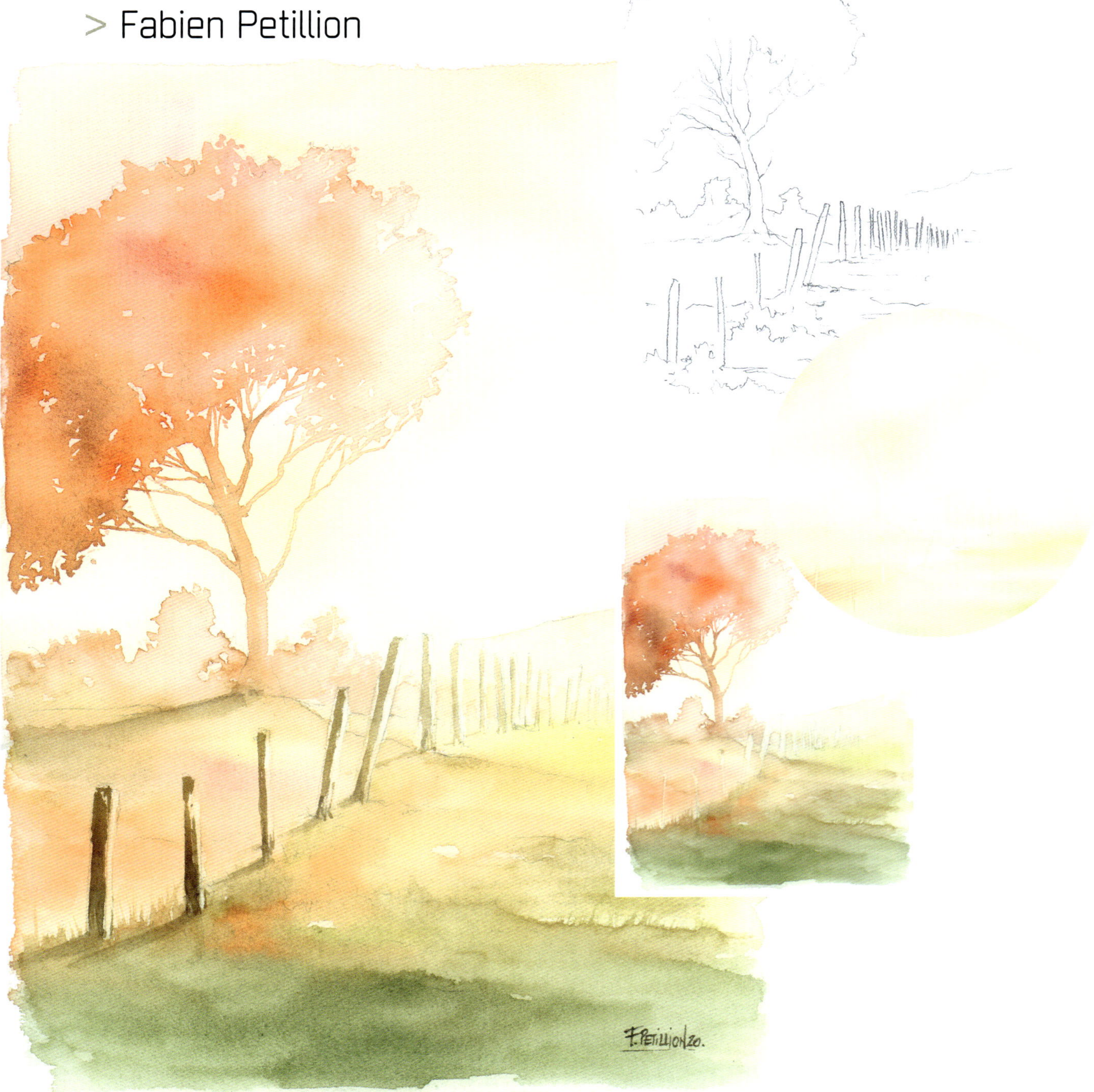

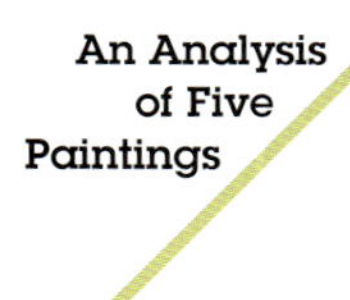

1.1/APPLICATION OF A FIRST WASH TO WET PAPER

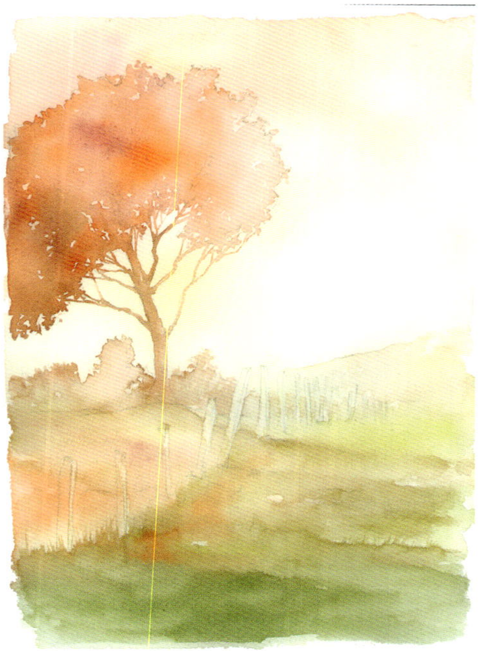

1.2/WORKING ON THE CONTRASTS AND THE FOLIAGE OF THE TREE

DRAFTING AND COMPOSITION

When you paint a landscape, it's important to ask yourself what it is that you want to highlight and where you want to direct the viewer's gaze.

The two-thirds rule continues to be a solid basis for choosing where to place the horizon line. If you want to emphasize the sky, plan for it to take up two-thirds of the picture. On the other hand, if it is the landscape that you want to highlight, then that is what should take up two-thirds of the picture.

Here, Fabien is working a little differently, because he has chosen to place his horizon line in the middle of the composition. However, he is using the two-thirds rule vertically. You can see that the tree in the foreground takes up two-thirds of the picture. However, it is not the tree that draws our gaze, but rather the light-filled area in the remaining third of the picture. This is not by chance: Fabien's entire composition leads us toward this point, which gives us a feeling of space and vast expanse.

COLORING

Step 1

After moistening the entire page, Fabien lays down a first wash using a base of yellow ocher (PY42), Isaro rose (PR122), and Chinese orange (see page 73; the formula using Isaro rose is the most suitable one here) in order to color his sky. This step is painted wet-on-wet so that the colors can fuse with each other. Two areas are left white to introduce light into the landscape: the first one at the horizon line and the second one to the right of the tree. The ground is also painted wet-on-wet, but here, in addition to the three colors of the sky, there are also chartreuse yellow (PY129) and olive green. This last helps to sustain greater intensity in the contrasts in the foreground.

Step 2

Using the same range of colors, once the paper is completely dry, Fabien uses layering to intensify the lower part of his landscape.

At the top of this watercolor painting, only the tree is reworked. First, Fabien moistens the trunk and the leafy crown, and then he lays down his three colors, which spread out there. Then, using a fine brush, the artist works on the outline of the foliage, tilting his paper slightly to the left. This tilt invites the colors to travel and to color the part of the tree farthest from the light most intensely. More generally speaking, this technique makes it possible to create shadings and to keep the light in a watercolor painting.

The tree has to blend into the landscape and harmonize with the background. If this tree had been painted using sharper colors and more intense details, it would undoubtedly have drawn the viewer's eye, and Fabien's watercolor would have lost some of its delicacy.

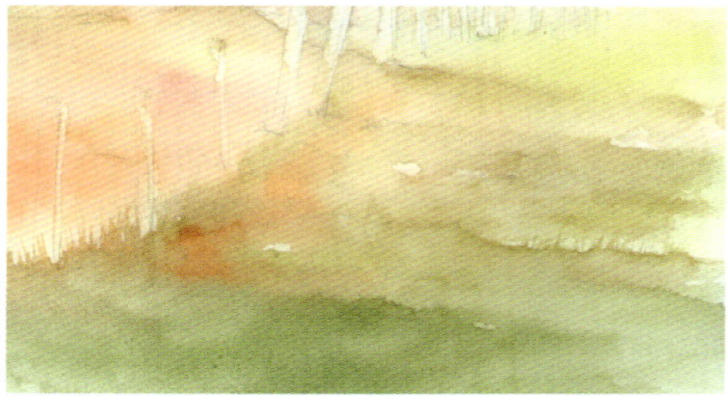

2.1 / CLOSE-UP OF THE LOWER PART OF THE LANDSCAPE

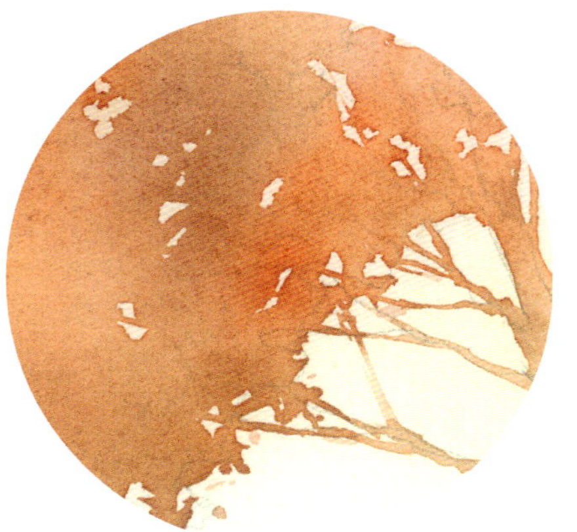

2.2 / CLOSE-UP OF THE LEAFY CROWN OF THE TREE

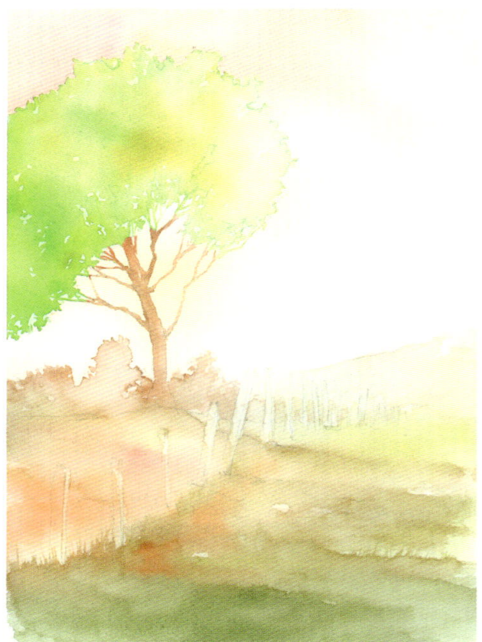

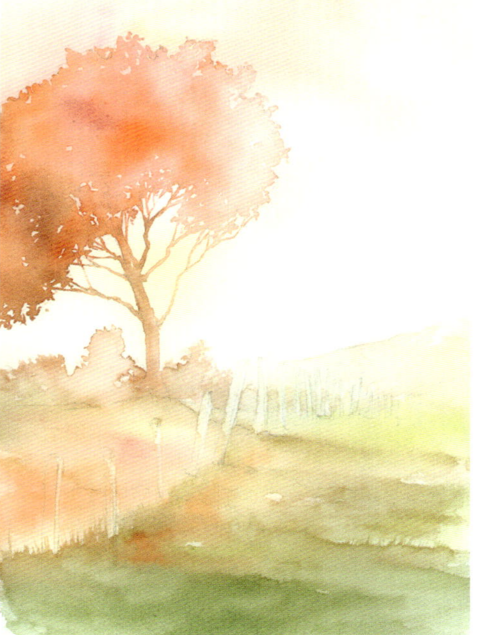

2.3 / FOR COMPARISON, ON THE LEFT, THE TREE HAS BEEN PAINTED IN A COLOR THAT DOES NOT HARMONIZE WITH THE BACKGROUND.

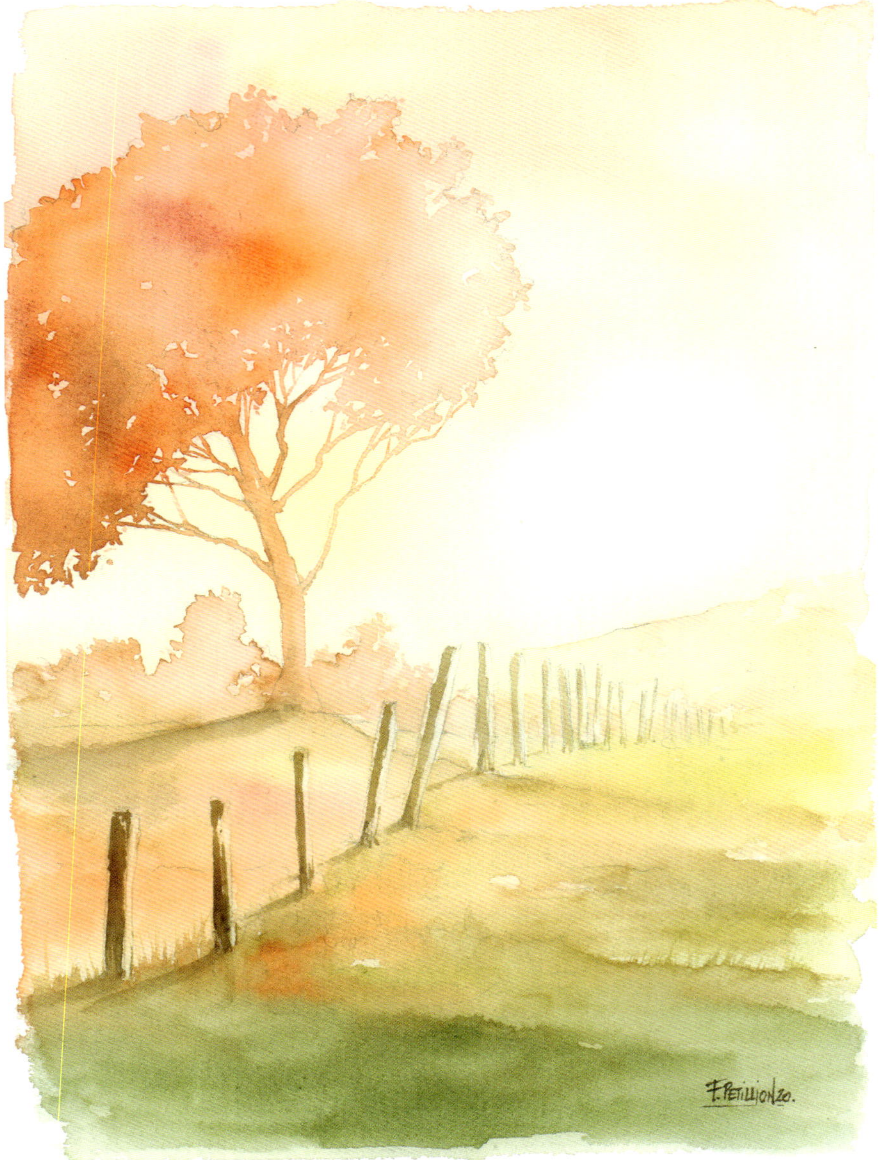

3.1 / THE FENCE PICKETS ARE
PAINTED USING DARK BROWN.

STEP 3

The last step consists of painting the fence pickets using a dark
brown, such as sepia. The closer they get to the light source, the
lighter the pickets have to become. Fabien obtains this shade by
increasingly diluting his dark brown. This last coloring stage is
important, because it finalizes the emphasis on the perspective
and guides our gaze toward the light on the horizon.

An Urban Setting

> Fabien Petillion

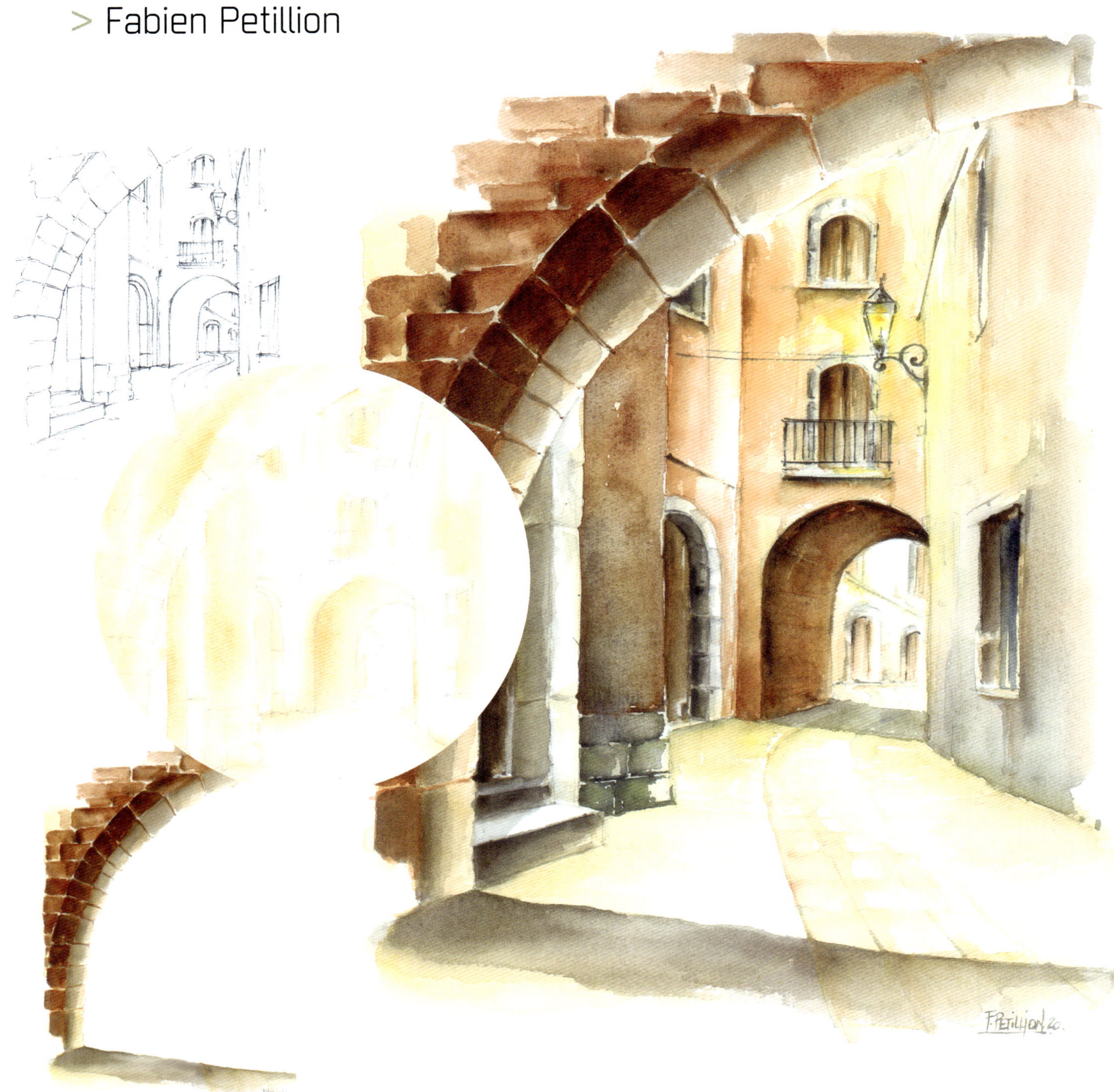

DRAFTING AND COMPOSITION

In this composition, the gaze is guided toward the end of the little street. This is achieved, first, by the brightness emanating from the street and attracting the viewer's attention, and, second, through the respect paid to perspective. In order to do this, you need to first draw your horizon line, which should be positioned at the spectator's eye level. Then, place a point on the page (called the vanishing point) toward which you make all the lines converge (these are called convergence lines). The aim is to force the viewer's attention toward the determining element in your painting, in this case the end of the street.

COLORING

Step 1

The first step consists of applying a yellow ocher wash. Using a broad brush and clear water, Fabien wets the entire page, following the movement of the buildings' lines. This technique allows him to create white areas at intervals across the page, correctly positioned, where the brush has not moistened the paper.

Then, using a yellow ocher wash, Fabien colors the whole drawing. He takes care to keep some of the areas lighter, while saturating the areas that are least exposed to the light. This step indicates the lighter areas to him for what comes next.

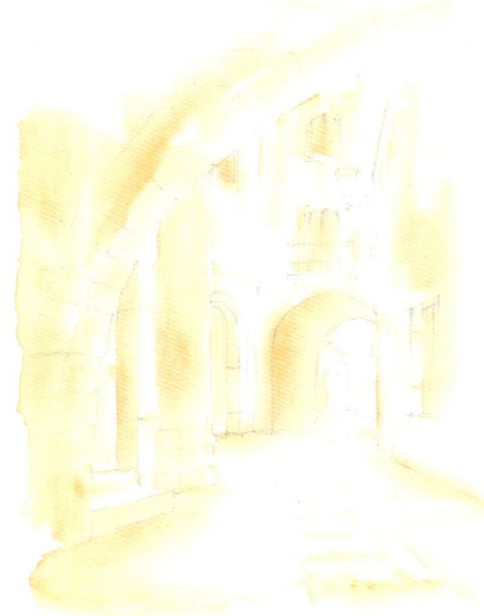

1.1/YELLOW OCHER WASH

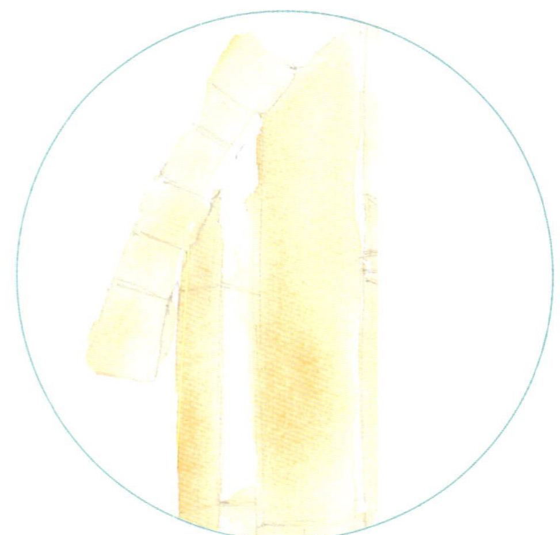

1.2/CREATION OF WHITE SPACES AT INTERVALS

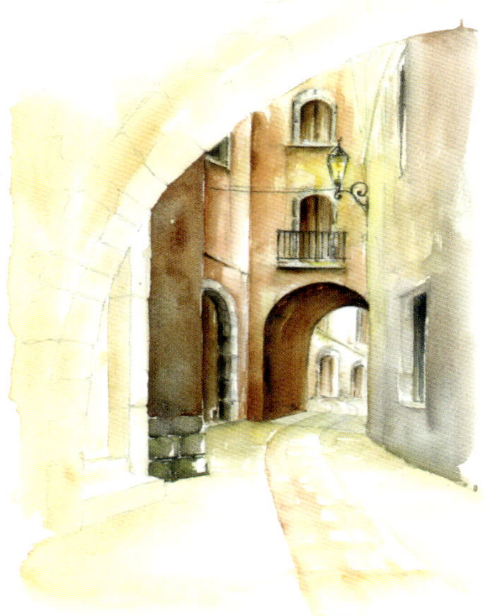

1.3/COLORING OF THE FIRST TWO AREAS

Step 2

Once the page is completely dry, Fabien reworks his watercolor, which can be divided into three areas:

• the area farthest from the viewer, which needs to be left light;

• the interior courtyard, a little less light;

• and the archway in the foreground, the darkest area.

Remember that in watercolor painting, it is easier to darken something than to make it lighter. Thus, it is always better to paint the lightest areas first, ending with the darkest areas. This is why Fabien begins by coloring the background, then the middle ground, and only at the end the foreground.

In order to keep harmony among all the colors, he chooses a range of warm browns. Burnt sienna is the dominant color in the interior courtyard, whereas the archway in the foreground uses burnt umber (PBr7) and a touch of Payne's Gray. The contrasts are painted using a very dark brown, like sepia (see page 71).

We have learned, throughout this book, to create various browns. They are perfect for painting this picturesque view. Nevertheless, it is also interesting to point out here that the natural earth tones, namely burnt sienna and burnt umber (PBr7) (see page 104), have a very interesting granularity. Although mixtures can allow us to approach their color, their unique granularity is inimitable and is particularly suited to representing the roughness of these old stones.

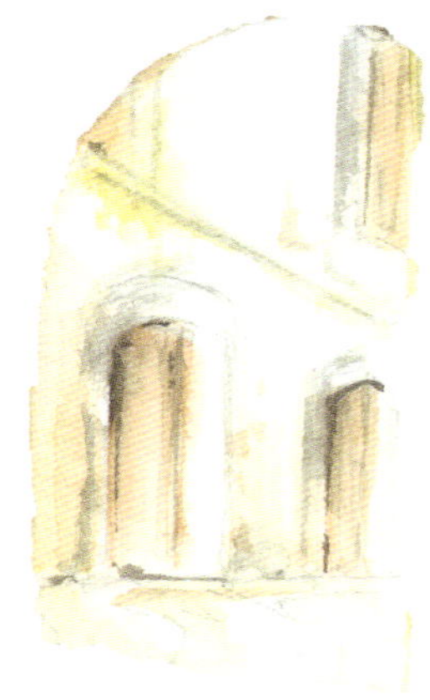

2.1/BACKGROUND—THE END OF THE STREET

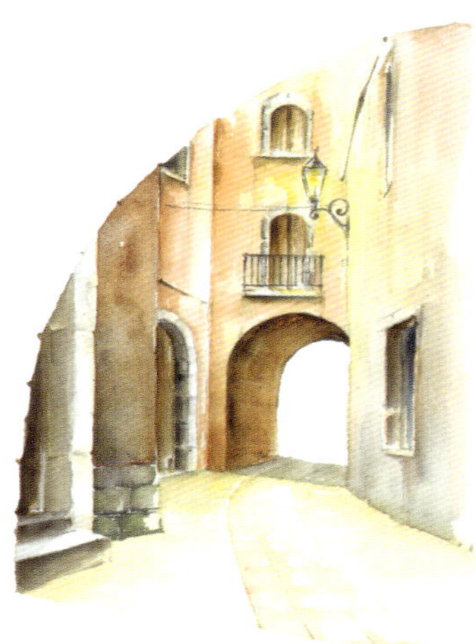

2.2/MIDDLE GROUND—THE INTERIOR COURTYARD

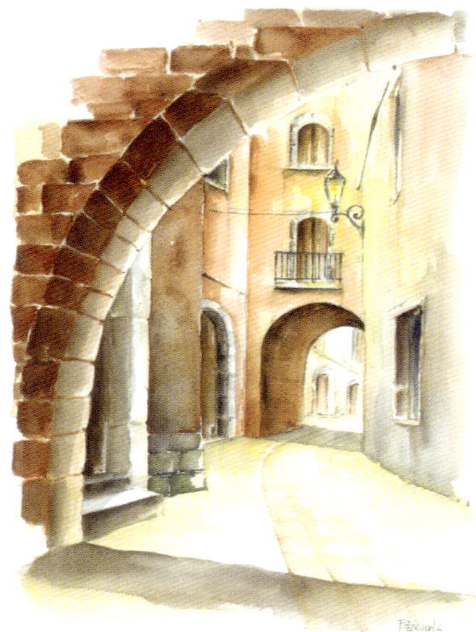

2.4/COLORING AND ADDITION OF CONTRASTS IN THE FOREGROUND

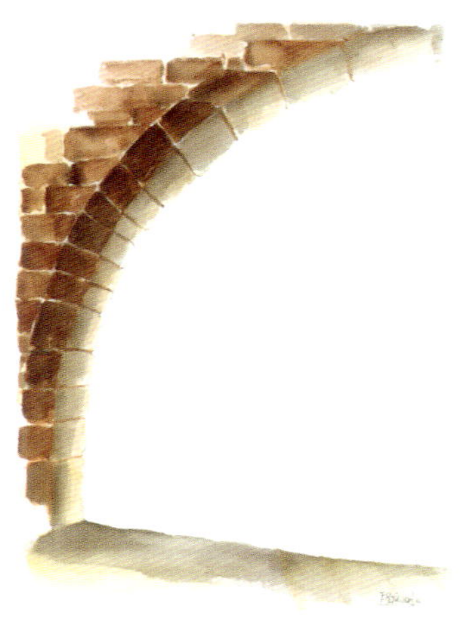

2.3/FOREGROUND—THE ARCHWAY

A Portrait

> Fabien Petillion

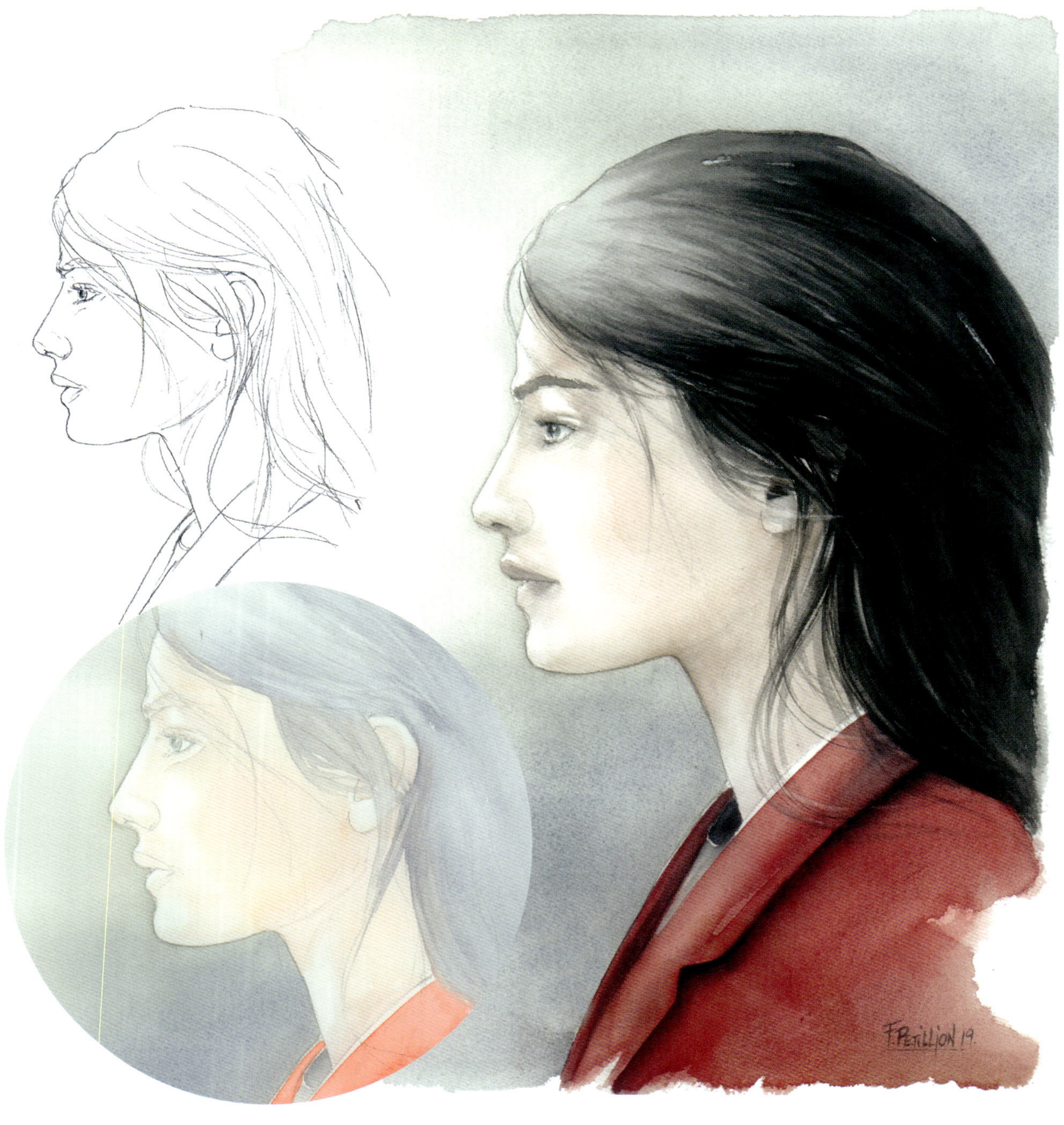

DRAFTING AND COMPOSITION

Painting a portrait is still a difficult exercise, because the drawing must be just right if you want to make sure the resemblance to the model shines through. And the proportions must be respected so that nothing will look jarring, because the smallest little mistake will alter the harmony and the accuracy of the portrait. If you are a beginner, you can work from a photograph and measure the distances between the various elements of the face, because the goal is to create accurate reference points. There is a good reason why the anatomy of the face, including the study of the facial bone structure and muscles, is taught in many drawing classes. The analysis of these formations allows you to better grasp the structure of a face and helps you to position each element in its proper place.

When you are positioning the face, it is also essential to leave some space where the person's gaze is directed. Based on Fabien's experience, the ideal is to leave at least 1/3 of the painting as empty space compared to 2/3 used for the drawing, up to a maximum ratio of 1/2 empty space and 1/2 drawing. If you use less empty space, the portrait appears locked in; if you use more, it seems lost.

COLORING

Step 1

Working on moistened paper, Fabien first paints his background with a neutral and not-too-strong color in order not to make the composition too dark. He keeps one part much lighter at the front of the face, which points us to the source of the light. Keeping part of the composition very light in his watercolors is an artistic maneuver that Fabien often uses. In this way, he invites the viewer's eye to travel across his work, in order to then lead it toward the light and suggest an exit. This is a visual game that is particularly interesting to carry out. Capturing your viewer's attention and succeeding in getting them to take the time to really contemplate the painting, rather than merely casting a distracted glance at it, is essential to a painter. It is a central goal of the painter's work, especially if they want to exhibit their work. Every professional artist has their own way of addressing this, and that is what defines each of them: It is interesting to pay attention to how they do this when you are visiting exhibits or salons.

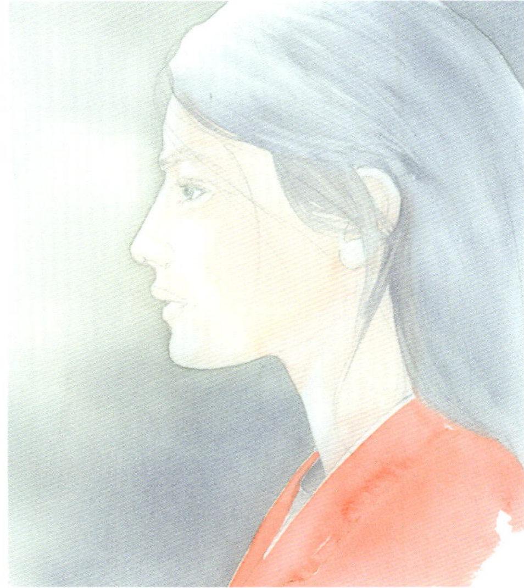

1.1/ APPLICATION OF A FIRST WASH IN THREE PHASES: FIRST THE BACKGROUND, THEN THE FACE AND HAIR, AND THEN, FINALLY, THE JACKET

When the base layer has dried, Fabien moistens the face while leaving a few areas in pure white by keeping them dry, particularly at the top of the forehead, the cheekbone, the underside of the eye, and the bridge of the nose. Then he colors the face using a mixture of yellow ocher (PY42) and Isaro rose (PR122) (see page 103) in a relatively intensive way to build up the volumes. Once this step has dried completely, Fabien paints the hair in wet-on-wet, using an initial Payne's gray wash. This wash is applied in the direction of the hair. He finishes by coloring the jacket, still working wet-on-wet, using pyrrole red deep (PR264) and scarlet red (PR255). Thus, the application of the colors takes place in four distinct stages. And because the various stages are applied wet-on-wet, in each case it is essential to make sure that the area that was previously painted is completely dry before beginning to paint the next one. If you work too quickly and do not respect the time needed for drying, the colors will merge with those that were applied previously, and the outlines will lose their sharpness. Remember that a watercolor travels where there is water and stops where the paper is dry.

Step 2

Fabien finalizes the young woman's skin tone using a very light carbon-black-based wash that he uses for shading (see page 107). This allows him to reinforce the shadowed areas at the neck, the nostrils, and the brow bone.

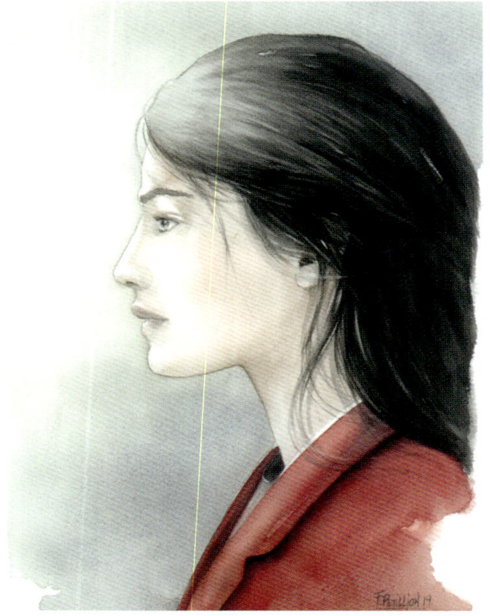

1.2/PAINTING OF THE SHADOWS ON THE FACE AND THE MOVEMENT OF THE HAIR

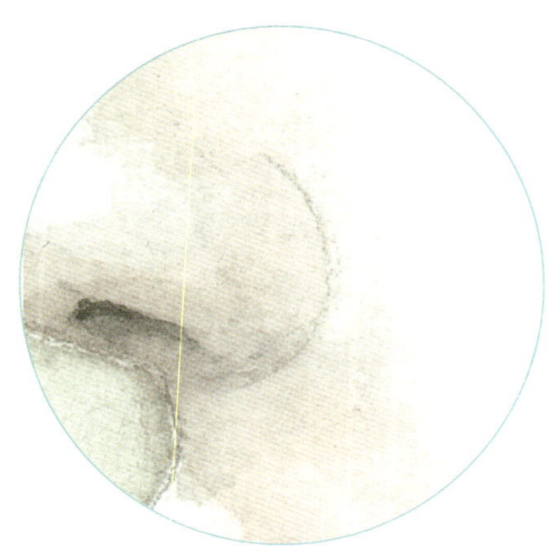

2.1/CLOSE-UP OF THE NOSE AREA WHERE A FINE WASH BASED ON CARBON BLACK (PBK6) HAS BEEN APPLIED

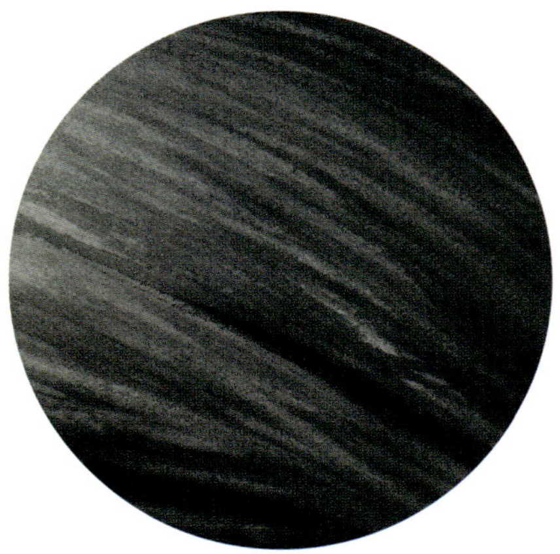

2.2/CLOSE-UP OF THE HAIR

Next comes the painting of the hair. Fabien paints it using carbon black (PBk6). As we explained earlier, he prefers a pure black to a black obtained by mixing colors, which runs the risk of being less neutral. Over his gray wash, he applies the carbon black. While the color is still wet, he then uses the method of withdrawing the color to draw the movement of the hair and to allow the color underneath to show through. This technique is a very good way to render the reflections that show on a head of hair. Then, still working by withdrawing color, he does more detailed work on the hair, using a fine wet brush. Finally, he draws a few individual locks with a thin brush, using black.

In a portrait, the coloring of the eye is very important. The eye should ideally be darker at the top than at the bottom. If you pay attention to it, you will notice that the eyelid lightly shades the top of the iris. Therefore, it is not enough just to color the iris, you also have to give it subtle nuances, working with a more diluted color on the bottom than on the top. The white of the eye should also be slightly grayed in its upper section. You must also make sure to retain a flash of white in the pupil by leaving it white when you apply the watercolors or, failing that, by adding a touch of white acrylic or gouache. As for the eyelashes, it is better not to draw them as straight little lines but instead to paint them less methodically, for a more natural look.

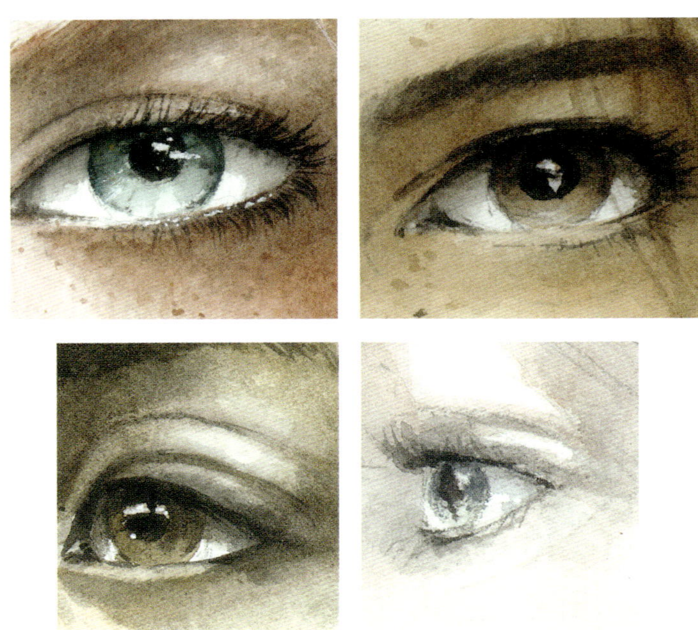

2.3/CLOSE-UP OF THE PAINTING OF THE EYE IN THE FOUR PORTRAITS PRESENTED IN THIS BOOK

An Animal Portrait

> Fabien Petillion

DRAFTING AND COMPOSITION

For the portrait of this tiger, seen in 3/4 profile, the main difficulty is drawing the foreshortened right eye. Drawing a shortened version of the curves often turns out to be a delicate task. The eye that is farther away needs to be smaller, and the angle of its curves sharper, compared to the closer eye. Your draft needs to do this correctly so as not to disrupt the perspective and accuracy of the drawing.

It is also essential to think about what will be placed where so that there will be enough room around the tiger's head that it does not feel constricted. Thinking this through will keep you from having to bend or shorten the tiger's ears, a classic mistake that would make you have to start all over.

As in all portraits in full or 3/4 profile, it is a good idea to leave enough empty space where the gaze is directed (see page 132). In this composition, Fabien leaves 1/3 of the page empty in front of the tiger.

COLORING

STEP 1

The background of this painting involves a neutral and relatively cool color. It is neutral so that the background does not take over the focus from the portrait, and it is cooler than the portrait in order to give depth to the composition. Because the tiger's orange coat is very warm, the artist can allow himself to work with a relatively warm background color. Fabien chose a light gray, with indigo added (see pages 66 and 68), for the darker areas. Because the light is coming toward the tiger, it is logical that the background area will need to be the lightest.

In order to create a diffuse background, Fabien moistens his page before applying his colors. He doesn't hesitate to move the paper around and play with the movement of the colored water in order to delicately fuse the colors. However, he is careful not to moisten the portrait of the tiger, otherwise the colors would travel across the whole painting.

Still using the color of his background, Fabien builds the most shaded areas of the cat's head. This includes the inside of the ears and nostrils, the underside of the mouth, and the outline of the eye. In this way, Fabien creates a connection between the color he has chosen for his background and the cat itself, uniting the subject with the background.

1.1/ BACKGROUND USING A BASE OF LIGHT GRAY AND INDIGO BLUE

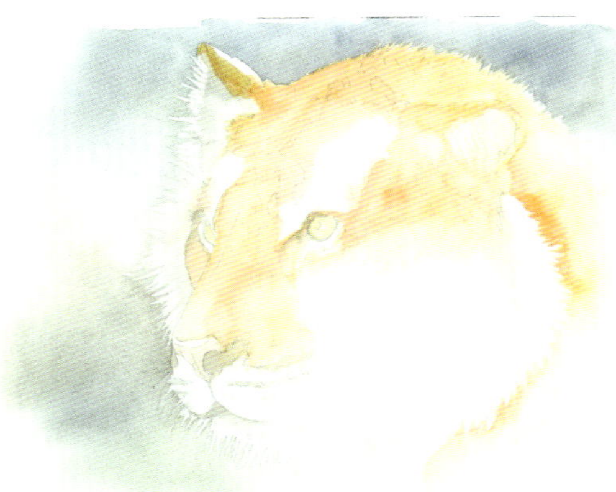

1.2/ BACKGROUND WORK AND FIRST WASH USING A BASE OF YELLOW OCHER AND CHINESE ORANGE

Unlike the background, the head of the tiger is built on dry paper. The color, a mixture of yellow ocher (PY42) and Chinese orange (see page 73; the formula using dark brown is the most appropriate here), is laid down using a water-reservoir brush, which is a brush with bristles that can hold a large amount of water. A relatively thick and pointed squirrel-type brush is particularly well suited for this.

The hairs of the thick white fur that form the tiger's collar are created with negative painting (see box below).

Step 2

Fabien accentuates the red of the tiger's fur by layering over the first coat a layer of Chinese orange. In places, he adds a touch of burnt sienna to gently deepen it, indicating the darker areas, such as the cat's ears. He keeps the lighter areas as is, the ones previously colored with yellow ocher (PY42) or left white, such as the top of the eyes and the muzzle. The collar is reworked using negative painting.

Then, Fabien accentuates the volumes in the fur by adding new touches of gray. This is always in the same shade as his background.

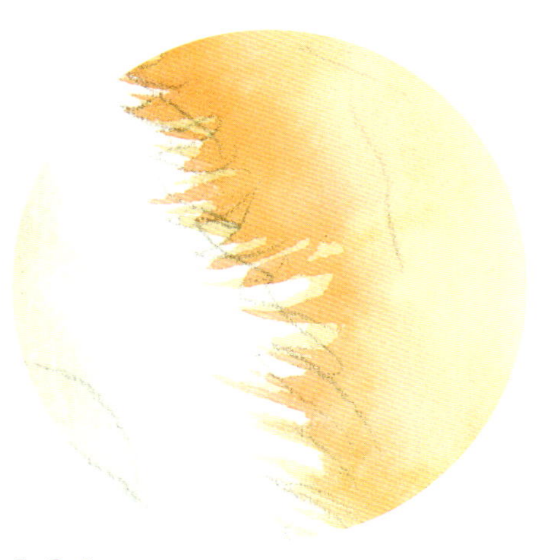

1.3/CLOSE-UP—NEGATIVE PAINTING

Negative Painting

This means that what you have to do is not to paint the individual hairs of the tiger's fur but to build these by painting the spaces between the hairs. The goal is to maintain the pure white spaces of the paper.

As previously mentioned, in watercolors, we use the white of the paper and we avoid painting with pure white.

White watercolor paint is in fact not opaque enough to cover what lies below, so the final effect is unsatisfactory.

When it is well mastered, the technique of negative painting is foolproof, but it does require a certain amount of practice, because it goes against how our brain sees things.

Finally, he paints the eye of the tiger, using carbon black (PBk6) that he superimposes on the previously applied gray. One might be tempted simply to paint the outline of the eye in black, but layering it over a gray wash makes it less harsh.

STEP 3

To paint the tiger's stripes, Fabien chooses a neutral black. From our studies of black earlier in this book, you will recall that it is hard to get a clear, neutral black. This is why Fabien chooses to work with carbon black (PBk6). If you want to use a black that you mix yourself, make sure that it is a warm one so that it will remain within the tonal harmony of the painting. It is not enough simply to color the stripes black; you also need to make sure that they are tied in with the rest of the coat in such a way that visually, they make up a connected whole. Thus, the stripes need to be painted in the direction of the fur, using a deep black.

Then, this black has to be shaded into the cat's fur in order to work in the gradations of gray. The hairs that catch the light therefore have to remain very white, while those that add dimension are made gray, to varying degrees, by the overlay of a black wash that starts from the stripes. The artist can use the various shades of gray to create the shadows and pull together the entire coat in a natural way.

The iris of the tiger's eye is done in chartreuse yellow (PY129), tinted with a hint of Chinese orange.

The whiskers are painted with white acrylic or using a fine white permanent marker pen. You could also keep the whiskers in the white of the paper, using a masking fluid. However, it is so risky to try to get fine, elegant lines using this method that, in the end, the entire composition could be ruined by it. In addition, white acrylic or gouache creates a less distinct and thus more natural final product because of their very light transparency.

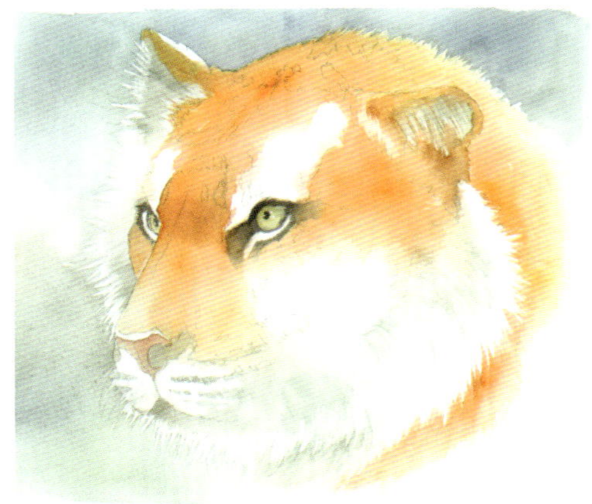

2.1/CREATING THE CONTRASTS

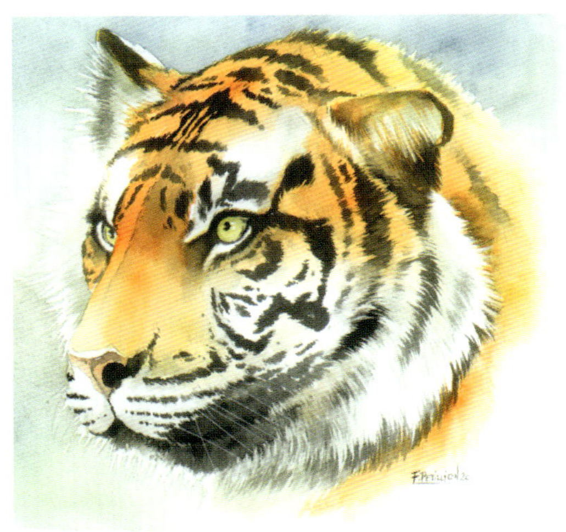

3.1/WORKING ON THE TIGER'S STRIPES

Resources

From the French edition, provided in English

Supplies

www.isaro.be/shop/gb/

shop.kremerpigments.com/us/

www.blockx.be/en/accueil/index.asp

www.royaltalens.com

danielsmith.com/watercolor

www.schmincke.de/en/

www.sennelier-colors.com

Colors

colour-index.com

okhra.com/en/accueil/accueil-english/

Other Resources

www.jacksonsart.com/blog

www.janeblundellart.com

www.handprint.com/HP/WCL/water.html

www.desireherman.com

Bibliography

Taken from the original French edition.

/ Bower, Stephanie. *Comprendre la perspective [Understanding perspective]*. Éditions Eyrolles: Paris, 2017.

/ Clinch, Moira. *Le nuancier de l'aquarelle: Petit guide des mélanges de couleurs [The watercolor color chart: Little guide to mixing colors]*. Éditions Eyrolles: Paris, 2010.

/ Coles, David. *Chromatopia*. Éditions Eyrolles: Paris, 2019.

/ Goethe, Johann Wolfgang von. *Traité des couleurs [Theory of colors]*. Éditions Triades: Paris, 2000.

/ Itten, Johannes. *Art de la couleur [The art of color]*. Éditions Dessain et Tolra: Paris, 1990.

/ Morelle, Jean-Louis. *Aquarelle: l'eau créatrice [Watercolor: Creative water]*. Éditions Fleurus: Paris, 2015.

/ Pastoureau, Michel, and Dominique Simonnet. *Le petit livre des couleurs [The little book of colors]*. Éditions Points: Paris, 2014.

/ Perego, François. *Le dictionnaire des matériaux du peintre [The dictionary of painting supplies]*. Éditions Belin: Paris, 2005.

/ Rainey, Jenna. *Mon cours d'aquarelle en 30 jours [My watercolor course in 30 days]*. Éditions Eyrolles: Paris, 2018.

/ Roelofs, Isabelle, and Fabien Petillion. *La couleur expliquée aux artistes [Color explained to artists]*. Éditions Eyrolles: Paris, 2012.

/ Saint Clair, Kassia. *La vie secrète des couleurs [The secret life of colors]*. Éditions du Chêne: Vanves, 2019.

/ Wilton, Andrew. *Venise: aquarelles de Turner [Venice: Turner's watercolors]*. Éditions Bibliothèque de l'image, 1996.

/ Yvel, Claude. *Peindre à l'eau comme les maîtres. Dessin, lavis & détrempe, techniques anciennes [Painting with water like the masters. Drawing, washes, and wet-on-wet, ancient techniques]*. Edisud Éditions: Aix-en-Provence, 2006.

The Authors

Isabelle Roelofs is the founder of the Isaro brand, which specializes in manufacturing colors for artists. Her family has maintained and passed down this specialized know-how for four generations. Isabelle is passionate about the history of colors and about pigments, and she has developed a range of extra-fine watercolors, which she has been marketing since 2011. Isabelle personally guarantees the production of all of her colors because, as an artisan, it is the very essence of her profession.

She listens to artists so that she can use their feedback to keep evolving her range of colors, and she enjoys sharing her knowledge with them.

Follow Isaro online:
Website – isaro.be
Instagram – @isaro_watercolors_oil_paint
Facebook – ISARO:Aquarelles et Couleurs à l'huile

Fabien Petillion is a graphic designer by training, a painter, illustrator, and watercolor artist. He moves easily among the universes of watercolor, oil painting, pastels, and colored pencil. In 2005, the challenge of watercolor drew him in and he very quickly developed a technical mastery that brought him international recognition. Today, he is regularly invited to take part in prestigious exhibits. At the same time, he also teaches watercolor and drawing and runs workshops. His works are exhibited in Belgium and abroad.

Follow Fabien online:
Website – fabienpetillion.com
Instragram – @artiste_fabienpetillion
Facebook – Fabien Petillion - artiste peintre,
aquarelliste, portraitiste

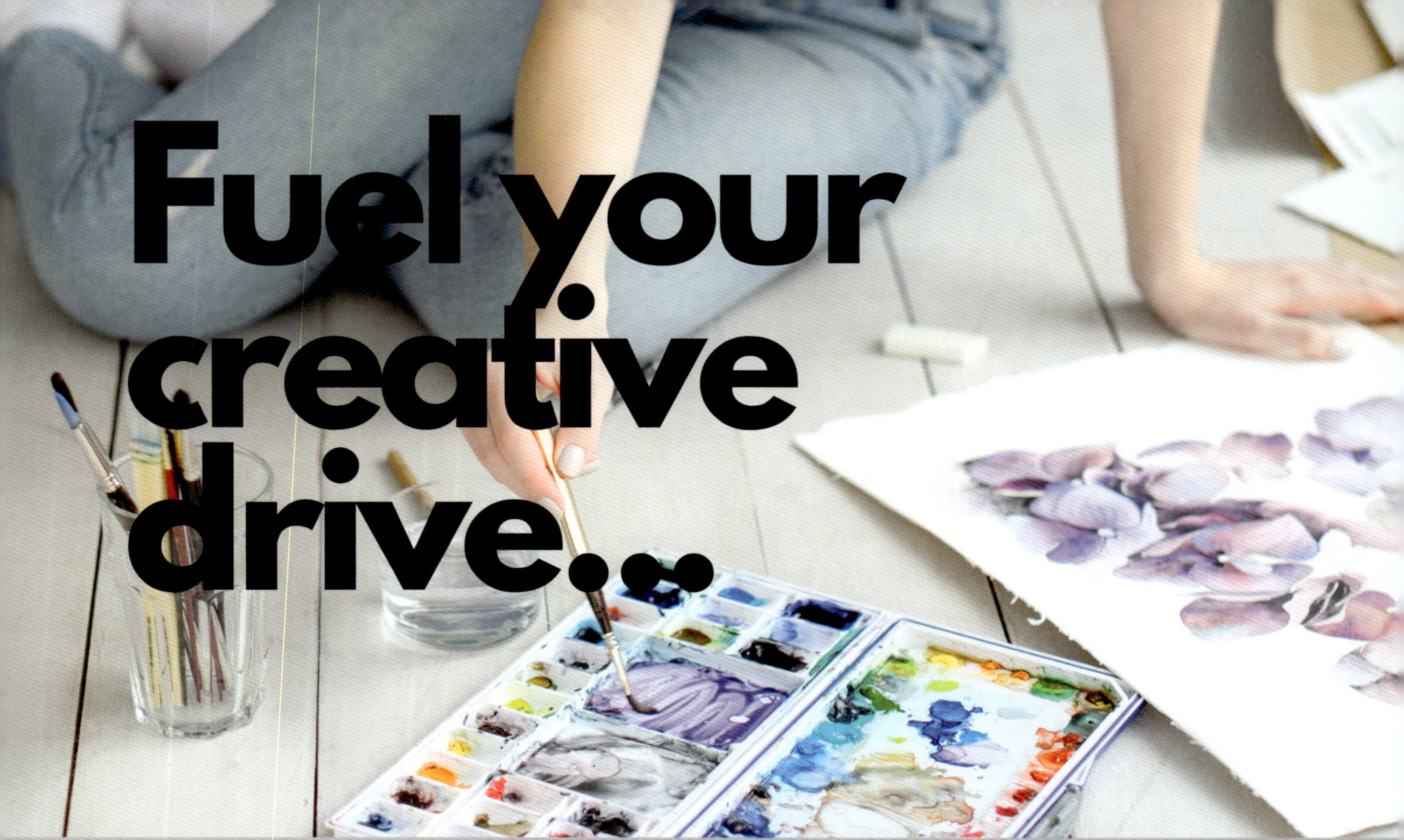

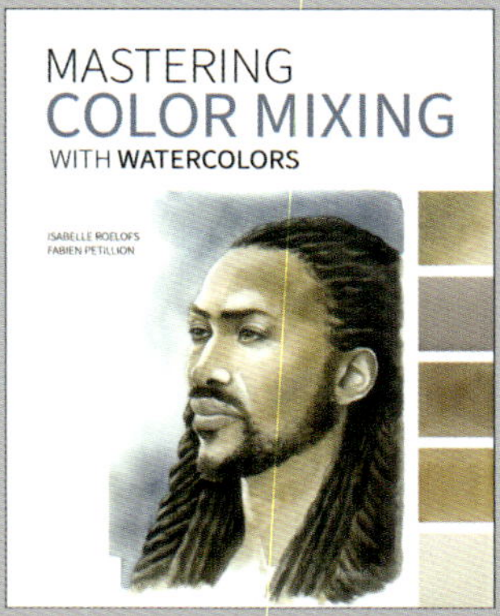

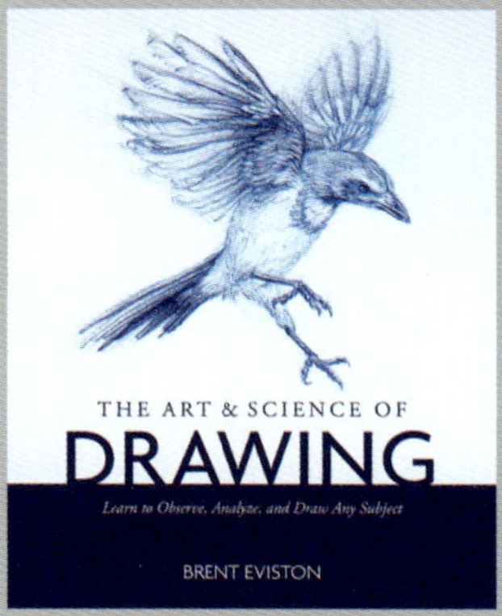

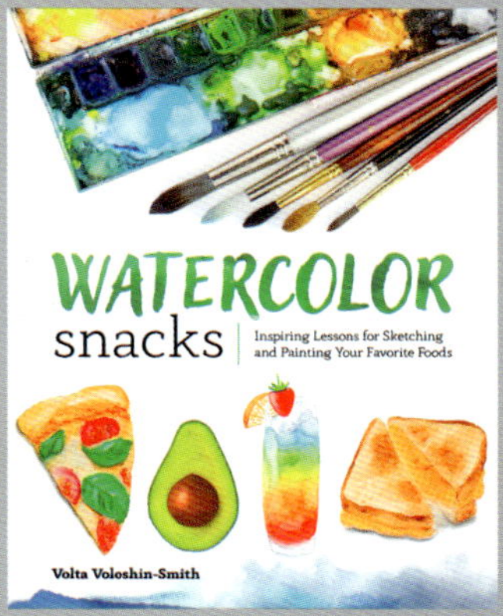

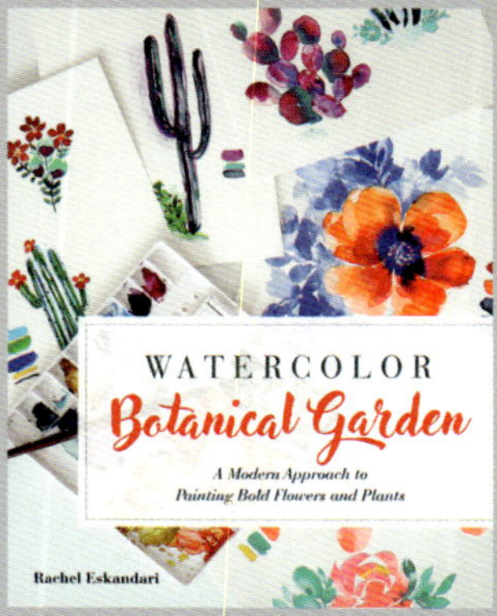

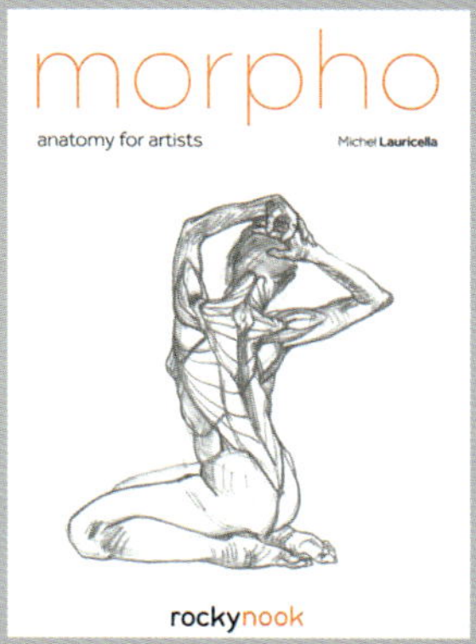

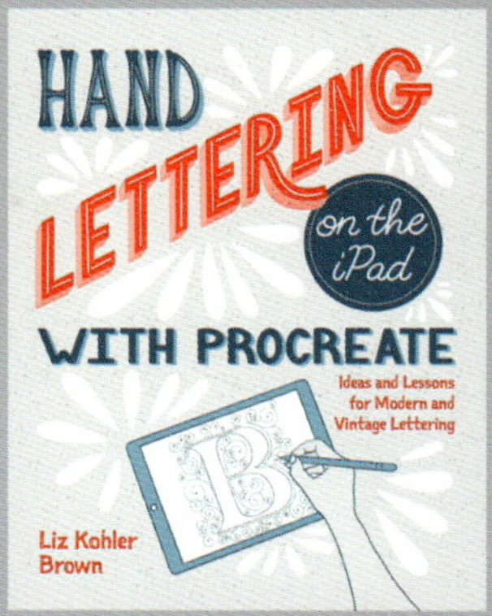